Volume One

The
Female
Alcoholic

Judith Goodman Ph.D.

Women and Addiction Counseling and Educational Services

Santa Cruz, California

Volume One
The Female Alcoholic

Judith Goodman M.A., CADC, ICADC, Ph.D.

Published by:

Women and Addiction Counseling and Educational Services (WACES)
111 Donna Court • Santa Cruz • CA • 95060 • (831) 426-6636 Ext. 4
www.women-addiction.com • FAX # (831) 426-6636 • e-mail: info@women-addiction.com

First Printing February 1998
Second Printing March 1999
Third Printing July 1999

Cover by Donald F. Van Selus

Library of Congress Catalog Card Number: 98-60139
ISBN 0-9663144-0-9 Softcover

To the Oldtimers Group
for teaching me the true meaning of sobriety.

To my wonderful husband Don
for helping me live it.

And to my children
for making it worth something.

Table of Contents

Part 2: WOMEN, ALCOHOLISM AND RELATIONSHIPS

Part 3: WOMEN, ALCOHOLISM AND PARENTING

Part 4: WOMEN, ADDICTION AND MENTAL ILLNESS

Part 5: WOMEN AND TREATMENT

Acknowledgements

To everyone who made this book a possibility, I wish to express a debt of gratitude. I had talked about writing such a book for years because I felt it was greatly needed in the field. However, it was not until my friend Donald Van Selus suggested that I purchase a computer to write it that I began to take the idea seriously. I wish to thank him for his many hours of support, his contribution to the cover design and his careful editing of the entire manuscript.

I also wish to thank two other supportive friends and colleagues. Claudia Alonzo, a Marriage, Family and Child Therapist in private practice gave feedback and ideas for the chapter on alcoholic mothers and edited several other chapters of the book. Lynne Wittenberg, a Health Educator who specializes in women's reproductive health and perinatal substance use issues, contributed a great deal of information for the chapter on the pregnant alcoholic. Without their help, these chapters would have been difficult to complete.

Others who have added much to the content of this book include my colleagues in the field. Many of them work in treatment centers and private practice with female alcoholics and were able to provide an inside view of the treatment issues faced by their clients. Others offered opinions about twelve step programs and dual diagnosis. Dr. Jim Ferrell was particularly instrumental in helping with the chapter on dual diagnosis by providing valuable feedback as well as insight from his work with clients. I also appreciate the many women in Alcoholics Anonymous meetings that were willing to talk to me about their experiences of the twelve step program.

Finally, I wish to thank my own clients who agreed to let me tell their stories. Working with them inspired me and kept me focused on this project. Their willingness to share their experiences has offered a rare opportunity for others to really understand the disease of alcoholism from those who suffer from it. Without their candidness, this book would not have been possible.

Introduction

Purpose of this Book

Alcoholism is gender-blind, but the research on it has not been. Most of the studies done on alcoholism have been about men. Yet, men and women are introduced to alcohol under different circumstances, choose to drink for different reasons and become addicted in different ways. Alcoholism is a psychobiological disease that has different ramifications for men and women. Until recently, little was known about alcohol's effect on the female body. However, the female body undergoes physiological changes in response to alcohol in the system that contrasts remarkably to men. Adaptations in tolerance level, functioning ability when alcohol is present and withdrawal symptoms that set the stage for addiction follow a different course for women.

Even so, this does not explain why women pick up a drink in the first place or why they continue to drink before the body becomes addicted. The fact that physical, financial, social and psychological factors influence the course of the disease in women, their access to treatment and their chances of success with abstinence have been largely ignored. In addition, society's attitudes on female alcoholism or women's roles have not been considered in the equation of why women become addicted and why they stay addicted.

Volume One: The Female Alcoholic confronts this dearth of information and provides concrete facts as well as personal stories of women's experiences with alcoholism. Few researchers have examined how women begin drinking, how they become addicted to alcohol or how the disease progresses in them. This information however, is important in the treatment of women alcoholics. Society, family and husbands' responses to female alcoholics severely limit women's choices when it comes to treatment. Women face very different negative consequences from their drinking and different obstacles in their recovery primarily because of the roles they play in our society.

As a Certified Alcohol and Drug Abuse Counselor, I am continually being asked by clients and colleagues to recommend reading material that gives them information on how:

> * the stages of alcoholism progress in women in contrast to men
> * drugs play a part in women's alcoholism
> * eating disorders and other addictions reinforce women's alcoholism

* ACA issues can increase the likelihood of women becoming alcoholics
* alcoholism impacts women's marriages and relationships
* relationships impact women's alcoholism
* alcoholism affects women's ability to mother their children
* alcoholism sets women up to be abused, battered and raped
* alcoholism and mental illness interact
* women feel in Alcoholics Anonymous, and
* about treatment options, issues and relapse prevention triggers specific to women.

Volume One: The Female Alcoholic was written in response to these frequently asked questions. This volume is based on 15 years experience working with female alcoholics and extensive research on alcohol and other addictions. Therapists, other clinicians, clients, family members of female alcoholics and members of Alcoholics Anonymous were also interviewed while researching for this book. Factual information is used to eliminate the myths and stereotypes surrounding alcoholism and personal renditions are told from recovering alcoholics to give the disease a "human face".

In Alcoholics Anonymous meetings, women tell the newcomers to stick with the women. It is believed that other women have a shared experience and understanding that helps strengthen the newly recovering female alcoholic's resolve for sobriety. It is through other women's stories that an understanding of what alcoholism means for women in general is possible. The women in this book are recovering alcoholics and addicts who have chosen to share their stories.* Their goal as well as mine is to eliminate the mystery and misinformation of this disease. Their hope is to give the female version of what women face as alcoholics and possibly reduce the loneliness and isolation felt by those trying to seek help.

For counselors, medical staff and mental health professionals, this book will outline the specific issues women alcoholics face as they go into recovery. To develop an appropriate and effective treatment plan, healthcare professionals must have an understanding of how alcoholism impacts a woman's life, what obstacles they face when attempting abstinence and the specific relapse issues unique to women. *Volume One: The Female Alcoholic* offers a comprehensive account on alcoholism in women and is an excellent reference source for those trying to help this particular population.

Volume One: The Female Alcoholic is the first in a series of five books written specifically for clinicians, female alcoholics and their families that addresses alcoholism in women. The first volume focuses exclusively on the disease process and provides an overview on the stages of alcoholism, drug addiction, other addictions, mental illness, treatment options, recovery issues and relapse triggers specific to women.

* The names of the women and their families, as well as any identifiable features, have been changed to protect the privacy of those concerned.

The second volume, *Counseling the Female Alcoholic* examines the role of the counselor, the diagnostic criteria of alcoholism, the intervention process, how to work with defense mechanisms and the first thirty days of sobriety. *Volume Three: Recovery Issues of the Female Alcoholic* offers more detailed information for developing a treatment plan for maintaining sobriety and teaching relapse prevention skills. The final two books in the series, *Volume Four: Relationship Skills for the Recovering Female Alcoholic* and *Volume Five: Parenting Skills for the Recovering Female Alcoholic* explore the two greatest relapse triggers for female alcoholics and provides a complete treatment plan for both issues.

For simplicity sake, the terms "counselor", "healthcare professional" and "clinician" are used in all five volumes to include a variety of medical and mental health experts such as doctors, nurses, licensed marriage and family therapists, licensed clinical social workers, certified addiction counselors, psychologists, psychiatrists and other medical staff members. In the same light, the pronoun "she" is used for the counselor where it was impossible to remain gender neutral. This is not to negate however, the many male healthcare professionals who have devoted their careers to helping female alcoholics.

Part 1:

Alcoholism, Drug Addiction and Women

1

The Disease of Alcoholism

Description of an Alcoholic

In an exercise designed to describe what an alcoholic looked like, most people imagined a middle-aged, dirty, unkept man, who had lost his job, his home and his family. He lived on the streets, drank from a brown paper bag and owned nothing but the old torn clothing on his back. The participants of this exercise expressed little respect or sympathy for this man and in fact, regarded him with contempt. He was viewed as pathetic because he "could not hold his liquor." Few wanted to know him let alone be a relative or friend. It was expected that he would be ignored and avoided if seen on the street. This stereotype of the classic alcoholic rang true no matter how often the exercise was done.

The picture of a drug addict was even more disparaging. A popular story in 12-step meetings tries to describe the difference between an alcoholic and a drug addict. "When you're missing $20.00, the alcoholic will lie and say s/he didn't take it. The addict on the other hand, will also lie and deny taking it but then will offer to help you look for it." Now imagine you have just been told that you are an alcoholic. What would be your response? If you believe the stereotype just described, your first reaction would probably be to exclaim in horror "No, I am not!"

Surprisingly, our culture continues to be amazed and critical at the tenacity of many alcoholics/addicts to deny their problem. Yet I have never met a single person who would want to believe that the above description applied to them. Our denial system kicks in when information presented to us is too painful, frightening or ugly to accept. The alcoholic label would certainly qualify. It is no wonder that even the alcoholic does not want to be an alcoholic. The diagnosis of alcoholism automatically comes with preconceived notions and baggage of what it means to be an alcoholic.

It is true that with the advent of programs like Alcoholics Anonymous the definition of an alcoholic is changing. More people recognize it as a disease like diabetes that requires treatment. Society has even expanded its view of the alcoholic to include a wider variety of people from different cultures, religions, socioeconomic backgrounds and an assortment of family structures.

It is now more widely accepted that alcoholism afflicts the young, the elderly, the educated, the uneducated, the executive, the blue-color worker or the unemployed alike. However, the old stereotype rears its ugly head when society reluctantly comes to terms with the concept of alcoholism in women.

Women as Alcoholics

A double standard exists in our society. A woman diagnosed with alcoholism is the target of negative labels about her mothering, femininity, and sexuality in a way that is not true with a male alcoholic. Because of these prejudices not accorded to her male counterpart, women are faced with different obstacles and an even stronger reluctance to give up their denial system and seek help. Financial difficulties, child care issues and the absence of addressing women's issues as a part of recovery helps to explain why fewer women obtain medical assistance. Women alcoholics often stay "in the closet" to protect themselves, their reputation, their children and their families.

When describing a male alcoholic the image that comes to mind is a man who has lost control of his drinking. The description of a female alcoholic however, includes more than loss of control over how much she drinks. In our society, female alcoholics lose their status as women, mothers and wives as well. This judgment creates obstacles for female alcoholics in accepting responsibility for their addiction and in getting treatment. Women, by virtue of being alcoholic are judged as bad, neglectful and abusive mothers. Male alcoholics are rarely questioned about how their drinking affected their children. Treatment issues preclude concerns about the father's drinking on the children. The focus is primarily in helping the entire family support the man's sobriety.

Mothers, on the other hand, are admonished for causing great harm to their children. Female alcoholics are seen as bad, not sick as male alcoholics are perceived. Since women are the primary provider for their children, mothers are the ones held accountable when their addiction makes them too sick to fulfill their role. Even when not drinking, mothers are held responsible for their children's' shortcomings or problems. When the woman drinks, it is automatic proof of her incompetence as a parent in a way it never is for the man. Fathers are rarely even considered an option when it comes to child care and caretaking responsibilities. When his drinking prevents him from meeting his children's needs, he does not experience the same level of criticism for not fulfilling his parental duties.

This stigma of the bad mother further reduces the likelihood that the woman will take responsibility for her addiction. To do so places her in a position to be blamed for what the addiction has done to her children rather than helped with the disease that threatens both herself and her children. She is a woman with a disease, not an abusive mother. However, the public continues to have difficulty seeing women alcoholics as sick as their male counterparts.

Women's sexuality is also called into question when they are diagnosed as alcoholics. The labels that come to mind often include "slut", "whore" or "prostitute". Men's sexuality again is not even brought up for debate or included as part of the description of alcoholism. When drinking, women are considered unlady-like, vulgar and disgusting; men are seen as having a good time. Male alcoholic behavior is seen as an extension of what our society considers acceptable masculine behavior. This exacerbates the shame and embarrassment female alcoholics experience when seeking help. They are not given the same support needed to confront the disease of alcoholism.

Another obstacle women face when confronting their alcoholism occurs during treatment when staff define the disease. In the United States, studies of male alcoholics have determined both the definition and the description of the course of the disease. Few studies have observed the different types of alcoholism experienced by women. Even fewer have revealed the unique stages of alcoholism women progress through as they become addicted. However, these are important considerations when it comes to diagnosing women.

Different Types of Alcoholism

E. M. Jellinek, a pioneer in alcoholism research, published a study in 1952 that charted the symptoms and progression of the disease (Kinney et al. 1991). It was the first of its kind to identify alcoholism as a disease with a specific course, symptoms and patterns. Jellinek based his findings on a survey of 2000 Alcoholics Anonymous (AA) members and came up with four phases of alcoholism; prealcoholic, prodromal, crucial, and chronic. Later in his research of alcoholism in other countries, Jellinek discovered that there was more than one type of alcoholism. The four phases he had discovered described only one type of alcoholism which he named Gamma Alcoholism. He believed that this type was the most common in the United States. However, his early studies focused primarily on men.

Female alcoholics show more variety in the types of alcoholism they experience. Although many women do follow the drinking patterns of Gamma Alcoholism, others diagnosed with alcoholism experience the progression of the disease according to the Alpha, Beta and Delta types of alcoholism.

Alpha Alcoholism according to Jellinek describes a psychological but no physical dependency on alcohol. This person does not have difficulty with loss of control or in abstaining but when drinking is identified as a problem drinker. Significant of this type of alcoholism is the person's reliance on alcohol to deal with stress, conflict or crisis. Many women who use alcohol to cope with their relationships and sexual problems may be identified as this type of alcoholic. This alcoholic drinker may never progress beyond problems at work or with family.

Beta Alcoholism describes the drinker who has physical problems such as cirrhosis but does not have a psychological or physical dependency on alcohol. Women tend to experience more physical problems at a much faster rate than their male counterparts.

Gamma Alcoholism describes the progression from psychological to physical dependence. It is marked by loss of control, changes in tolerance and withdrawal symptoms. This was the type of alcoholic most commonly seen in the United States and AA meetings at the time of the study. Jellinek described the progression of this disease in the four phases: prealcoholic, prodromal, crucial, and chronic. In the prealcoholic phase, the person drinks socially, seeks out situations where drinking will occur and eventually begins using alcohol to relax and deal with stress. Many women begin their drinking with their partners (see Chapter 2 for more information).

The prodromal phase is marked by a need for alcohol and by blackouts. (Blackouts occur when the person appears to be functioning normally but cannot later remember anything about that period of time.) This need leads the person to sneak drinks, gulp them down, and lie about the amount drunk. Drinking before an event (that serves alcohol) occurs more frequently in order to get enough alcohol in their system to be able to function.

The third or crucial phase is marked by loss of control over how much alcohol is consumed once drinking begins. Control over whether or not to start drinking is still present. Defense mechanisms are consistently triggered. Attempts to quit or change the drinking pattern is evident. Nevertheless, the drinker's world has begun to center around alcohol and the consequences of this evolution increases.

The final or chronic phase is marked by daily drinking and intoxication. The circle of friends changes for the worst.   Tolerance drops sharply, tremors develop, and simple tasks seem impossible to do in the sober state. The drinking has interfered with daily functioning and created numerous consequences.

Delta Alcoholism is similar to the Gamma type in that there is psychological and physical dependence. However, there is no loss of control. On any particular drinking episode, the amount consumed can be controlled but withdrawal symptoms are inevitable if the person does not drink. She can control dose and frequency to maintain a certain level of intoxication but she cannot remain abstinent. Women who work in the home tend to exhibit these symptoms. They practice maintenance drinking to ensure a steady blood alcohol level but do not become so intoxicated that they can not take care of the home or their children (Sandmaier 1992).

Epsilon Alcoholism is marked by periodic, unpredictable binges or drinking sprees that may last days and sometimes weeks. This person can control when she drinks and at times can maintain long periods of abstinence. However, there is difficulty in controlling how much she drinks once drinking begins.

There is a tendency in the treatment field to diagnose women as alcoholics when they have features of Gamma alcoholism when in fact, there is evidence that women often exhibit very different drinking patterns from their male counterparts. In AA meetings and clinical settings, women frequently describe drinking as a way to feel connected to a partner and eventually as a way to cope with stress. These women develop a psychological dependency on alcohol described in Alpha alcoholism because of their need to drink with drinking partners. If the man stops drinking, many of these women stop as well. Other women use alcohol as a coping mechanism to deal with poverty, abuse issues, loneliness, single parenting, environmental stress, poor living conditions, economic hardship and conflicts in their relationships. These women follow the drinking pattern of Delta alcoholism. There is a psychological and physical dependence but no loss of control.

Definitions of Alcoholism

Over the years, alcoholism has undergone many definitions in an attempt to address the different types discovered by Jellinek. For most of the United States, alcoholism can be described as "a chronic, primary, hereditary, eventually fatal disease that progresses from an early physiological susceptibility into an addiction characterized by tolerance changes, physiological dependence and loss of control over drinking" (Mueller et al. 1987, p.9). In twelve step programs like Alcoholics Anonymous (AA), "an alcoholic is a person who cannot predict with accuracy what will happen when he takes a drink" (Kinney et al. 1991, p.54).

It is widely accepted in the medical field that alcoholism is a biogenetic disease progressing from an early, middle to late stage. By the late stage, the disease eventually effects the physical, psychological and social life of the alcoholic. According to the fourth edition of the Diagnostic and Statistical Manual (DSM-IV), alcoholism is divided into two syndromes. The early and middle stages of alcoholism are referred to as alcohol abuse. Alcohol abuse is diagnosed when there is significant impairment with the individual's health, family relationships, job performance, financial difficulties or legal problems due to the persistent and excessive use of alcohol. The later stages of alcoholism in the DSM-IV is called alcohol dependence. Alcohol dependence is marked by increased tolerance, loss of control over how much and whether to drink, physiological and psychological dependence on alcohol and an increase in negative consequences as a result of the drinking.

The medical field has not yet found a cure for alcoholism. Presently, the disease requires a specific course of treatment to recover or go into remission. There has been a great deal of controversy over whether an alcoholic can be taught to drink properly. The debate over controlled drinking versus abstinence still rages on in the field and there are studies to prove both sides. The most likely conclusion is that it depends on the type of alcoholism and the stage at which treatment is sought that determines the necessary course.

Finally, for women, the definition of alcoholism must include impairment that prevents women from making safe and healthy decisions that insures the welfare of themselves and their children. Alcoholism prevents women from protecting themselves from physical abuse, rape and becoming involved in battering relationships. It prevents them from protecting their children from being witnesses and/or victims of abuse. Alcoholism impairs a woman's judgement in how to properly care for her children and in permitting or introducing their children to alcohol and drug use.

Course of the Disease

For women, drinking and using drugs often starts out as fun and as part of a relationship. At first, there are few consequences to drinking. Alcohol and drugs act on the central nervous system (CNS) to create a pleasant sensation. Most women begin using alcohol in response to their partner's drinking. Many times, the woman is introduced to it by a date, boyfriend or husband making it a social and sometimes, sexual lubricant that only adds to this pleasant sensation. In his book *I'll Quit Tomorrow*, Vern Johnson (1973) describes this stage as the first one of four phases that lead to addiction.

In contrast to Jellinek's prealcoholic phase, Johnson names this phase "learning the mood swing" because the woman is discovering that drinking consistently makes her feel good. She is not physically or psychologically dependent on the alcohol. In fact, she feels normal or like her old self after a drinking episode. There is no pain from withdrawal or any remorse for how she behaved while drinking. The woman learns she can control how good she feels by varying the amount she drinks. It becomes predictable. She learns to trust that it works. This trust blossoms into a relationship where the woman perceives that alcohol is an effective coping mechanism.

In Johnson's second phase, the woman actively "seeks the mood swing." She is now using alcohol exclusively to feel good, especially when she is down. It works the best and most consistently. Over time, she chooses friends that drink because they are more interesting. They are doing the same thing she does (drinking), share in the same interests (drinking) and understands how she feels (drunk). Eventually, her social life revolves around drinking activities. She consciously chooses alcohol as her way to handle stress, negative feelings and difficult situations. In this way, she creates a support system or social circle that works to reinforce that use of alcohol as a coping mechanism.

As this stage progresses, the woman starts experiencing some negative consequences from her drinking. She may experience a hangover or embarrassment with how she acted while she was drinking. The association between alcohol and feeling good however continues to dominate. At this stage, her drinking begins to slowly increase as she develops a tolerance for it but she can still control the amount she drinks. Her faith in alcohol as a viable coping mechanism grows.

As the woman moves into phase three, she crosses the line between social drinking and a dependence on alcohol. Over time, repeated exposure to the alcohol allows the CNS to adapt to its presence. It can tolerate more alcohol and still maintain normal functioning. This tolerance means that the woman cannot feel the same pleasant sensation any more on the same amount of alcohol. Her physiological dependence requires her to use larger quantities of the alcohol to produce the same results she once felt on smaller doses (Kinney et al. 1991). This larger quantity sets her up to experience negative consequences such as hangovers, financial difficulties, and shame at behavior engaged in when intoxicated.

To complicate the process, the woman has developed a psychological dependence on alcohol as the only coping mechanism for pain even if that pain is a result of drinking. She is no longer choosing whether to drink. She now feels a need to drink. Conflict develops between the need for more of the drug to feel good and the resulting negative consequences of drinking. This conflict triggers the woman's defense mechanisms. Unable to abandon alcohol, the woman must find a way to minimize the negative or harmful impact drinking now has for her. To avoid the painful information that alcohol is creating its own set of problems, a number of cognitive distortions develop. It is largely an unconscious process that works in preventing the woman from recognizing that alcohol is now responsible for creating the problems. It has long ago stopped being the solution. This phase marks the onset of the disease of alcoholism.

The Denial System of the Alcoholic

By the time the woman reaches phase three, significant changes in drinking, thinking and behavior have occurred. At this point, there is a heavy reliance on a number of defense mechanisms to protect the woman from seeing the truth about her drinking. The most common defense mechanism for the woman to maintain is denial. She either denies that she drinks at all (or that much) or denies that her drinking is a problem. As her need for alcohol increases, so does her need to deny that need. She rejects any information that might prove her wrong. She may go to great lengths to explain her drinking in a way that maintains her belief system that it is harmless. The woman becomes preoccupied with proving that she is not an alcoholic even while her focus on alcohol grows. This makes it impossible for her to ask for help as she spirals out of control. It also makes it difficult for those around her not to buy into her denial system and deny her drinking problem to themselves.

Denial is one of the strongest defense mechanisms of alcoholics. It is an unconscious process used to avoid knowing something considered unacceptable or uncomfortable. This may be to avoid:

* pain (physical or emotional)
* negative information about oneself
* negative information about loved ones
* negative feelings such as disappointment, frustration, anger, fear, hurt
* feeling helpless, powerless and/or hopeless
* taking action that one is afraid or uncomfortable to take
* taking risks
* fear of the unknown
* making painful decisions
* rejection and/or abandonment
* loss/grief (i.e. triggered by giving up the alcohol)
* looking bad, sick, stupid or wrong
* seeing a loved one look bad, stupid or wrong
* feeling guilt, shame or remorse
* negative consequences of one's behavior
* taking responsibility
* changing behavior
* hurting a loved one

The alcoholic develops an accounting system as a way to maintain her denial that she is not an alcoholic (Brown 1985). She creates her own version of what an alcoholic looks like and then uses it to compare herself to it. For example, she may tell herself that an alcoholic is an alcoholic when that person drinks before noon. Since she does not drink before lunch herself, she is reassured that she is not an alcoholic. However, as the disease progresses, the woman finds herself doing those behaviors she identified as alcoholic. It becomes necessary at that point for the woman to change her stereotype of what alcoholism looks like and begin using the new version to disprove her own alcoholism. She will find other behaviors that she does not engage in as proof of alcoholism. The image must change in order for her to successfully continue to deny the truth about her drinking.

The female alcoholic rationalizes and projects onto others reasons for why she drinks without ever realizing how absurd her explanations are. She may blame her husband, her children, her job, her parents or life situations for driving her to drink. She cannot take responsibility for it herself. When stopped for a speeding ticket, the woman will insist (and believe) that the officer just did not like her. It is inconceivable to her that her drinking may have impaired her driving and that the officer was simply responding to the way she was speeding. Blaming others for their problems is one of the most common defense mechanisms for alcoholics.

A popular defense mechanism for women alcoholics is compensating for some shortcoming in one area by overachieving in another area. An example of this is seen when the alcoholic mother creates a huge homemade breakfast for her children when she was too drunk to prepare dinner the night before. She offers no explanation for the missed meal and will act as if making an elaborate breakfast is normal and an every day occurrence. Many women will also project what they are feeling onto someone else in order to avoid facing reality. Alcoholic women frequently blame their husbands for their lack of interest in sex when it is the women who have lost interest because they would rather drink.

Minimizing how her behavior impacts others and isolating from loved ones to avoid painful confrontations are also common ploys to protect the woman from the truth about her drinking. Others use anger, suicide threats, depression or tears to distract family members from seeing her drinking as the real problem. Women are particularly good at talking incessantly to prevent people from bringing up uncomfortable accusations or fears. This behavior is very confusing to friends and family. The woman they love is becoming unpredictable, dishonest and difficult to understand. It is often at this stage that family members question the woman's sanity. They know something is wrong but they do not know what it is.

Joe Perez (1994) discovered that female alcoholics have a rich fantasy life that is supported by these defense mechanisms. Alcoholic women develop a world focused on themselves, their feelings and reactions to others. A great deal of time is devoted to fantasies that are dominated by themes of being rejected. Feeling rejected in relationships justifies for these women the need to drink. Society often supports these fantasies of rejection with real examples of women being discriminated against. In addition, the women's own beliefs that they will be rejected becomes a self-fulfilling prophecy. Even when an interaction occurs where they are not rejected, these women often test and test until they succeed at alienating themselves. This supports their belief that they get rejected. Eventually, female alcoholics become adept at destroying relationships rather than building them. This self-fulfilling prophecy enables them to succeed at isolating themselves as they enter the later stages of the disease.

Final Stages of the Disease

During the third stage of the disease, the woman needs to drink more to feel the effect. When she does sober up, she suffers many consequences associated with her drinking. Her defenses become fine-tuned as she makes excuses for the price she is paying to drink. There is a growing preoccupation with alcohol and the woman makes constant adaptations to her lifestyle and means of coping to support her use of alcohol. Being able to drink becomes the dominant force in deciding what social events to attend, which friends to socialize with and even whom to marry. Her whole life revolves around the availability and use of alcohol. A vicious cycle develops as alcohol is used to emotionally cope with the negative consequences of using alcohol. She has lost control. She has developed a relationship with alcohol that now evolves into a way of life.

At this point the woman has reached phase four, the final stage of the disease process. When sober she feels pain and drinks to feel normal or to be able to function. It is almost impossible for her to complete tasks unless she maintains a certain blood alcohol level. When the woman's blood alcohol level is climbing there is more impairment then when it is dropping even if both measures are the same. The body seems to adapt to the alcohol and learns to function normally in its presence (Kinney et al. 1991). This sets up the woman to need to drink to maintain the blood alcohol level the body is accustomed to and experiences as normal. This level is needed to manage the day to day responsibilities and to prevent symptoms of withdrawal and therefore, pain.

Unable to admit this to herself, the woman has a multitude of excuses for why she drinks the way she does. The most common being that others drive her to it. She lies and then lies again when she is caught. Others see her as financially irresponsible when she buys expensive gifts while bills go unpaid. The woman displays mood swings and a considerable amount of time is organized around when, how and where she will drink. Her behavior becomes even more erratic. Promises are constantly broken. Excuses are made for reasons other than the alcohol. By this time, there are physical, mental, emotional and social problems occurring. It is at this final stage that the symptoms of alcoholism are most notable.

Symptoms of the Disease

Alcoholism as a disease has identifiable symptoms. Not every female alcoholic experiences each of these symptoms and they may vary in terms of the progression they take. They include:

* Craving for alcohol/other drugs
* Blackouts
* Loss of control
* Changes in tolerance
* Withdrawal symptoms
* Compulsion to drink/use
* The use of denial or other defense mechanisms
* A preoccupation on alcohol/drugs
* Mood swings
* Poor eating and sleeping habits
* Behavior changes
* Lifestyle changes to adapt to using alcohol and other drugs
* Harmful consequences related to alcohol/chemical use (physical/mental, marital/family, social, job, financial, legal, spiritual)

Women typically experience the mood swings, poor eating and sleeping habits, behavior changes, lifestyle adaptions and harmful consequences with family. In addition, symptoms for women must include being in a battering relationship, sexual abuse and an inability to protect her children. Finally, women experience more medical problems at a faster rate than their male counterparts especially with reproductive problems, cirrhosis, malnutrition and anemia.

Genetic Factors

There is mounting evidence that alcoholism is hereditary or at the very least has a genetic component. Goodwin traced male children born to alcoholic and non-alcoholic parents who were then adopted by the age of six weeks by non-alcoholic parents. Boys with a biological parent who was an alcoholic had a higher tendency to develop the disease than those who did not (Kinney et al. 1991). Research done on half siblings reared together demonstrate that the child of a biological parent with alcoholism was more likely to develop alcoholism than the half sibling who did not share the alcoholic parent. In some cases, these half siblings were adopted by a family with alcoholism. In other cases, the children were adopted by a non-alcoholic family. These research findings suggest growing up in an alcoholic family did not increase the risk of developing alcoholism for either half sibling (Kinney et al. 1991).

In another study, identical twins of biological parents who were alcoholics had a higher tendency to develop the disease themselves. Identical twins were also more likely to have a higher incidence of alcoholism than their fraternal twin counterparts. Even so, not all the identical twins were both alcoholics. This indicates that there is a strong genetic correlation but the fact that not every identical twin became an alcoholic suggests that there is something more involved than just genetics.

Controversy over whether alcoholism is genetic or environmental escalates when studies are done on women. Most of the research has focused on men and those that include women are often inconclusive. Some of the research on women has pointed to a significant increase for alcoholism among daughters of alcoholics. Other studies cite environmental factors such as parental role models, abuse, economic barriers, and societal prejudice. These factors lead to lower self-esteem (Finklestein et al. 1990) which make women vulnerable to developing the disease.

A combination of genetics and social factors seem to be the most obvious cause of alcoholism in women. Although children of alcoholics tend to be more vulnerable to inheriting the disease, it does not explain the reason they pick up the first drink and continue to drink long before they become addicted. More is being uncovered on how personality traits, bodily response to alcohol or drugs, social support of heavy drinking, stressful events and conflicts within the individual's life help to contribute to some women's vulnerability to the disease. Many recent studies have discovered a link between low self-esteem and women's initial use of alcohol and drugs (Perez 1994). Women with higher self-esteem may have better coping skills to resolve their problems without drinking. For most women drinking is somehow connected to their need to being attached in a relationship (Finklestein et al. 1990). Drinking is part of their relationship. It is how they are introduced to it and it is often their reason for continuing to drink.

2

The Female Alcoholic

Factors That Affect Alcoholism in Women

Men and women drink, suffer the course of the disease and experience treatment very differently. Physical, social, economic, cultural and psychological factors influence the way women are introduced to alcohol, under what circumstances they drink, the way their bodies respond to it and how they attract attention from the medical and mental health field.

In the first place, physical differences between men and women have a profound influence on how the female gender experiences the course of the disease of alcoholism. Body weight, the menstrual cycle and hormones play an important role in women's greater sensitivity to alcohol and to the increase in the number of medical problems associated with alcoholism. Women tend to visit doctors and therapists more often and with more complaints. Depression being the most common presenting problem associated with alcoholic women (Finklestein et al. 1990).

Secondly, women's social status negatively affects society's attitude toward female alcoholism in a way it does not for men. In our society, drinking in men is accepted and even encouraged through various customs such as stopping off after work for a beer with co-workers. Drinking is part of the social fabric of most men's lives both on the job, where alcohol is served at meetings, business lunches and company parties, as well as in the family, where beer is served to buddies that come over to watch the football game.

Although some women also drink after work with co-workers, most are introduced to alcohol by husbands, boyfriends or lovers. In this context, alcohol is seen as a "social lubricant" primarily used to create the illusion of intimacy and to loosen a woman up to be sexual. The message given to women is that their drinking is associated with promiscuity and not seen as part of a business meeting or luncheon. This connection between women's drinking and their sexuality creates, for the female alcoholic, a stereotype of the "drunken slut". As a result, women are more likely than their male counterparts to be stigmatized by their alcoholism (Blume 1988).

Consequently, women will go to even greater lengths than male alcoholics to deny and hide their drinking (Blume 1988). When they do ask for help, female alcoholics focus on the underlying symptoms rather than admit that their drinking is a problem (Perez 1994). In contrast to the widely held belief that female alcoholics are promiscuous, most tend to experience various types of sexual dysfunction and difficulty with intimate relationships. Initially, alcohol is often used as a way to cope with these difficulties (Finklestein et al 1990 & Perez 1994) but eventually alcohol creates the problems it was meant to solve.

Thirdly, most female alcoholics have had a dysfunctional, abusive childhood and have experienced a loss of one or more parents either through divorce, abandonment or death (Sandmaier 1992). This chaotic childhood is often the result of having at least one alcoholic parent, usually the father (Sandmaier 1992), and a cold, domineering mother (Perez 1994). When these women grow up to form their own families, they tend to marry an alcoholic (Finklestein et al. 1990) only to face their own abandonment by these partners. These men often leave their wives either because of the alcoholic drinking or when the women decide to become abstinent (Blume 1988).

Women often begin their alcohol and drug use for a variety of reasons. As noted earlier, most women begin drinking as part of a relationship with a man. Other women start using alcohol as a coping mechanism during periods of emotional distress (Blume 1988), to self-medicate a psychological diagnosis such as depression or to alleviate premenstrual symptoms (Finklestein et al. 1990). Many drink to deal with the confusion surrounding their identity as women (Perez 1994) and to cope with the proscribed roles assigned to them in our society (Sandmaier 1992). The associated low self-esteem that follows such confusion and conflict is the predominant characteristic of alcoholic women (Perez 1994 & Finklestein et al. 1990).

Women seek treatment for alcoholism for very different reasons than men. While men are usually confronted with problems on the job or trouble with the law (as in drunk driving), women are motivated to get help when their health or the welfare of their family is at stake (Blume 1988). Nothing convinces women to get help faster than the fear that they may be harming their children. This can be a valuable piece of information for counselors and family members trying to make an intervention. While treatment staff focus their efforts on how a male alcoholic's drinking is creating negative consequences at work, women are more likely to respond when confronted with facts on how their drinking is affecting their children and partner.

Physical Factors

A number of physical factors affect the course of alcoholism in women. Although as a group, women tend to start drinking later, their need for treatment emerges at about the same age as male alcoholics (Chiauzzi 1991, Finklestein et al. 1990). The reason for this disparity is that alcohol is metabolized very differently in women. Women have lower levels of gastric acetaldehyde

(ADH) which accounts for the metabolism of up to 30% of the alcohol ingested by men (Kinney et al. 1991). As a result, less alcohol is metabolized by the stomach. Instead, the alcohol is absorbed by the body when it passes on into the small intestine, increasing the amount of alcohol circulating in the bloodstream.

In addition, women have more fat cells and less muscle tissue containing the body fluid that dilutes alcohol (Finklestein et al. 1990). Since alcohol is water soluble, less fluid means less dilution. Therefore,a woman drinking the same amount of alcohol as a man with the same body weight will become more intoxicated for a longer time (Kinney et al. 1991). For women, absorption is faster and metabolism slower, making them far more vulnerable to the effects of alcohol and the need for treatment.

Women also demonstrate greater variability in their response to alcohol due to hormonal fluctuations associated with their menstrual cycles. Research on women drinking the same amount of alcohol throughout their cycle measure higher blood alcohol levels during the premenstrual phase than at any other time of the month (Kinney et al. 1991). This can have dire consequences for the many women who start out using alcohol to medicate premenstrual symptoms (Finkelstein et al. 1990). These women are at greater risk for later addiction because of the way their bodies deal with metabolizing the alcohol at this time of their cycle.

Recovering alcoholics who have stopped drinking are also more vulnerable to relapsing right before their period for the same reasons (Kinney et al. 1991). Cravings are stronger during this time due to hormonal factors and once drinking has begun, women tend to become intoxicated faster. Finally, there is also some evidence that taking birth control pills can raise the blood alcohol level in women by affecting their metabolism of alcohol (Kinney et al. 1991).

Faster absorption, slower metabolism and higher fat to muscle ratio in women severely affects the way the woman's body can respond to the alcohol ingested. Compared to the male alcoholic, women experience more health complications in a much shorter period of time in their drinking career. Known as telescoped development, this process forces many women into treatment after fewer years of abusive drinking. They are susceptible to more of the physical consequences of late stage alcoholism earlier in their drinking career (Finkelstein et al. 1990). Women run a higher risk of developing liver disorders, cirrhosis, hypertension, anemia, malnutrition and gastrointestinal hemorrhage then men at lower levels of alcohol intake and with fewer years of drinking. For African-American and Native-American women (between 15-34 years old), the risk is 6 times and 36 times greater respectively, of developing cirrhosis in comparison to Caucasian women (Finkelstein et al. 1990).

Alcohol acts on the stomach lining by stimulating secretion of hydrochloric acid. This acid irritates the lining and inhibits the muscular contractions (peristalsis) that moves the food along the intestines. This can lead to irritation of the mucous membranes, bleeding and difficulty with absorbing nutrients. Loss of appetite, frequent belching, diarrhea, constipation, nausea, vomiting and a higher risk for cancer can also occur (Kinney et al. 1991). Female alcoholics die 2.7 to 7 times faster than non-alcoholic women from the numerous complications associated with the body's response to abusive drinking (Finkelstein et al 1990).

Alcoholic women have more infertility, miscarriages and still births than women who do not drink alcohol. Alcohol depresses the hormones and adrenal gland levels which causes a loss of sexual arousal, lack of interest in sex, and interference with the rapidity and intensity of orgasm. Women in one study reported that although they expected greater desire and enjoyment of sex when drinking (Blume 1988), they found they experienced less. Contrary to the myth that women are more sexual when drinking, researchers found that alcohol abuse produces depression, low self-esteem and conflicts in relationships that work to disrupt sexual functioning not increase it (Finklestein et al. 1990).

Social Factors

Studies indicate that the rules society expects women to follow make them vulnerable to using alcohol (and drugs) to cope (Sandmaier 1992). Instead of protecting women, the role of wife and mother is an incredible burden that forces many to turn to chemicals for relief. This relief is short-lived, however. When the line is crossed to abusive drinking, women are attacked for not fulfilling their roles properly. Female alcoholics are automatically stigmatized as sluts and bad mothers. It is considered part of the diagnosis.

Although there is little evidence that women alcoholics are promiscuous, the myth is a strong one. It is reinforced by the small number of women who use sex to hang onto a relationship or as a way to obtain alcohol and drugs. Far from becoming more sexual, the truth is that alcohol creates a variety of sexual problems including a decrease in desire. For the vast majority of women, alcohol is actually used to deal with pre-existing sexual problems or to help cope with the anxiety around being sexual (Covington 1991).

According to society's standards of what is appropriate female behavior, women do not have permission to be sexual unless they have been drinking. This permission however, does not exempt them from any responsibility. When some women use alcohol in order to be sexual, it perpetuates the belief that all women are consenting to sex when they drink. This belief that sex is mixed with alcohol every time is so widespread in our society that it sets women up to be victims of physical and sexual abuse as opposed to consenting sexual partners.

Men exposed to these myths believe a woman is agreeing to have sex with them once she agrees to a drink. It is not considered taking advantage of a woman when she is drunk because society has already dictated that drunk women want to be sexual. Alcohol provides an excellent excuse for those men who want to act inappropriately and get away with it. They are not held accountable for raping or sexually abusing a woman. For men whose inhibitions are lowered by the effects of alcohol, they may simply be acting in ways they would never act when sober. Because the myth that sex naturally follows alcohol is so ingrained, society offers forgiveness for these men when they are so impaired. It is considered inevitable. Society does not however, offer the same excuse for women.

Women are victims of these myths once they begin to drink. Alcohol does not offer women the same alibi as it does men. Society views women drinkers as asking to be raped and sexual abused because they agreed to drink and therefore agreed to be available for sex and sexual abuse. Whether women realize it or not, their dates have assumed that the decision to drink with them includes being sexual with them. In addition, drinking impairs women's ability to protect themselves, lowers their inhibitions, impairs their judgement and encourages them to socialize with people in drinking situations that are not safe. While her risk factors go up with every drink she consumes, his go down.

Alcoholism severely damages the woman's reputation as a mother as well. While a man's job may suffer because of his drinking, a woman's child may suffer when she is too drunk to do her job. In our society, it is women who are solely responsible for their children's welfare. It is therefore, women who fail and are blamed when they become too sick to parent. Although children are deeply affected by either parent's drinking, men are seldom held accountable and tend to experience less guilt and shame over its impact on them. Women, on the other hand, have difficulty forgiving themselves (as society does) and tend to view their alcoholism, not as a disease, but as a failure in their responsibilities to their children (Finklestein et al. 1990).

Women in their roles of wives tend to take care of, and ultimately slow down, the damaging consequences of the disease in their alcoholic husbands. They will call work for him, make meals for him, watch over his health, dress him in clean clothes, make sure he looks presentable, and cover for him with family and friends. Men on the other hand, often abandon their alcoholic wives or continue to enable the women's drinking in order to cover their own alcoholic behavior. Men, as a group, do not make sure their drinking wives eat regularly, have adequate childcare when they are drunk, or get to the doctor when they are ill. For those women who primarily work in the home, the course of the disease can be kept hidden for a much longer time. There are more places to hide the bottles, more opportunities to drink alone and fewer people to see the aftermath of the drinking.

Homemakers are able to maintain a steady blood alcohol level because of their tendency toward maintenance drinking (Sandmaier 1992). Maintenance drinking is drinking smaller amounts throughout the day rather than large quantities in a short period of time. This allows these women to continue functioning at a fairly normal level (due to the body's ability to adapt) and making it more difficult for family members to recognize the addiction until it progresses to the later stages.   Women who work in the home are also more likely than their employed counterparts to abuse prescription drugs because of the convenience of being alone. There is no one available to monitor behavior or evaluate work performance (Sandmaier 1992).

Women who practice maintenance drinking make it harder for their husbands to detect a problem. Many work-at-home mothers avoid detection by waiting to drink alone after their children are dropped off at school or have gone to bed (Blume 1988). This isolation decreases their chances for an intervention. Job problems, suspicions by boss or coworkers and trouble with the law as in drunk driving arrests are more prevalent for male alcoholics. These problems attract attention from those in a position to help. Women are not exposed to the large number of people associated with employment. Bosses, co-workers or other employees may become suspicious of alcoholic behavior in their male employee but homemakers usually answer only to themselves, their children and their husbands.

Family members often have a lot invested in covering up for their mothers, wives and daughters' drinking because of the stigma associated with being a woman alcoholic. Children are often in a position to know there is a problem but lack the power to confront what is happening. In alcoholic families, members rarely talk outside the home let alone to each other about what is going on. And if they do, they are often not believed. This is particularly true if the children are young and don't have the language or credibility to describe what is going on.

As a child of an alcoholic mother described it;

> I would wait after school with my younger brother for my mother to pick us up. When she didn't show up, we would walk home only to find her drinking in her bedroom. My father never believed me when I told him what happened. My brother just wouldn't talk about it. When my Dad finally did realize what was happening, he took to picking us up himself. But he never confronted her or explained why he was doing the driving now. We just never discussed it.

Wives and mothers who work outside the home often face the same wall of denial from family members as their at-home counterparts. Their income may be critical to the family's welfare, making it too threatening to confront the behavior. This is especially true for children in the homes of divorced and single parents. They have fewer resources, no one else at home to make an intervention and a great deal of fear around further loss. Women working low-paying jobs deal with financial insecurity, boredom and frustration. The stress of trying to make ends meet in supporting themselves and their children can be overwhelming. When these women turn to alcohol as a way to cope with stress, their co-workers, bosses and employees may associate the accompanying erratic behavior as a result of this stress and not associate it with the drinking.

For those struggling with careers, many find themselves dealing with situations that offer drinking as a way to belong.   This is especially true if the work environment is a hostile one. Studies indicate that women in some male dominated jobs may be particularly vulnerable to heavy drinking and alcohol problems.   Wives and mothers in the work force are more than twice as likely as single working women to have drinking problems (Sandmaier 1992).   Exhaustion from working two jobs and guilt about abandoning their children can increase relationship conflicts and sexual problems.   Many women facing this kind of stress in their families turn to alcohol for the solution (Finklestein et al. 1990).

Female alcoholics avoid detection and therefore access to help in one other way.   Because women addicted to alcohol tend to experience anxiety and depression and lower self-esteem, when they do attract attention, it is for a referral to the mental health field instead of an intervention for alcoholism (Blume 1988).   Doctors and counselors exposed to the same stereotypes as the general public face their own denial system when confronted with the alcoholic woman.   They tend to focus more on the presenting emotional symptoms rather than the underlying cause.

Economic Factors

Society's lack of tolerance, acceptance and understanding of the nature of alcoholism in women restricts access to proper treatment by not providing appropriate childcare, a nurturing support system or financial assistance.   Women typically earn less money and have fewer opportunities for education and on-the-job training. As a group, they tend to work minimum wage jobs and do not benefit from adequate insurance coverage or Employee Assistance Programs (Finklestein et al. 1990).   They cannot afford the huge costs of a 28-day treatment program, counseling appointments or medical care. Women's financial restrictions not only prevent them from getting the help they need, it prevents them from paying for the childcare needed while they are gone.   Women must remain with their children instead of obtaining the necessary treatment that would allow them to become better mothers.

Treatment for alcoholism is expensive.   Child care is expensive. Without the support of the children's father or other family members, mothers are often hard-pressed when faced with a costly bill for treatment and the impossibility of leaving their children for any length of time.   Many alcoholic women come from alcoholic homes themselves so family members are often not considered an option (Finklestein et al. 1990).   Frequently divorced by the time they reach the later stages of the disease, women often have few options for a safe place to leave their children. Others, fear losing their children permanently if the father or other relatives view a diagnosis of alcoholism as an opportunity to sue for custody.

Treatment centers co-sign these belief systems when they do not provide childcare as part of the program, do not schedule outpatient programs around children's and work schedules or provide space for children to live with their mothers while she is in an inpatient program.   While male alcoholics leave their children with their mothers, most women lacking the father's physical support forfeit help rather than abandon their children.

Another option for these women is to take advantage of the no-cost 12-step programs. However, for full-time workers time to go is difficult to arrange especially if they have children. Without financial support to pay for child care, many women have been forced to bring their children to meetings. Unfortunately, a woman entering a meeting with one or more children is not always greeted with enthusiasm as children can be very disruptive to the group. Often, women are criticized and reprimanded for not finding child care. Sometimes they are fortunate to be told secretly by other women in the group which "women's meeting" will be more sympathetic and understanding.

Cultural Factors

Cultural factors influence the course and treatment of the disease as well. Minority women are not only stigmatized for being female alcoholics but face racism associated with their ethnic background. Economic issues are even more pronounced. Women of other nationalities are at the bottom of the pecking order when it comes to access to education, safe childcare, adequate health care, housing and job opportunities (Sandmaier 1992). With fewer resources, there is a higher rate of maternal mortality, less prenatal care and fewer available preventive services. Latino women are less likely to drink than African-American women who are less likely to drink than Caucasian (Sandmaier 1992). However when they do, the consequences seem to be much greater.

Physically, minority women seem to be at tremendous risk to the effects of their addiction. One study of 700 women in a ten year period showed that 36% of Caucasian women and 71% non-Caucasian women died of alcoholism (Sandmaier 1992). A report on Native Americans from the National Center for Health Statistics found that women account for almost half the total deaths from liver cirrhosis. In contrast, about one third of the deaths from cirrhosis in the African-American and Caucasian populations are women (Sandmaier 1992). Native American women are also more likely to die at a younger age; at nine times the rate between the ages of 35-54 and 37 times the rate of Caucasian women between the ages of 15-34 (Sandmaier 1992). In Latino women, 8% used alcohol heavily compared to 4% of African-American women and 9% of Caucasian women (Sandmaier 1992).

Self-esteem is even lower for these women who struggle to survive in a society that judges them harshly on two accounts; for being women and for being minority women. Low self-esteem is the predominant characteristic of alcoholic women. At first, alcohol and drugs offer some relief from the economic and physical hardship of being single parents, oppressed and women.   In the end, it keeps women trapped.

Psychological Factors

A woman's primary source for self-esteem comes from her role as wife and mother. From an evolutionary perspective, a woman's need to be in relationships makes sense. It ensures the survival of the next generation and consequently our species. If this attachment was not such a basic need, women would not be so committed to the well-being of their children even to the point of making great sacrifices for them. Society reinforces women's biological tendencies by granting greater responsibility to them for their sexuality and their children.

The stigma associated with alcoholism of being promiscuous and a bad mother sets women up in a spiral of negativity that corrodes their identity. The predominant trait in alcoholic women is low self-esteem (Finklestein et al. 1990). This low self-esteem is reinforced by a society that insists that alcoholic women have failed their proscribed roles. It does not perceive these women as being sick and in need of treatment.

Self-esteem is severely damaged when women have difficulty forming relationships. This difficulty is exacerbated when these women form relationships with male alcoholics. It may have been the way they were introduced to the alcohol and drugs in the first place. If they do not drink with their partners or attempt to stop drinking with them, they risk abandonment.

Unlike a man whose primary source for self-esteem is through his job, a woman's self-esteem is derived from her attachments to relationships with partners and children. While men will often go into treatment when their job is threatened, women tend to go for help when their marriages or children are jeopardized. Unless to do so would put the marriage or children at greater risk. This can lead to a common catch-22 for alcoholic women in two ways; abandonment by husbands because of their drinking and abandonment by alcoholic husbands because of their decision to stop drinking.

Most women stay with their alcoholic husbands. They offer financial and emotional support, seek out medical help for them and cover for them at work. They will protect them in front of friends, family and the children. If their husbands decide to quit drinking, wives will watch the children while they go to meetings, take over responsibilities for them while in treatment and often take on a second job to provide financial assistance. Husbands, in general, are not as supportive of their drinking wives. There is little sympathy for the female "drunk", who is often abandoned by her husband, family and community and forced to seek treatment alone. In addition, the woman faces the risk of losing her children if she is diagnosed with alcoholism because it is synonymous with being unfit mother (especially when considering leaving her children to go into treatment).

For the female alcoholic married to another alcoholic, the threat of abandonment comes from her decision to stop drinking. The man's denial system may prevent him from recognizing the extent of her addiction both because she often drinks less than he does (Blume 1988) and because it threatens to uncover his own drinking problem. Confronting his wife's drinking would force him to reveal his own problem with alcohol. Wives who choose sobriety on their own frequently jeopardize their marriage to husbands who may not want clean and sober wives. Women often get sober when their husbands do. If they try to do so without him it may mean a "choice" between sobriety and her marriage. Many women will do anything to keep the marriage (Finklestein et al. 1990).

Familial Factors

Research supports that alcoholic women have more dysfunctional childhoods than male alcoholics. Studies show that up to 50% of female alcoholics come from homes where one (more often the father) or both parents are alcoholics. An alcoholic home can include separation, divorce, death, emotional inaccessibility of parents, inconsistent parenting, incest and family violence. This is particularly traumatic for women whose development depends on an ability to form relationships. As a result, women tend to be more effected by a parent's drinking than men are and more likely to have a deeper attachment to the alcoholic. For the most part, the alcoholic is the father whom the daughter gravitates toward and emulates.

Female alcoholics frequently report that their mothers had more physical and psychological problems, were emotionally unavailable and difficult to connect with. In contrast, alcoholic fathers are often able to be more affectionate. This increases the likelihood that their daughters will grow up in search of a relationship with a man who drinks just like her father. Unable to understand the dynamics behind the alcoholic marriage, daughters had a tendency to misinterpret their mothers angry, bossy and negative attitudes toward the fathers and themselves (Sandmaier 1992).

Sexual Orientation

Lesbian women tend to abuse alcohol and to use prescription drugs more than any other group (Sandmaier 1992). A study done by Marcelle T. Saghir found that 35% of lesbians had drinking problems compared with 28% of homosexual men and 5% of heterosexual women. Faced with homophobia in addition to the second class status of being a woman, lesbian women must find safe, alternative ways to meet other women. The gay bar functions as a place to meet friends, find potential partners, and to socialize. It creates a safe haven while at the same time, encouraging drinking. This haven provides relief from the oppression felt by women whose sexual preference gets them fired from their jobs, expelled from schools, thrown out of their homes, and threatens their custody of their own children.

The fear and hate society feels for lesbians threatens women's self-esteem, their economic security, ability to form relationships, connection to their children and access to treatment. Homophobia in our society affects alcoholism programs by creating yet another obstacle to a woman's ability to afford treatment, find appropriate childcare, and help for the specific issues that led to and exacerbate her alcohol abuse.

3

The Female Alcoholic
and Chemical Dependency

Multiple Drug User

The days have gone when alcoholism meant abusing alcohol exclusively. Treatment centers are seeing a growing number of female alcoholics dependent on other chemicals (Blume 1988). Many of these women are abusing prescription drugs. Research shows that, in comparison to women holding jobs outside the home, women working in the home are more likely to abuse drugs than alcohol (Sandmaier 1992). These women tend to be over 30 and are more likely to use prescription drugs (Finklestein et al. 1990).

The most popular "drugs of choice" accessible through the medical field are minor tranquilizers, barbiturates, diet pills (amphetamines), controlled narcotics and antidepressants (Sandmaier 1992). Mixing these medications with alcohol further exacerbates the effects of alcoholism on women (Blume 1988).

In contrast, other studies reveal that abuse of illegal substances is fast becoming a major problem for women between the ages of 18 and 34 regardless of their occupation. In the United States, one in four drug abusers is a woman (Finklestein et al. 1990). The most popular illicit "drugs of choice" are stimulants such as cocaine and crack, opiates such as heroin and morphine, and marijuana or hashish. The most startling increase in drug use for women is heroin and marijuana. Heroin use in women is excelling at a rate greater than men and women's use of marijuana has reached the same level as men (Finklestein et al. 1990).

The National Institute on Drug Abuse (NIDA) found that 70% of African American women, 65% of Latino women and 35% of Caucasian women abused opiates. While African American women were more likely to use heroin, they also used marijuana and cocaine. Caucasian women, on the other hand were more likely to use prescription drugs in addition to some heroin use (Finklestein et al. 1990). African American women tend to use at older ages than Caucasian women, use depressants rather than stimulants and use fewer types of drugs (Finklestein et al. 1990).

Prescription Drug Abuse

It is estimated that about 2 to 4 million women are addicted to legal drugs obtained by a prescription from a licensed physician (Finklestein et al. 1990). Women become addicted to these medications in a number of ways. Many receive a prescription for another physical or emotional condition that is believed to require drug treatment. Others, seek out medical help for the symptoms of alcoholism that their denial system convinces them is unrelated to their drinking. Finally, newly sober women are vulnerable to prescription drug addiction when they seek out medical alternatives for withdrawal and other physical symptoms associated with early recovery. Even recovering alcoholics who are sober for years are susceptible to cross addiction to such drugs as Librium, Valium and Xanex. These drugs have a similar pharmacology to alcohol and when prescribed can set up the recovering alcoholic to become addicted to a new "drug of choice" or act as a pathway toward relapsing back to alcohol (Blume 1988).

In our society, it has become acceptable if not an expectation to treat most problems, especially emotional ones, with drugs. Doctors are under enormous pressure to take some kind of action whenever a patient comes in with a complaint. This pressure often comes in the form of the patient demanding relief from pain. The expectation of most patients is that tests will be done, a diagnosis made and medication prescribed. An example of this belief is evident in the thousands of dollars spent each year on cold remedies that are relatively useless (Schmitt 1991), all in an attempt to feel better.

Women, in general, are more vulnerable to abusing prescription drugs because of their greater socialization to visit doctors and take medication rather than tough it out as men are expected to do. This expectation stereotypes women as weak and fragile. Since this stereotype lends itself to view women as having more emotional problems that are in need of medical help, they are often the ones exposed to such interventions (Blume 1988). Women are given antidepressants, tranquilizers, barbiturates and amphetamines two times more often than men (Blume 1988, Finklestein et al. 1990). Even if the complaint is physical, the medical field's adherence to the stereotype of women being weak and emotional increases the likelihood that she will receive some type of drug treatment. In addition, many of these women find that they can continue to get prescriptions from other doctors long after their original complaint and treating physician is gone.

An example of this dynamic was given by one husband who described how his wife started taking pain medication after back surgery and was able to continue getting pills long after the original problem subsided;

> I got a phone call one night from the police saying they had just arrested my wife for writing a fraudulent prescription. All I knew was that she was having back pain and had gone down to the drug store to get her prescription filled. I had no idea the number of

doctors she had seen over the years to get prescriptions. When that stopped working, she stole a prescription pad and began writing her own. She had also taken money from our savings account so I wouldn't know how much she was spending on drugs. I had no idea how much she was taking or how dependent on the pain medication she had become until I got that phone call.

Many women become addicted unexpectedly when they seek out treatment for a legitimate physical or emotional complain. Running up against the stereotype of women and society's expectation that medication is the preferred course of treatment, these women take the prescription on faith only to find themselves craving it later on. The woman alcoholic coming in to complain about problems associated with her drinking benefit from this stereotype in that it is easier for them to get the prescription. Lack of knowledge about addictions coupled with the physician's own denial system prevent many from recognizing a patient's alcoholism. The assumption is that the anxiety, depression or insomnia must be an indication of mental illness.

A referral is usually given for psychiatric help where, again, medication is frequently administered (Finklestein et al. 1990). Physicians see alcoholism as a man's disease. When the complaints are coming from a female patient, doctors are more likely to believe the stereotype that the woman is experiencing emotional problems. This stereotype is supported when medical staff dispense medication for the woman's symptoms instead of doing an intervention for addiction (Blume 1988).

Finally, the pharmacological similarities between some of these drugs and alcohol allow many women to substitute prescription drugs in their attempts to abstain from drinking (Blume 1988). Rather than confronting their addiction to alcohol, women medicate their withdrawal symptoms and cravings with doctor-approved chemicals. However, cross-addiction to these drugs prevents women from actually achieving sobriety. Most female alcoholics do not need medications to help with the symptoms of withdrawal. Anxiety, sleeplessness and depression are a normal part of early recovery (Blume 1988, Finklestein et al. 1990). Those that do use such drugs may become just as addicted to them as they were to the alcohol (Finklestein et al. 1990). This vulnerability to cross-addiction to other drugs remains throughout recovery.

Medical Factors

The medical and mental health field prescribe drugs to female alcoholics for a variety of reasons. As noted earlier, society believes in the stereotype that women suffer from emotional problems and that these disorders warrant medication. In addition, drugs are prescribed because alcoholism can be notoriously difficult to diagnose. The symptoms of alcoholism can be easily confused with other mental illnesses. It is often impossible to tell if the woman's depression is a coexisting disease, a symptom of abusing a depressant such as alcohol, or the original diagnosis that the woman is self-medicating with alcohol for relief (Blume 1988).

Physicians often lack adequate training in addictions and therefore are not very knowledgeable about the symptoms of alcoholism or the different stages of the disease (Wholey 1984). Society's denial that alcoholism can affect both genders prevent many physicians from recognizing that their female patients may be suffering from an addiction. In addition, the denial systems of the physicians may be influenced by their own drinking patterns or alcoholism in their families (Blume 1988). It is believed that the rate of alcoholism for people in the medical field is 35 times higher than that of the general population (Wholey 1984).

Furthermore, alcoholism is a difficult diagnosis to make and treat. It is complicated by the fact that every alcoholic is different and comes into the system at various points in the progression of their disease. Many patients strongly deny their symptoms, their drinking and their consequences making it impossible at times for physicians to get enough facts to determine the nature of the problem. Furthermore, even when a diagnosis is made, scores of alcoholics refuse treatment. Those that do enter treatment often fail to abstain. Others may relapse numerous times, sometimes for years. These factors make alcoholism a very unpopular and frustrating illness to treat.

Finally, alcoholic women in denial about their own drinking welcome a prescription for medication rather than face the truth. The doctor reinforces the denial by appearing to deal with the emotional issues that both doctor and patient agree are unrelated to alcoholism. The medication the doctor prescribes can be taken without guilt because it is not an illegal drug. The process of administering medication for a variety of emotional problems confirms for the woman that she does not have a problem with alcohol or an addiction but a legitimate illness. For the most part, a woman would rather be ill than diagnosed an alcoholic. Once the symptoms are explained as another illness, the woman's drinking can now continue undisturbed albeit exacerbated by the additional drugs she is taking. Or she can substitute the prescription drugs for alcohol and believe the illusion that she has solved her drinking problem.

Prescription Drugs

The most frequently abused prescription drugs are the minor tranquilizers, barbiturates, sedative-hypnotics, nonbarbiturates), antidepressants and amphetamines (Finklestein et al. 1990). The minor tranquilizers include Valium, Librium Serax, Equanil, Miltown and Xanax. Valium is one of the most popular drugs prescribed to women. It is often given for the emotional problems associated with alcoholism. These drugs serve to relieve anxiety and are frequently prescribed as muscle relaxants. Many female alcoholics substitute these drugs for alcohol because of the strong potential for cross-addiction.

Barbiturates such as Amytal, Butisol, Nembutal and Seconal are used to treat insomnia and anxiety. They are extremely addictive and can be deadly when mixed with alcohol. Quaaludes, Dalmane, Doriden, Noludar are the most commonly prescribed sedative-hypnotics for inducing sleep and carry the same addictive potential as barbiturates. Examples of amphetamines include Benzedrine, Dexedrine, Preludin and Ritalin. These drugs are prescribed as appetite suppressants to women who want to control their weight.

Although the antidepressants, Sinequan, Tofranil, Elavil, Norpramine, Pertofrane and Aventyl are not considered physically addictive, they can have adverse effects if mixed with alcohol. They have the potential to increase the level of intoxication if taken with alcohol and can create a life-threatening condition if mixed with red wine (Finklestein et al. 1990). Other side effects include confusion, delirium, reduction in central nervous system functioning and hypertension (elevated blood pressure).

All of the above drugs have the potential to be life-threatening when mixed with alcohol because of the synergistic qualities of such chemicals. Synergy means that the combination of, for example, a minor tranquilizer like Valium and a glass of wine is more than double the effect of either substance alone. "Alcohol potentiates the effects of these drugs such that even small combinations of alcohol with low doses of medication causes a chemical interaction that can lead to serious and even fatal outcomes" (Finklestein et al. 1990, p. 117).

In addition, women are vulnerable to overdosing on these medications because alcoholics develop a tolerance level for drugs that are pharmacologically and chemically similar to alcohol. Known as cross-tolerance, the female alcoholic is immediately able to cope with higher doses of the medication and often needs more of the drug to produce the same effect. As a result, the woman becomes dependent on higher levels of medication and a belief system that tells her that she is capable of handling such doses. A situation that can be fatal if she takes the higher dose after a period of sobriety (when the body's tolerance level for alcohol has decreased).

Suzanne's Story

After the delivery of her second child, Suzanne needed back surgery. At that time, she was given Vicodin for the pain. It offered immediate relief and Suzanne became quite vocal in insisting her doctor continue to prescribe it long after he thought she should have needed it. What Suzanne found was that she was in constant pain unless she was on the medication. She eventually began to use more than was prescribed. Over the years, she accrued several doctors who agreed to give her Vicodin whenever she suffered from other ailments or injuries. Her husband became concerned at the number of accidents she was having but attributed it to her inability to balance herself as she gained additional weight.

Eventually, Suzanne became desperate as it became more difficult to convince the doctors that she had a real need. One day, when leaving a doctor's office, she stole his prescription pad. Later that evening at the pharmacy, she was caught trying to fill a phony prescription. At that point, she entered into a treatment center for alcohol and drug addiction. She successfully completed the program and remained abstinent for a little over a year. Some time after celebrating her first AA birthday, she injured her arm. Suzanne made sure she told the treating doctor that she was a recovering addict.

Once again, she was given a prescription for Vicodin to help with the pain. Confident that she had her addiction under control and that the doctor wouldn't give her pain pills unless he thought the same, she took the medication. The cycle began again. She found herself asking for pain medication for an ear infection, her twisted ankle and finally, when she got bronchitis. This time her husband found the bottle of pills in her bathrobe pocket. He had become suspicious when he saw her resorting to lying, sneaking and manipulating doctors again into giving her more and more pain medication.

After her husband confronted her, Suzanne began the road to abstinence again. However, she continued to have difficulty with the relative ease doctors had in their willingness to prescribe medication even when she told them she was an addict. To protect herself, she asked her husband or trusted friend to accompany her to the doctor's office in order to help her say No and insist on alternatives to drug treatment for her physical ailments.

Women's Introduction to Illegal Drugs

Although many women are introduced to drugs through the medical and mental health field, women are primarily exposed to illegal drugs through a relationship (Blume 1988). While it is somewhat acceptable for men to use illegal substances, women usually rely on male contacts to obtain heroin and cocaine.

A study done by the Women's Drug Research Project found that one third of the African-American men and one fourth of Caucasian men were living with women who were not abusing illicit drugs. Only 15% of African-American women and 7% of Caucasian women were living with men who did not abuse illegal drugs (Finklestein et al. 1990).

Ironically, women begin using drugs as a way to connect with their partners only to discover, as the disease progresses, that it destroys their capacity to maintain these relationships. The lives of these women become more disrupted as the disease and the ramifications of surviving in a drug environment take its toll. For mothers, drug addiction threatens their ability to care and retain custody of their children.

According to the authors of *Getting Sober, Getting Well*;

> An alcoholic woman who uses illicit drugs may be doing so to mask her alcoholism, to manage it, to substitute for alcohol or because she is dually addicted. For many addicted women, alcohol and illicit drugs are used in a variety of patterns with one drug being the 'drug of choice' at any given time. A woman many drink to 'dull' the edginess caused by cocaine. She may smoke marijuana when alcohol is unavailable. She may drink alcohol or smoke marijuana when cocaine is too expensive or otherwise undesirable. She may use different drugs at different times: cocaine and stimulants to feel 'up', alcohol and marijuana to mellow out and relax. A woman may quickly develop cross-tolerance and cross-dependence so that even if she never drank alcoholically while she was using opiates, for example, should she cease them and turn to alcohol, she will develop a dependency and tolerance for alcohol (Finklestein et al. 1990, p. 300).

The Drug World

The drug environment has certain characteristics that become part of the female addict's world. Deception, danger, secretness, fear, and an obsession around obtaining her supply dominate the woman's reality. Experts believe these factors force the progression of the disease to accelerate in women who abuse drugs. Female addicts in the early stage of the disease frequently display behaviors common to the middle stages of alcoholism because the substances are not legally available (Finklestein et al. 1990).

The drug world is not a safe place for women (or for men, for that matter). Drugs can be cut with a number of toxic substances (Finklestein et al. 1990) and violence is rampant. The possibility of drug overdose from mixing a variety of drugs with alcohol and the exposure to AIDS or other sexually (or intravenously) transmitted diseases is extremely high. The life of an addict in this world is one ruled by danger, fear and a concern for obtaining the needed drugs. Women often make decisions based on their need for drugs instead of their own or their children's well-being. Decisions that frequently lead to an exposure to abuse, disease, prostitution, and an inability to care for children or themselves. When reality revolves around shooting heroin, everything else is inconsequential. Her job, children, partner, basic needs or the safety and well-being of the woman's own body are far lower priorities.

An addict's world changes when drugs and alcohol become a problem (Evans 1990). Friends who complain about the addict's drinking or using (or do not use themselves) are dropped for those who support the use of drugs and alcohol. Social functions that do not include alcohol and drugs are avoided in favor of those that do and often the addict will drink or use prior to the event. The value system of the addict is compromised as she begins to act out in ways never seen before. This includes acting out sexually, lying, hiding, sneaking, stealing, driving while intoxicated, driving recklessly, and selling drugs.

Family problems in the drug world include an increase in conflict between the spouses and other family members, neglect and abuse of children, sexual dysfunction and financial problems. Avoiding contact with family members, especially those that confront the addiction become a way of life for the addict. One heroin addict describes how she has to live a double life. "I tell my mom I'm clean because that's what she wants to hear. But the truth is, I shoot up every chance I get."

Women also experience more physical illness due to the harsh conditions of the drug world. They are far more likely to be victims of physical and sexual abuse, malnutrition, and lack of good medical care. Poverty and the ravages of the drug abuse on the human body takes its toll on the female addict as well. These women suffer from depression, anxiety, sleep disturbances, malnutrition, hypertension, gastritis, ulcers, heart disease, intestinal difficulties, emphysema, diabetes or hyperglycemia, and hepatitis (Evans 1990).

If the woman works outside the home, she will often hoard her money to pay for her supply. The heroin addict mentioned earlier felt an incredible amount of shame over taking money that her children needed for clothes to pay for drugs . "I feel I've spent thousands of dollars on heroin. Money that should have gone to my kids. Now I don't think I can spend a dime on treatment because its money that belongs to them. My husband tells me that all the time. Of course, he doesn't want me to stop using 'cause that means he has no one to get his dope for him. No one to blame for his using."

Drug addicts have a tendency to get into conflicts with their co-workers and have inconsistent work patterns. Medical problems, use of sick time, Monday and/or Friday tardiness or absenteeism and over sensitivity to feedback by a supervisor are other indicators that the woman's drug addiction is progressing (Evans 1990).

Finally, the greatest damage the drug world has on the female addict is the prevalence of AIDS. Unprotected sex and intervenous drug use exposes women to the HIV virus at a far greater rate than women in the general population. Women are more vulnerable to the transmission of this virus in much the same way as they are for most sexually transmitted diseases. However, children of these women are at an even greater risk for exposure to the HIV virus than any other disease.

> The majority of women with AIDS are drugs abusers or the sexual partners of drug abusers. Nearly 75% of AIDS cases in women are associated with intravenous drug abuse. Over 80% of children who contract AIDS are born to drug abusing mothers or mothers who have had sexual partners involved in drug abuse (Finklestein et al. 1990, p. 302).

Although it would be impossible to discuss every drug, or drug combination, an overview of the more popular ones follows. Women use of heroin, cocaine and marijuana is increasing. Therefore, some information about these drugs would be helpful in understanding the dynamics of addiction in women.

Heroin Addiction

As noted earlier, heroin use by women (of color in particular) is continuing to rise. The death rate from heroin addiction is also increasing. "The health risks to a woman who is heroin addicted and to her children not only involve the drugs themselves, but the lifestyle and dangers of the drug subculture in which heroin exists" (Finklestein et al. 1990, p.304). Poor hygiene, lack of good medical care, bad nutrition and the effects of the drug on the body can have devastating consequences for the woman. So can living in the drug world itself. Many women are forced to trade sex to support their habit. Street life and prostitution increase the risk of infections, sexually transmitted diseases, AIDS and physical and sexual abuse. Heroin addicted women are frequently unable to care for their children. Infants born to these women have a much higher death rate than infants born to non-addicts.

Women who use heroin have extremely low self-esteem. Society views them as the worst possible drug addict. As with alcoholism, women heroin addicts are judged more harshly than their male counterparts. As a result, they are frequent victims of abuse, prejudice and ostracized from family and friends. They are reluctant to ask for help and will often lie about the heroin use while focusing on their drinking or other drugs they abuse. One heroin addict described the hierarchy of drugs in the world when she explained that "even among addicts, heroin is considered the drug at the bottom of the heap".

Jenny's Story

Jenny had been using heroin since she was a teenager. Now at forty, she looked ten years older than her age, and felt a great deal of shame that she was still hooked. She believed heroin was a drug for the young and she should have been able to "kick it by now". Currently on a methadone treatment plan, she still craved the heroin and sometimes used it in addition to her dose of methadone. She felt she could not tell her husband that she was on methadone because she used the heroin with him. She could not tell the treatment center about the heroin or they would stop giving her the methadone. She knew her mother would be horrified to find out she used heroin so she did not tell her the truth either.

Her greatest shame, though was that she has tried to hide her addiction from her children and was not sure she had been successful. She described her life as one huge lie. Her energy was spent on keeping track of who knew what and on how to get what drug. "Heroin is the drug for the lowest class of drug addict. You don't brag about it to no one."

Cocaine Addiction

Unlike the negative vision society has of heroin, cocaine has been seen as the "drug of choice" for the affluent and upper class. Female addicts are frequently introduced to cocaine through relationships with men and at an earlier age than for other drugs. Women addicted to cocaine however, often also turn to prostitution when there is no other means to support their habit (Finklestein et al. 1990). As with heroin, infants are at risk for spontaneous abortions, stillborns and fetal death at a greater rate than the general population (Finklestein et al. 1990).   "Fetal cocaine syndrome has been identified in babies of cocaine abusing women. The signs include congenital abnormalities, minor strokes, visual problems, erratic and unresponsive behavior" (Finklestein et al. 1990, p. 307).

Since most women do not use cocaine exclusively, the life of the mother and infant is in jeopardy from mixing alcohol with other drugs. Many use prescription drugs to deal with the insomnia, depression, paranoia, agitation, irritability that comes from using cocaine.

> Moreover, cocaine abusing women may not only be abusing alcohol but also heroin or prescription opiates. Some intervenous drug using women may do 'speed balls', injecting combinations of heroin and cocaine, a potentially fatal mix. Dual or triple physical dependence on alcohol, cocaine and heroin presents a serious threat due to complications and severity of withdrawal" (Finklestein et al. 1990, p. 308).

Cocaine can be taken intranasally, injected intravenously, or smoked freebase in the form of crack. Crack has made the drug more affordable, and therefore, more available to the general public. It is also more addictive than cocaine in other forms (Finklestein et al. 1990).

Marijuana Addiction

Marijuana is often viewed as a harmless recreational drug much in the same way as alcohol. In fact, marijuana is an addictive drug with identifiable symptoms of withdrawal. Weeks after women have stopped using it, they may experience sleeplessness, irritability, appetite changes and a persistent craving for the drug. Many women who begin by using marijuana and alcohol eventually end up using other drugs.

> Ninety percent of young adults who reported using cocaine, hallucinogens and other drugs reported first using marijuana on a regular basis. Marijuana may be a substitute or

secondary drug of abuse and is not usually described as the 'drug of choice' (Finklestein et al. 1990, p. 310).

Marijuana addiction leads to mental confusion, inability to concentrate, poor attention span and difficulties with memory. As the addiction progresses, there may be paranoia, suicidal and self-destructive behavior. Marijuana irritates the lungs, depresses the immune system, interferes with cognitive functioning and increases heart rate. In women, marijuana can cause irregular ovulation and lead to difficulties with reproduction. It can affect the regularity of menstrual cycles and travels through the placenta causing complications in pregnancy (Finklestein et al. 1990).

The most common complaint about marijuana however, is its ability to take away the addict's motivation to do anything else in her life. One smoker described her life as a nothing. She did not feel like going to work, taking care of her children or going out of the house. She just wanted to sit, smoke and "veg". Eventually, it led to using other drugs.

Rachel's Story

Rachel began drinking alcohol and using marijuana when she was an adolescent. She quickly graduated to doing speed intravenously (needles) with her husband and continued to do so throughout her pregnancy. When her son was born prematurely, the doctors gave him less then twenty-four hours to live. The baby was withdrawing from speed and alcohol and fighting for his life on severely undeveloped lungs. Somehow he survived the first night and it began to look like he would make it.

Rachel felt guilty about her drug use and what it was doing to her son. She made all kinds of promises to God to stop the "junk" if her son lived. Her son did but she did not keep her promise. As soon as he came home from the hospital, the stress of being a single parent (while her husband served a drug-related sentence in prison) was more than she could handle. Soon she was back on alcohol and drugs. In addition, she frequently gave her baby alcohol to subdue him.

By the time he was a toddler, the boy was known to sip his parents and their friends' beers. They thought it was adorable when he stumbled around obviously inebriated. Rachel had forgotten all about her promises to God or the terror of almost losing her son to drugs and alcohol. She thought it normal that he sought out her drinks. It never occurred to her that she might be helping him become addicted in the same way she was.

Part 2:

Women, Alcoholism and Relationships

4

The Female Alcoholic
in Relationships

The Codependency Controversy

Many counselors have labeled women's fears of abandonment and the ensuing behaviors used to hang onto a relationship as a disease called codependency. Codependency like any addiction, describes an extreme form of relationship neediness and dependency (Wegscheider-Cruise et al. 1990, Beattie 1987, Lerner 1988). Women who place the importance of a relationship over their recovery, health, safety and the welfare of their children have crossed the line into addictive behavior.

The fact that women need relationships to feel good about themselves however, is not dysfunctional in itself. It is an evolutionary truth, that the human species has survived and reproduced because of women's ability to put aside their own needs for the sake of their offspring. Women also increased the likelihood of their children's survival by attaching themselves to men who were able to protect and provide for them. This partnership ensured the perpetuation of the human race. For women to form such attachments to children and men, they had to develop an ability to make sacrifices to preserve this connection. Most importantly, they had to be willing to consider the relationship above all else.

Although it is an evolutionary strength, women's skill at maintaining relationships does place them at risk for becoming dependent on a partner and not being able to make healthy decisions on their own. Many female alcoholics believe that they cannot take care of themselves and are terrified to be alone. They have turned to their partners to take care of them, for financial support and for making decisions. Their dependency can be so great that these women tolerate abusive and unhealthy relationships. When it reaches this level of dysfunction, a woman's need to have a relationship is considered codependent.

Women and Self-Esteem

Women tend to get their self-esteem through relationships by feeling connected to others. Since relationships are so important to women, it can leave them vulnerable to being influenced by their partners. As noted earlier, a woman's introduction to alcohol is often facilitated by a male partner and will often follow his drinking pattern (Finklestein et al. 1990). The importance of relationships in a woman's life is evident when a woman is confronted by her alcoholism. Women often continue drinking in spite of negative consequences in order to maintain the relationship rather than risk abandonment. Almost every alcoholic woman faces the prospect of abandonment (Finklestein et al. 1990). Some because of their drinking. Others because of their decision to get sober. The same is not necessarily true for men. Most wives stay with their alcoholic husbands both while they are drinking and when they go into recovery (Finklestein et al. 1990).

Many female alcoholics have trouble asserting themselves with partners. Dependent on a man for financial, physical and emotional support, women are powerless to make decisions that are in conflict with their partners' needs. Women's fear of abandonment can trap them in violent and abusive marriages or place them at risk for exposure to sexually transmitted diseases. Many women face unwanted pregnancies because of their codependent need to please their men despite the consequences to themselves (Finklestein et al. 1990).

Research has found that women use alcohol to cope with unhappy marriages and to help them be sexual. Unfortunately, the drinking that is supposed to help them cope eventually results in shameful and embarrassing behavior that leads to more drinking. Self-esteem deteriorates because of the behaviors associated with both the women's attempts to maintain their relationships and their drinking. Even with sobriety, women face anxiety trying to maneuver sex and a relationship without alcohol (Turner et al. 1982). Many are ill-equipped, after years of drinking, in understanding how to relate to others without alcohol as a lubricant.

Sex and Alcohol

For centuries alcohol has been heralded as the great aphrodisiac of all time. This expectation is responsible for perpetuating the myth that female drinkers are automatically promiscuous because they are using alcohol. It is true, that in small amounts, alcohol can serve to decrease inhibitions and anxiety concerning sexual activity (Griffitt et al. 1985, Mueller et al 1987). However, alcohol is anything but an aphrodisiac. Alcohol use may begin as a social lubricant but often ends in sexual dysfunction, abuse, loss of libido and a breakdown in relationships. The association between alcohol and sex can have damaging consequences for the alcoholic woman.

Female alcoholics often begin their use of alcohol to deal with their conflicting feelings about their sexuality. As a central nervous system depressant, alcohol acts on the reticular activating system in the brain stem and affects the judgment center. This allows female drinkers to be sexual while intoxicated and maintain their sexual innocence by blaming the alcohol. However, in larger amounts, alcohol depresses the nervous system to the point that it reduces the sensitivity in the areas essential to sexual functioning (Turner et al. 1982, Griffitt et al. 1985, Mueller et al. 1987). Alcohol depresses reflexes and dilates blood vessels. This interferes with a man's ability to have or maintain an erection or a woman's ability to produce vaginal lubrication (Turner et al. 1982).

Alcohol is responsible for decreasing the secretion of follicle-stimulating hormone and luteinizing hormone which results in skin, hair and menstrual changes. The female alcoholic is more susceptible to vaginal infections, a reduction in libido, infertility, and repeated miscarriages (Drews 1986). She may also experience a number of menstrual disorders (Drews 1986) and in some women menstruation may cease altogether (Mueller et al. 1982). Finally, because alcohol is a depressant, a woman may become unresponsive to stimulation even to the point of failing to achieve orgasm (Turner et al. 1982).

In addition to the physical limitations of alcohol, the female alcoholic is at equal risk for participating in degrading sexual behavior. The drug's ability to release inhibitions finds women lacking discretion regarding sexual partners (Turner 1982). She may engage in sex with many partners or practice sexual behaviors that she is embarrassed or ashamed of after the effects of the alcohol have worn off. Many women use alcohol to overcome these feelings of shame and to help them become aroused.

For many female alcoholics, their partners may be alcoholics as well. Alcoholic men experience sexual dysfunction, erectile difficulties, a reduction in libido and retarded ejaculation (Jensen 1981). Faced continually with their husbands' impotence, lack of interest, or inability to ejaculate, wives of alcoholics, as part of this sexual union, are at risk for being blamed by the alcoholic for the problem. Since the nature of the disease does not allow the man to make the connection between his inability to perform and his use of alcohol, he naturally assumes it must be his wife's fault.

If the woman is an alcoholic and experiencing her own sexual dysfunction, she may blame herself as well. These women may double their efforts to "fix" the problem instead of confronting their men on the drinking. They may also go to great lengths to avoid sexual encounters altogether and therefore not risk failure.

Sexual abuse is not uncommon in alcoholic marriages and this certainly affects the healthy sexual functioning of the couple (Woititz 1979, Coleman 1988, Schaefer et al. 1988). Sometimes women are powerless to protect themselves from drunk, violent men. Other times, women submit to behavior out of fear of abandonment or when drinking impairs their ability to assert themselves.

Finally, sexual functioning may be impaired if women are no longer aroused by their husbands because of the smell of alcohol on their breath, their vomiting, or because they have passed out (Drews 1986). As the disease progresses, husbands may simply be focused on drinking rather than interested in sex or their wives (Turner et al. 1982).

Women's Alcoholism and Relationships

Alcoholism profoundly influences the structure of a marriage. In the later stages of the disease, alcoholics often abdicate their roles and responsibilities in the family to their partners and children. They prefer to focus their energy on drinking and drinking activities. This places family members in a position of having to adapt their behavior and needs to the alcoholic. In some cases, this allows the alcoholic a position of power such as when dinner and other routines are scheduled around the drinking. In other cases, the alcoholic has very little power as the spouse takes over making decisions, controlling schedules and determining what role the alcoholic has in the family.

Typically, the gender of the alcoholic has a great deal of influence on whether the alcoholic maintains power in the relationship. Generally, men come into the marriage with more power as defined in their ability to determine how decisions are made, the level of independence they experience, and how successfully they get their needs met from their partner. Women tend to have less power in their relationships. When the woman is an alcoholic, she has even less control, makes fewer decisions and experiences more difficulty in getting her needs met by her partner.

In the alcoholic marriage, drinking husbands frequently feel threatened by their wives attempts to get sober. They fear that their own drinking will be confronted or that they will lose a drinking companion. Alcoholic couples have marriages that revolve around drinking activities, drinking friends and drinking customs. If one partner stops drinking, it can disrupt the equilibrium or balance of the marriage. The old rules of the relationship no longer apply.

It is difficult for women to sit and watch their husbands continue to drink when they are no longer able to themselves. Newly sober wives often can not tolerate their husbands' late nights out drinking, responsibilities not met, commitments broken or social events that involve heavy drinking. This can create so much conflict in a marriage that the woman will refuse help for her alcoholism in order to reduce their husband's anxiety and to stabilize the marriage.

For women involved with non-alcoholic spouses, there is the strong possibility that the men have been comfortable with their wives' drinking because they like the way their marriages are structured and do not want them to change. These men frequently enjoy more power in the relationship. Their wives' drinking may have allowed more freedom in making decisions, to pursue other interests (including affairs), to have less involvement in the marriage and less intimacy between the couple.

In sobriety, the marriage changes. Sexuality, power, finances, decision-making, marital roles, relationships with children, boundaries, behaviors and feelings are defined, developed and acted out differently. When she drank, the woman's husband may have handled the money, made most of the decisions, found child care for the children and initiated sex. However, when the wife stops drinking, she may want to be involved in decisions, have more access to the family's finances, take over caring for the children and begin asserting boundaries around sex. He may be unprepared and even not like all of the changes that come with recovery. Few women are aware of how much alcoholism plays a role in determining the nature of their relationships.

Katie's Story

Katie and her husband, Stan came to couple's counseling because of her drinking. Stan complained that Katie would go out drinking with her friends and not come home when she said she was going to. Sometimes, she failed to do household chores, would forget to lock the front door or not follow through on a promise because she was too drunk. During the session, it became clear that Stan's drinking was also out of control but there was agreement between the couple that he was not going to stop and it was not to be addressed.

At the second session, Katie brought up her concerns that Stan would be upset if she stopped drinking. "I'm afraid you'll leave me," she told him. He assured her that he would not leave. However, when she made the commitment to quit, he seemed very critical about how they were going to spend time together if they were not doing something that involved drinking. He also accused her of focusing attention on his drinking insisting that they had agreed he would not stop.

By the third session, Katie was attending counseling alone. She had cancelled the last session and was about to cancel this one. She had continued drinking with Stan and explained that it was not possible for her to stop drinking. No matter how much Stan complained about it, she felt her marriage would end if she really did stop drinking. She also felt that she did not want to stay with Stan if he continued drinking after she stopped. As far as she was concerned, she was choosing her marriage over abstinence. Both needed the other to drink to continue the alcoholic marriage and their own drinking.

Alcoholic Women as Enablers

Women's natural tendency to sacrifice for the sake of the relationship makes them vulnerable to enabling their husbands' drinking. There is a fine line between helping someone and enabling them to continue acting dysfunctionally. Enabling means doing something for someone else that they should theoretically be able to do for themselves. Specifically, it refers to the behaviors spouses engage in to protect their alcoholic partners from the negative consequences of their drinking. Over the years, the addiction field has acknowledged that alcoholics can enable one another in a conspiracy to avoid detection of alcoholism in either spouse. By preventing partners from recognizing their own addictive drinking patterns, alcoholics ensure continued drinking without interference.

Although it may appear that enabling is a purposeful endeavor, it is really behavior initially motivated out of a desire to protect a loved one. It is human to want to help family members. With alcoholism, the problems are slow to develop and their connection to drinking is at first, difficult to identify. Offering help seems to be a valid solution to each unrelated incident. Initially, this help comes in the form of trying to get the alcoholic to control the drinking and in trying to minimize the negative effects of that drinking (Roche 1990). This process can take months or even years before it is realized that the problems are increasing rather than being resolved.

A good analogy to describe the way family members go from helping to enabling can be seen in the example of rescuing someone who is drowning. Picture a scenario with a man named Mark who is discovered in the lake flailing his arms and screaming for help. The family's initial response is to jump in and pull Mark to safety. Time is not taken to think of the appropriate action to be taken concerning these particular circumstances. No one questions why the individual is drowning in the first place. The immediate concern is to pull him out of the water.

Similarly, alcoholics are drowning from problems associated with their drinking. It could be a bill that has not been paid, too many sick days taken at work or a phone call for a ride home from the bar. The spouse or family member responds to the present crisis without thought as to the nature of the true problem. No one questions why the problem even exists. The bill is paid, the boss is provided with a reasonable explanation or the ride given. The denial associated with the disease of alcoholism infects the entire family and it is rare that the drinking is blamed for the crisis until much later. As with the drowning swimmer, the focus is on solving the immediate problem.

As time goes on however, something unpredictable occurs. In spite of his near fatal drowning, Mark insists on going back into the water. Family members are confused and then eventually become suspicious. They request that Mark learn how to swim if he is going back into the water. Some try to keep him out of the water altogether. Each time, they discover Mark back in the water, they feel obligated to pull him out. Resentments build as family members blame and make accusations over the reasons the problem exists in the first place.

Family members question why Mark places himself in danger by returning to the water or not learning how to swim. Some members of the family become so angry that they withdraw completely. Others feel an even greater obligation to jump in out of fear that they are the only ones left available to help and that they will be blamed if Mark drowns. Responsibility has shifted from Mark to the people who have been rescuing him. Family members become divided about how best to approach this issue and as a result feel isolated from each another.

Alcoholism has a similar dynamic to Mark's compulsion to jump back into the water. The alcoholic seems to insist on drinking despite the consequences. Family members try to stop the drinking, ask the alcoholic to learn how to drink socially or attempt to control access to the alcohol. The blackouts, denial and distorted thinking that accompany the disease, however, prevent the drinker from realizing that alcoholism is the true cause of the problems. The family may become suspicious of the alcoholic's continual insistence to drink, but like Mark's loved ones, the family will become divided and isolated. Some family members will withdraw completely, refusing any assistance, while others take on all the responsibility. Instead of an intervention, loved ones will vacillate from blaming, accusing and abandoning the alcoholic to making excuses, taking responsibility and enabling.

Definition of Enabling

According to Helena Roche (1990), a psychiatric social worker,

> The term enabling is used to include any behavior by family members or friends which aims to contain or limit drinking, drug-taking or gambling or to shield the dependent person from the familial, legal, social or work-related implications of ongoing excessive use. Although based on a desire to resolve problems, enabling actually worsens the situation in the long term. It removes responsibility from the person whose drinking, drug-taking or gambling is creating difficulties. It, therefore, slows down his recognition of the illness which is developing and the need to seek help (p. 5).

She continues by saying that enabling can be motivated by any number of the following factors (p. 7):

* a sense of loyalty to the alcoholic
* a constructive desire to cope with the difficulties posed by the alcoholic's behavior
* a sense of personal responsibility for creating or contributing to the alcohol problem
* concern for the good name of the family
* the desire to prevent damage to others when the alcoholic is intoxicated
* the survival needs of the family unit
* a desire to prevent a deterioration in the alcoholic's social position or employability
* fear of loss or damage to the relationship with the alcoholic
* fear for the alcoholic's physical safety
* fear of confronting the alcoholic
* pressure to stand by the alcoholic from family members, friends or in-laws

* a desire to defer or avoid seeking outside help with a problem
* a lack of awareness of alcoholism as an illness
* an unrecognized personal desire to be needed by the alcoholic
* an unrecognized personal desire to have power over the alcoholic
* a sense of responsibility for the alcoholic

The Need to be Needed

It has been established that women derive self-esteem by being successful in relationships. Evolution has benefitted from women's strength in their ability to connect to others and society has reinforced the belief that women are solely responsible for maintaining their marriages. This adds up to a basic need to feel important, valued and loved when needed in a relationship. It is also the basic formula for enabling. The alcoholic husband's preoccupation with alcohol makes him less responsible to the relationship and family. As the disease progresses, the alcoholic needs his wife to perform daily tasks for him. She feeds him, provides him with clean clothes, pays his bills, creates excuses to the boss for his behavior and maintains the family for him. During this time, the wife feels special and important to her husband. He needs her.

This need serves an even more crucial service. As long as he needs her, he will not abandon her. Most female alcoholics experience some form of abandonment from friends, parents, family and partners. To avoid further rejection, wives of alcoholics know they must take care of their husbands to prevent them from finding someone else who will. Wives try to control the drinking, the negative consequences of the drinking and the events that lead up to a drinking episode in order to maintain their relationships. According to Roche (1990, p. 14-18), some methods women use to monitor their husbands' drinking is to:

* control the amount of money available to buy alcohol
* physically preventing the alcoholic from getting to the source of supply
* emptying bottles and disposing of drugs
* accompanying husbands to drinking events in order to control consumption
* monitoring the alcoholic's free time
* avoiding social events that include drinking
* requesting family members, friends or suppliers not to provide alcohol
* begging the alcoholic not to drink
* using humor, making deals, and extracting promises not to drink
* using sex as a distraction
* making demands for drinking behavior to change
* setting limits on how much the alcoholic can drink
* using silent treatment as punishment for drinking
* threatening separation or other sanctions without follow through

* confronting with rage, accusations or blame
* threatening

Unfortunately, women in alcoholic marriages eventually face the truth about their husband's drinking. They may not recognize that their husbands are alcoholic but every woman, at some point in her marriage, realizes that her husband's priority is drinking and not her. This painful awareness creates resentments and hostility toward her husband. She increases her efforts to control his drinking; believing that he will then be more available to the relationship. The husband instead feels misunderstood and frustrated by her attempts to interfere with his drinking.

The Alcoholic Marriage

The development of the alcoholic marriage is largely outside the woman's control, though she plays a central role in maintaining it. Since women derive self-esteem from having successful relationships, they place a great deal of importance and energy onto their marriages. Society reinforces the importance of relationships in women's lives by telling them that it is the wife, not the husband, who fails when the marriage ends. For many women, husbands provide financial support and are the fathers of their children thereby increasing their sense of failure and fear if they should lose the man. The children might blame them for their loss of a father and for their lifestyle deteriorating. Many women experience poverty after ending an alcoholic marriage.

Finally, women fear that they will be abandoned if they interfere with their spouses' drinking. This leads to a need to develop a pattern of relating that maximizes the woman's chances of staying married. The behaviors she develops to cope with her husband's alcoholism have been labeled as enabling and have been identified as creating the perfect environment for the alcoholic to continue drinking. It is a no-win situation; further exacerbated when the woman becomes addicted herself.

As an alcoholic, the woman is stigmatized by the stereotype of promiscuity and a bad mother. She struggles with low self-esteem and no doubt has a history of being abandoned. It is highly likely that if in a relationship at all, it will be with another alcoholic. The fact that both partners have the same disease, coupled with the woman's investment in maintaining the relationship, ensures a certain level of denial and support of each other's drinking. The woman cannot risk confronting her husband without risking a confrontation of her own drinking so she learns to adapt. This adaption comes from her own needs to stabilize the marriage, loyalty to her husband, genuine concern for his and the family's well-being, a need to protect her own drinking and a belief that she is responsible for her husband's behavior. Her husband supports her fears that his drinking is somehow her fault by blaming her each time he drinks. His mood, his behavior and his beliefs dominate the family.

How the alcoholic marriage develops is determined largely by the couple's involvement with alcohol when they met. Some couples meet, date and socialize with other couples at drinking events. Their marriage may have been predicated on their mutual bond with alcohol. In this kind of relationship, denial is strong and the unwritten agreement is that the marriage revolves around the couple's need to drink. Another factor that influences the successful adaption to alcohol in the marriage is the presence of alcoholism in the family of origin of the husband and/or wife (Steinglass et al. 1987). If both partners have learned how to support the behaviors associated with alcoholism from alcoholic parents, it makes it much easier to continue that support in their own marriage.

In their research on how alcoholic families adapt to the presence of alcohol, Dr. Steinglass and associates (et al. 1987) discovered that many families can do remarkably well in making alcohol central to their lives. In fact, the alcohol can be the glue that keeps the marriage together.

> We would contend that just as a family dynasty can be built around economic or political power, it can also be built around alcoholism. In this sense, alcoholism can have as powerful an impact on family members as community status in shaping their shared beliefs and sense of their role in life. Thus *alcoholic family identities* that have survived intact across multiple generations can produce alcoholic dynastic identities that demand the loyalty of each and every family member and, in interactive fashion, influence behavioral expectancies (e.g., that the next generation will, of course, include alcoholic members) (Steinglass et al. 1987, p. 61).

Problems arise however, when one spouse decides to get sober or recognizes that the alcoholism once seen in a parent is now being replayed by the partner. Not wanting to relive the childhood experience of alcoholism, the spouse confronts the drinking partner. This destroys the delicate balance created in the alcoholic marriage.

With other couples, alcoholism does not play such a central role in the beginning of their marriage. The disease may have been in the early stages for the husband and he introduces his wife to drinking. As the disease progresses, physical, psychological and behavioral changes occur that profoundly effect the stability of the marriage. Alcoholics are eventually unable to function normally with large quantities of chemicals circulating in the brain. Slurred speech, vision problems, blackouts and lack of coordination prevent the drinker from behaving in socially approved ways. Personal hygiene, nutrition, family schedules and responsibilities are neglected as the alcoholic becomes increasingly preoccupied with maintaining his drinking patterns.

Liver disease, heart disease and gastrointestinal problems become major concerns for the couple. In addition, neurological problems affect the alcoholic's thinking, emotions and judgement. Personality changes occur, values are no longer adhered to, behavior problems escalate and problem solving skills are lost. The husband no longer thinks, acts or feels the way he used to. He now lies to protect his drinking, may steal money for alcohol and shun most, if not all, his responsibilities. Alcoholics in the later stages of the disease can be so impaired that their only focus is the need to drink. Anything that interferes with this need is unimportant including the demands of their relationship with their wives.

Wives, in these marriages, work hard to take care of their husbands. They go to great lengths to compensate for their husbands' impairment and perpetuate the illusion of normalcy. Many neglect their own needs to structure the family schedule around their husbands' drinking. They make sure their husbands eat, are properly clothed, cleaned up and driven home safely after drinking bouts. Alcoholic husbands become children in the marriages as the wives take on more of the responsibilities. The men both welcome the reduction of the burden of daily care and resent it. Their self-esteem deteriorates and they resort to blaming their wives rather than confronting their need to drink. They deny that they have a problem with alcohol. In response, the wives become depressed, anxious, fearful, ashamed and hopeless to stop what is happening to their husbands.

Many alcoholic men try to preserve their self-esteem by controlling the family's moods, activities and attitudes toward him. They exaggerate their importance to the family and their contribution to maintaining it. They punish family members who do not take them seriously or who refuse to play the facade of the alcoholic spouses' value to the family. They blame everyone else for the problems that the family faces. The unpaid bills, broken promises, and the chaos in the household. Most of all, they blame their wives.

Wives of alcoholics blame themselves too. They know something is wrong but they often do not know what it is. These women become as adept as their alcoholic spouses at denying the problem with alcohol. Instead, they blame stress, job problems, the boss or whatever the alcoholic uses as an excuse to explain away the troubles. The wives experience physical problems of their own in response to the stress of the alcoholic marriage. Headaches, stomach aches, sleeplessness, anxiety and depression are some of the symptoms of living with an alcoholic. Smoking, drinking, using drugs, and eating disorders are some of the ways wives try to cope (Roche 1990).

Throughout this process, wives of alcoholics try to protect and take care of their husbands. Some out of love and loyalty. Others out of duty or pressure from other family members. Many women are financially dependent on these men or are so terrified of being abandoned that they cannot risk angering the alcoholic by confronting him about his drinking. Others stay because of their children or because it allows them the freedom to drink. In any case, the alcoholic marriage takes on a set of rules that clearly state that drinking is the most important activity. Family members take on specific roles to compensate for the alcoholic's behavior becoming isolated in the process. Communication, sex, intimacy, the physical and psychological well-being of the family members and the needs of the spouse become nonexistent in the face of alcohol's importance to the alcoholic.

The example of the drowning man used earlier describes the final stages of both the disease of alcoholism and the alcoholic marriage. Mark's compulsion to jump back into the water in spite of his inability to swim places his spouse in a difficult position. Unable to understand her husband's preoccupation with the water, she attempts to control his behavior. When that fails, she feels her only option is to save him each time before he drowns. Over and over again, she rescues him from certain death. Instead of gratitude and a new awareness of his predicament, Mark continues to act as if he can swim and blames his wife for her interference. Mark's wife, fearful that he will find someone else to tolerate his behavior and abandon her, learns to accept the behavior. Terrified that he will drown, she continues to rescue him and finds herself spending more time in the water with him. As far as she can see, there is no other choice.

Angela's Story

When I married my husband, our social life was spent hanging around bars and with friends who drank. We found an apartment and became friends with another couple across the hall who drank as often as we did. I never though there was anything wrong with it. We had been doing the same thing while we were dating. But over time, I found we didn't do anything else. My husband stopped going to work, going out or doing anything he used to like to do. He just drank more and more.

I would try to stay with him but I couldn't drink as much as he did. He took to drinking more on his own or with the friend from across the hall. I would come home from work to find he hadn't done anything all day on the apartment or with himself. He had just sat around with his friend who was also unemployed and drank. I was miserable but I didn't know why. He seemed happy to see me and I was always invited to join them but it was getting boring. There were bills to be paid and the house to clean. I didn't have the time to drink all day. He just got angry that I didn't want to spend time with him.

I wanted kids but he thought it was too much responsibility. I wanted to do other things but he just wanted to drink. I wanted to move but he wanted to stay near his friends. He started complaining that I wasn't much fun anymore and when I quit drinking, he moved out. A week later he called to say his friend had blown his brains out with a shotgun and he didn't know why. Before I knew it, I heard myself saying that the guy had no life. He just sat around at home all day drinking. I could have been talking about my husband.

5

The Battered Alcoholic

Definition of a Battered Woman

According to Lenore Walker (1979), a leading researcher in the area of battered women,

> A battered woman is a woman who is repeatedly subjected to any forceful physical or psychological behavior by a man in order to coerce her to do something he wants her to do without any concern for her rights. Battered women include wives or women in any form of intimate relationships with men. Furthermore, in order to be classified as a battered woman, the couple must go through the battering cycle at least twice. Any woman may find herself in an abusive relationship with a man once. If it occurs a second time, and she remains in the situation, she is defined as a battered woman (p. xv).

In recent years, it has come to light that lesbians are also being battered in their relationships (Finklestein et al. 1990). The defining characteristic of battering is that it is happening in the context of an intimate relationship. While involved in these relationships, women feel guilty and responsible for the abuse (Finklestein et al. 1990). Society reinforces the beliefs that women are to blame for the battering by focusing attention on why women stay instead of why men get away with the violence (Walker 1989). Women are blamed for encouraging the abuse, for accepting it and for not divorcing the batterer. Female alcoholics face the additional stigma of being "drunks" and therefore, deserving of the abuse.

Society's attitude toward battered women and women alcoholics influence the number of resources available to them. Convinced that they are responsible for what is happening to them, women believe they should be able to stop the battering (Walker 1979). This sets up a cycle where battered women put their energy into controlling the circumstances that lead up to the abuse rather than on ways to escape it. Despite their attempts to control the battering, women learn that they are powerless to stop it even while continuing to receive the message from society that they are responsible for the abuse.

However, in the same way no one can control the drinking of an alcoholic, no one can control the violent behavior of a batterer except the batterer himself. Nevertheless, women's self-esteem is severely damaged by society's messages; first by the abuse; second, by the belief that the abuse is their fault; and third, by their inability to stop the abuse. The alcoholic woman whose self-esteem is already low experiences even fewer options. Battered alcoholic women are disabled by their disease because of the stigma involved in being a female alcoholic. Losing control over their drinking is something else society tells women they are responsible for and becomes the fourth factor affecting their sense of helplessness.

Learned Helplessness

Experimental psychologist Martin Seligman's research on what is called "learned helplessness" best illustrates the battered women's experiences with relationships (Walker 1979). An experiment done with dogs shows how a sense of powerlessness can result in passive behavior under a number of different circumstances.

In the experiment, Seligman worked with a group of dogs and a room where only half the floor was wired to give an electric shock. The first group of dogs were placed one at a time on the side wired for shock. Researchers administered the electrical shocks at random and varied intervals. Predictably, the dogs tried to avoid the shocks by searching for an escape route. Once the side of the room that was not wired for electricity was discovered, the dogs would automatically move to the safer corner in the room. Eventually when the dogs were placed on the side that was wired for electrical shock, the dogs would immediately move to the other side of the room even before the shock was administered.

The dogs responses were not surprising. When they perceived that they were going to experience pain, the dogs would react by trying to avoid it. This same response is what is expected of battered women. If a woman knows her husband is going to abuse her, society expects that the woman will go to similar lengths (as the dogs) to avoid the relationship. However, Seligman and his researchers did not end their experiment at this point.

In the second set of experiments, access to the side not wired was denied by a barrier too high for the dogs to jump over. When the dogs were shocked this time, they discovered that they could not escape the pain by moving to the other side of the room. Although they tried to find other ways to avoid the shocks, they eventually gave up and endured the pain in silence. "When nothing they did stopped the shocks, the dogs ceased any further voluntary activity and became compliant, passive and submissive" (Walker 1979, p. 46). They had learned that they were powerless to control what was happening to them and instead, put their energy into surviving the experience.

Battered women experience the same sense of powerlessness in their relationships with abusive men. When overpowered and prevented from escaping the battering, women turn their focus on surviving the experience. These women are frequently dependent on men financially, lack the community resources or self-esteem to leave and have difficulty with persuading law enforcement officials to take action against the batterers. They know that there is no "other side of the room" to escape to.

The final set of experiments with the dogs, however, proved to be the most revealing. Returning to the room once more, the dogs were placed on the floor wired for electric shock. This time the barrier to the other side of the room was lowered so that the dogs could jump over it when the shocks were administered. Although an escape route was provided, the dogs did not respond. Even when the experimenters removed the barrier altogether and "the dogs were shown the way out they remained passive, refused to leave and did not avoid the shock" (Walker 1979, p.46).

Though conditions had changed, the dogs beliefs about their experience had not. Experimenters had to drag the dogs across the room to prove that the situation had changed. For some dogs, the earlier conditioning that they were helpless to avoid the shocks was so strong, that they had to be dragged across the room over 200 times before they realized they had an escape route. "The earlier in life that the dogs received such treatment, the longer it took to overcome the effects of this so-called learned helplessness. However, once they did learn that they could make the voluntary response, their helplessness disappeared" (Walker 1979, p. 46).

Similar experiments have supported the phenomenon of learned helplessness in other animals. An experiment with rats also showed that learned helplessness in one situation can be generalized to another condition. Experimenters took newborn rats and taught them that they could not escape being held. The rats were held repeatedly until they stopped squirming or wriggling to be released. Then the rats were placed in a pool of water.

> Within thirty minutes, the rats subjected to the learned helplessness treatment drowned. Many did not even attempt to swim, and sank to the bottom of the vat immediately. Untreated rats would swim up to sixty hours before drowning. The sense of powerlessness was generalized from squirming in order to escape handholding to swimming in order to escape death. Since the rats were all physically capable of learning to swim to stay alive, it was the psychological effect of learned helplessness which was theorized to explain the rats' behavior (Walker 1979, p. 46).

The rats, like the dogs, had come to believe that they could not change the conditions they were subjected to and therefore, did not attempt to exercise any control. Even when the situation changed to one where the animals have the ability to influence the conditions, their expectations that they could not control what was happening to them prevented them from taking action. "Once we believe we cannot control what happens to us, it is difficult to believe we can ever influence it, even if later we experience a favorable outcome. This concept is important for understanding why battered women do not attempt to free themselves from a battering relationship. Once the women are operating from a belief of helplessness, the perception becomes reality and they become passive, submissive, "helpless"' (Walker 1979, p. 47).

Battered women feel helpless in the face of the abuse. They learn that they cannot stop the batterers from abusing them. The men are physically stronger, the women frequently financially dependent, and the law often reluctant to take action. Women learn to accept the abuse as a way of life and become passive, submissive and "helpless" like the dogs in Seligman's experiments. Her belief system that she cannot influence or change what is happening to her generalizes to other aspects of her relationship. She fails to see any escape route, eventually gives up looking, and focuses her energy on surviving the battering.

According to Nicky Marone (1992) in her book on learned helplessness:

> Current research shows that this style of behavior systematically sabotages the very core of an individual's ability to cope with the rigorous demands of living in the world today. Learned helplessness corrodes self-esteem, blocks ambition, short-circuits motivation, and contributes to depression and panic disorders. People who suffer from learned helplessness are less likely to respond adaptively to change and more likely to avoid challenge and risk. They show low persistence in the face of obstacles and difficulties, exhibit deficiencies in strategic planning, and are often unable to assess the causes of both their failures *and* their successes (p.xiii).

The Victim Role

Women, who grew up in alcoholic homes have frequently experienced some type of emotional, physical and/or sexual abuse. They may be alcoholics as well. As children, they learned that they are not treated with respect, have no control over what happens to them and are told that the abuse is their fault. Alcoholics have a tendency to blame their children for both their drinking and their abusive behavior. These are the same elements present in the battering relationship and in the concept of learned helplessness. Daughters of alcoholics believe that they deserve the abuse because the people they loved and trusted decided to violate them.

An understanding of how learned helplessness impacts daughters of alcoholics explains why many girls grow up to marry someone who batters them. Not all women enter a battering relationship submissive and passive, but those that do frequently come from alcoholic homes. These women consider abuse a normal part of life and have come to expect to be treated that way. Women's expectations that they will be battered in any relationship lend themselves to acting out particular behavioral characteristics that actually attract abusive men. A behavior pattern described as the victim role.

Victims unconsciously set themselves up for a continuing pattern of victimization by acting passively in situations they believe are beyond their control. However, like the dogs in the Seligman experiments, it is obvious to others that the women have far more power than they realize. Abusive men recognize the passive response as a victim mentality. These men know the women will feel they have no control over what is happening and yet, be willing to take the blame.

Our media frequently reinforces the portrayal of women in trouble and needing to be rescued. Rarely is a woman seen taking care of herself and solving her own problems. In reality, women are often denied access to financial and physical resources to make changes in their lives. Many women are trained to believe that they need a man to take care of them and feel powerless to control their own destiny. Women are taught to focus their energy on obtaining a man and hanging onto him at all cost. This is ensured by meeting the man's needs rather than their own. If the women are from alcoholic homes, this training has begun early and like the dogs, makes it harder to change.

The Battering Relationship

Battering relationships are hard to identify. Many batterers do not begin the cycle of abuse until the couple are involved for a period of time. Batterers wait until there is a huge investment in the relationship such as moving in together, sharing finances, or children have arrived, before becoming violent. The men do not feel compelled to be on good behavior anymore and it makes it more difficult for the woman to leave. The dynamics of learned helplessness also explains why women are unable to leave battering relationships.

Battered women and battering men are represented in all racial groups, social and economical levels, religions and employment (Walker 1979). There is some association between alcohol and the battering though many men continue to be abusive after they become abstinent. Although there is a myth that the police will protect women, Lenore Walker's (1989) and Ann Jones' (1994) research on battered women found that the police were ineffective in most cases. In fact, many women were battered more severely after the police left (Walker 1979).

> A recently completed study in Kansas City and Detroit indicates that in 80 percent of all homicides in those cities, the police had intervened from one to five times previously. Thus, homicide between man and woman is not a 'crime of passion,' but rather the end result of unchecked, long-standing violence (Walker 1979, p. 27).

Children are also victims in battering relationships. Witnessing violence can be very traumatic for children, especially if the victim and perpetrator are loved ones. Many children are physically abused as well. In Lenore Walker's (1979) study of battered women, she found that about a third of the batterers and a third of the battered women beat their children. In addition, many of the batterers were suspected of sexually molesting their daughters.

Characteristics of Battered Women

Lenore Walker (1979) found that although battered woman come from all walks of life, they do share the following nine characteristics (p.31). Battered women:

* have low self-esteem,
* believe all the myths about battering relationships,
* are traditionalist about the home,
* strongly believe in family unity and the prescribed feminine sexual stereotype,
* accept responsibility for the batterers actions,
* suffer from guilt, yet deny the terror and anger they feel,
* present a passive face to the world, but have the strength to manipulate their
      environment enough to prevent further violence or of being killed,
* have severe stress reactions with psycho-physiological complaints,
* use sex as a way to establish intimacy, and
* believe that no one can help them resolve their predicament except themselves.

As a group, battered women believe that their men are the head of the household and that it is their place to cater to them. Many working women turn over their paychecks (and frequently their careers) to their husbands. Their primary focus is on making the batterers happy.

Many of the characteristics of battered women are similar to those of female alcoholics in general. Low self-esteem, using sex to establish intimacy and suffering from guilt are common in alcoholic women demonstrating their vulnerability in attracting men capable of battering them.

Characteristics of Battering Men

Batterers frequently report that, as children, they witnessed their fathers abusing their mothers. Many were beaten themselves or, at least, grew up in emotionally deprived homes (Walker 1979). Men who batter also share specific characteristics (Walker 1979, p. 36). They:

* have low self-esteem,
* believe all the myths about battering relationships,
* believe in traditional marital roles and male supremacy,

* blame others for their actions,
* are pathologically jealous,
* present a dual personality,
* have difficulty managing stress and use drinking and wife-battering to cope,
* frequently use sex as an act of aggression to enhance self-esteem and,
* do not believe their violent behavior should have negative consequences.

Male batterers often see their actions as an attempt to teach their women a lesson. Many are not violent in any other relationship and appear to be model citizens at work and in the community. However, battered women have reported that many husbands also beat their mothers and many abusive attacks were triggered by a visit to the batterer's mother (Walker 1979).

Batterers are not men who have lost their temper or under a great deal of stress. They are not being provoked by their victims or acting out their insecurity or lack of interpersonal skills. These men are intending to intimidate and coerce their women into doing what they want them to do (Jones 1994). At work, when the police arrive, or with friends, these same men are able to control their emotions and respond in appropriate ways. They know that society would not accept the violent behavior. Many use alcohol as an excuse for their behavior. Others are alcoholics in addition to being batterers.

The Battering Cycle

In battering relationships, the women are not constantly being abused. Walker's (1979) research proved that there was a predictable cycle with three distinct phases: the tension building phase, the explosion or acute battering incident, and the calm, loving honeymoon phase. These phases vary in time and intensity for every couple and even for the same couple as the relationship matures. The period for each stage is dependent on the relationship, how long the violence has been happening and how preceding episodes have been addressed.

The tension building phase is characterized by minor battering incidents. Batterers become irritable and the tension begins to build, independent of the women's behavior. The men blame the women for their anger and, in order to survive, the women take responsibility by trying to please them, take care of their needs and try not to upset them in any way. Nevertheless, the women are unable to control how their batterers feel. Their behavior only serves as a reinforcement that the battering is deserved and when the men explode, their wives often assume the guilt accordingly.

Women respond to the minor battering incidents in whatever way they believe will reduce the likelihood of further abuse. Although helpless to stop the abuse, they experience some sense of power in controlling when it will happen. Many women have been known to provoke an attack in an effort to shorten the first phase of the battering cycle. They know the men are going to escalate anyway and that the only thing the women can influence is when the attack will occur. Women also report that the earlier the man moves into the second phase, the more likely that the battering will be less severe (Walker 1979).

The anxiety and anger women feel during this phase must be denied so that she can focus on preventing further abuse. They minimize the battering incidents in phase one because they are aware of how abusive their husbands can be. If the man punches a hole in the wall, the woman is grateful that he did not punch her in the face.

This phase can last for days, months and even years. In some cases, the woman has become so adept at placating the man during this phase, the couple can successfully prolong it for years. However, the woman's passive acceptance of responsibility for both; trying to calm the batterer down and of the abusive behavior gives the batterer permission to escalate. Women do not cause the abuse, but the couple's belief system that the woman deserves it prevents the man from taking responsibility or control of his own behavior.

The second phase, or acute episode, is the most terrifying part of the battering cycle. Most women recognize that some external incident can trigger the move to this phase and will go to great lengths to control as much of the batterers' life as they can. In fear, the women tend to withdraw from the relationship. The men sense that the women are abandoning them, and retaliate with more abuse and possessive behavior.

This phase is marked by a loss of control and the severity of the abuse. It usually lasts from two to twenty-four hours. Women report that it is impossible to predict the kind of abuse the batterer will inflict and this unknown causes anxiety, sleeplessness, depression, eating disorders and other physical problems. Women are also aware that escape is not an option and all of their concentration is directed toward staying alive. After the battering, women are in a state of shock, denial, and disbelief that it has really happened. Most, do not seek any help for their injuries.

> A good many of the reactions battered women report are similar to those of catastrophe victims. Disaster victims generally suffer emotional collapse twenty-two to forty-eight hours after a catastrophe. Their symptoms include listlessness, depression and feelings of helplessness. Battered women evidence similar behavior. They tend to remain isolated for at least the first twenty-four hours, and it may be several days before they seek help. Mental health workers report that their clients frequently do not call them immediately after a battering incident but rather several days later. The same pattern occurs in seeking medical attention for nonemergency physical injuries. It is not uncommon for a woman with a broken rib to wait several days before she seeks medical attention. This delayed-action syndrome also prevails when battered women seek help from lawyers or any other source (Walker 1979, p. 63).

During this phase, women have little faith in law enforcement or any kind of outside help. Many women report that the violence increases after the police have intervened. Police officers become angry when attacked by the battered women after responding to the incident. They do not understand the women's terror in being seen as siding against the batterer and increasing their chances of further abuse. If the woman has been drinking, law enforcement officials tend to see the woman as part of the problem and unreliable as a witness. They believe she must have provoked him with her drunken behavior or that she has the facts distorted because she is inebriated.

The final stage, or honeymoon phase, is characterized by a period of calm and a great deal of loving, attentive behavior by the men. Batterers will apologize, show remorse, give presents, and often cry over their behavior. They make promises to change and beg others to talk their wives into taking them back. They constantly barrage their wives with requests for forgiveness and for the continuation of the relationship giving the women little time to be alone and think. Male batterers often agree to get help if the women will stay in the relationship. Many men work on their women's guilt about breaking up the family if they threaten to leave and make it clear that they cannot function without their wives. "It is also during this time that the battered woman realizes how frail and insecure her batterer really is. Included in his entreaties are threats that he will destroy his life if she does not forgive him" (Walker 1979, p. 68).

Most battering couples believe in the sacredness of marriage and the family. Women feel a responsibility in protecting their marriages and their husbands. It is terrifying to think that everything will fall apart if the battered women leave. "He reminds her how much he needs her and asserts that something awful will happen to him if she leaves him. Suicide is not an idol threat. Almost ten percent of the men who battered the women in this sample killed themselves after their women left them" (Walker 1979, p. 68). Many women reported that their husbands deteriorated after they left and they could sense the men's desperation and neediness directed toward them. It was also not uncommon for many of these women to feel their own lives had deteriorated once they separated from their husbands (Walker 1979).

According to Lenore Walker (1979),

> The couple who live in such a violent relationship become a symbiotic pair-- each so dependent on the other that when one attempts to leave, both lives become drastically effected. It is during phase three, when the loving-kindness is most intense, that this symbiotic bonding really takes hold. Both fool each other and themselves into believing that together they can battle the world. A sense of over-dependence and over-reliance upon each other is obvious at each phase of the cycle. The bonding aspects of it, however, are laid down during phase three (p.68).

Furthermore, being battered by someone they love, who is supposed to love them, can be such a shock that most women reject the truth. Their denial about what happens, their investment in the marriage, their love for their husbands and for many, their financial dependency on these men make it far too painful to believe the truth. Women are frequently convinced that the battering was an isolated incident, that it was their fault for provoking it, and that it will never happen again. If alcohol was involved, the woman prefers to blame the batterer's behavior on his drinking. If she was using alcohol, she may have difficulty believing her perceptions of what happened or blame herself for drinking too much and upsetting him. Denial is particularly strong in female alcoholics who use this defense mechanism to protect their drinking.

Battered women's desire to love and trust their men is far stronger than their belief that they have to protect themselves because it will happen again. Although it is unlikely that the batterer will get help if the woman stays, she believes her staying will encourage him to go for treatment. She knows it will keep her husband alive and the marriage intact. During this phase, the woman sees the man as he was when they first dated. The loving, attentive and caring man she fell in love with and married. She wants to, and needs to, believe that this is who her husband really is.

Although the battering cycle has three distinct phases, the time frame of each stage changes as the relationship matures. In the beginning of the relationship, the man may be very charming and the woman may not suspect the possibility of abuse. The couple are in love and the man is focused on impressing his partner. When the relationship moves toward a more permanent commitment, the man may still be only verbally abusive during the acute phase. The honeymoon phase may last longer than any other stage of the cycle. In addition, many women become quite adept at prolonging the tension-building phase allowing for more spacing between battering incidents.

However, like the disease of alcoholism, the battering cycle progresses over time. Eventually, the honeymoon phase may be all but nonexistent. By this time, the battering has been reinforced by the woman's inability to protect herself. Both partners believe the man has the right to beat his wife and that she deserves the abuse (Walker 1979). They see it as the husband's right to discipline his wife. The violence becomes more intense and the woman's life is frequently in greater danger in relationships with a history of violence, especially if she tries to leave. Many women face the possibility of being killed if they leave (Walker 1979, Jones 1994).

Why Does the Woman Stay

Battered women do not stay in these relationships because they like being beaten. Many try to leave only to be confronted with obstacles that prevent them from being successful. Many of the reasons women are forced to stay include (Walker 1979, Jones 1994):

* financial dependency on batterer,
* no legal recourse for protection from batterer,
* no safe place to go,
* police, courts, hospitals and social service agencies do not offer adequate protection,
* therapists often counsel women to keep the family together,
* family members ridicule women's fears and side with the batterer,
* the batterer and battered woman's fear that they cannot survive without each other,
* battered woman fear of being alone,
* battered women's fear of being responsible for taking children away from their father,
* women are socialized to believe they are responsible for the marriage,
* society blames women for their own battering and convinces them they can stop it,
* women lack skills to pursue jobs that will support them,
* learned helplessness
* low self-esteem further eroded by the battering
* the batterers need to feel powerful by dominating her prevents her physically from leaving,
* the batterer's threat of suicide or mental breakdown if she leaves,
* the batterer's threat that he will kill her or her children if she leaves, and
* inadequate child care, homelessness and poverty when the woman leaving is forced to go it alone.

The woman's alcoholism can also prevent her from leaving. Community services often show little interest in helping alcoholic woman. The women are usually afraid to ask for help out of fear that their children will be taken away from them. Treatment centers may be ill-equipped to provide shelter to a battered alcoholic and her children or to deal with the numerous issues the woman presents with. Finally, her drinking may distort her thinking and her ability to make sane decisions or to take appropriate action. It can seem easier for some women to "hide in the bottle" than face the truth about their marriages.

In her research on battered women who try to leave, Ann Jones (1994) found that many women are blamed for staying because of the belief that shelters, community resources and police officers are an available resource. This is frequently not true. More often the battered woman is on her own. "Today, experts name battery as a 'major cause' of homelessness; large numbers of the nation's growing band of homeless are women on their own with children--women and children who, despite the social and economic obstacles, ran from male violence at home" (Jones 1994, p. 201). These women are denied medical services, legal services, social services, child care, child support, affordable housing, convenient public transportation, a decent job free of sexual harassment, and a living wage (Jones 1994).

Female alcoholics are even more vulnerable to being blamed for the abuse and abandoned by the system. Stigmatized for being alcoholics, women are easy marks for continual rejection of help. They may be blamed for the abuse because of their drinking. Alcoholic women also risk losing custody of their children to the batterers if they use the alcoholism as an example of the women's unfit status as mothers. Finally, many women in the later stages of alcoholism are too sick to pursue what little resources are available. Although the woman may have started drinking out of a desire to bond with the batterer if he drinks, she may continue drinking to cope with the abuse. It is also not uncommon for batterers to insist their wives drink with them and the women do so because they are too fearful to refuse.

One of the most important reasons for a woman's inability to leave can be the dynamic of the relationship itself. These women have often been with their husbands for years before the first episode of abuse. A power imbalance, a history, the woman's love for her husband and a trust have been built into the relationship. Women are shocked the first time they are battered. It is incomprehensible. These women are traumatized that it happened--let alone that it will happen again. This shock serves to paralyze them long enough for the man to return to his loving old self and convince them that it was an anomaly. It is easier to deny that it happened; that it had to be an isolated incident.

Women believe that it will never happen again or that they can prevent it by changing what they are doing. Denial sets in to help women cope with their struggle over their feelings of betrayal, hurt, and fear that something is wrong. It is less painful to deny or minimize the level of abuse than to believe that their ideal marriage and husband are gone. For women alcoholics, denial is an already common defense mechanism used to avoid the truth about their drinking. As a result, it can be an automatic process to deny the abuse as well.

She Does Leave

Despite the immense achievements in the battered women's movement in the past fifteen years, those who work to stop violence against women--those who staff the hotlines and the shelters and the legal service centers, those who press to make law enforcement and criminal justice act responsibly, those who lobby for legislative reform-- know that the next time a woman is battered in the United States (which is to say within the next twelve seconds) few people will ask: What's wrong with the man? What makes him think he can get away from that? Is he crazy? Did the cops arrest him? Is he in jail? When will he be prosecuted? Is he likely to get a serious sentence? Is she getting adequate police protection? Are the children provided for? Did the court evict him from her house? Does she need any other help? Medical help maybe, or legal aid? New housing. Temporary financial aid? Child support?

No, the first question, and often the only question, that leaps to mind is: *Why doesn't she leave?* (Jones 1994, p. 131).

Society focuses so much blame on the victim, that very little responsibility is directed at the batterer for not controlling his own behavior. The truth is, only the batterer can stop his behavior. No one can control the behavior of another person. Women cannot stop alcoholic husbands from drinking and they cannot stop abusive ones from battering them. In both situations however, society faults the woman for not controlling either. Male alcoholics and/or batterers are offered excuses for their behavior. The most popular being that their women caused, provoked and forced them to drink and batter.

When women do leave, they are accused of staying when it is the batterer who continues to hold onto the relationship. Numerous women are stalked, discovered and attacked by the batterer long after they have physically and emotionally left (Jones 1994). In fact, women's lives are frequently more in danger when they leave the batterer than if they stay. Women are battered *because* they leave (Jones 1994).

One woman described how her batterer followed her from work after she moved out to find out where she now lived. Phone calls, letters and unannounced visits ensued. Sometimes she came home to find he had broken in and had gone through her belongings. Often, he would wait out in the bushes until she had to leave for work and then jump out and harass her. She got a restraining order that he violated, almost lost her job from a boss that repeatedly called the police on the man and risked a current relationship when her boyfriend fought with the batterer. After repeated arrests, the batterer was finally sent to jail when a witness testified that she heard the man threaten to kill this woman.

The batterers attack when they find the women in their hiding place. They take advantage of times when the women visit family members or during the exchange of children when fathers are exercising their right to joint custody or visitation. The women know there is no place to hide. If the batterer wants to find them, he will. The truth is that women do leave. The men just do not let them go.

Part 3:

Women, Alcoholism and Parenting

6

The Pregnant Alcoholic

The Effects of Drinking and Using Drugs on the Developing Fetus

Years ago, a woman drinking a glass of wine never thought she might be harming her fetus. The placenta, it was believed, prevented any foreign or harmful substance from passing through to the fetus. It is now an established fact that the placenta is not a barrier of any kind. Virtually all drugs cross the placenta to some degree (Niebyl 1982). The concern has now turned to the examination of how and to what extent the fetus is affected by chemicals such as alcohol.

Studies determining these effects however, are difficult to obtain for a number of reasons. Ethics negate the possibility of administering any drug to human subjects solely for scientific research. Studying drug-using populations who self-administer, use a variety of different substances and purchase their supply from dealers who mix it with other unknown chemicals make accurate interpretation of the results impossible (Kreek 1982). In addition, the unpredictable dosage schedule of street drug users results in periodic episodes of withdrawal or overdose (Finnegan 1982).

Any research done on a drug dependent population must also factor in that people consumed by an addiction have difficulty obtaining adequate sleep, appropriate nutrition and regular prenatal care (Finnegan 1982) which affects fetal development. Research that relies on people reporting accurately on their own drinking can be unreliable due to the enormous stigma placed on women who drink at all, let alone drinking while they are pregnant. Denial, guilt, blackouts and "too inebriated to count accurately" cloud results as well.

Another important consideration, is that a substance does not necessarily affect every fetus in exactly the same way. Timing, dosage and length of exposure are deciding factors. "Some women who took but a single dose of thalidomide produced malformed babies: others took the drug without any recognizable defects in their babies. In this latter group, the fetuses were spared during the critical period of chemical or cellular growth" (Shukey 1972). The unpredictability of nature makes it difficult to ascertain the exact effect of each drug on the developing fetus.

A major pitfall in studying the effects of certain substances on the fetus is the harsh reality that abnormalities occur spontaneously in nature itself. "About 2% of all pregnancies result in the birth of a child with major malformations; about 10% born have major or minor malformations and more than 10% have developmental and/or behavioral problems" (Blake 1982, p. 158). It is difficult therefore, to determine if the abnormality is a result of a harmful substance or the fault of nature. Furthermore, the elimination of other variables as possible causes of infant abnormalities is virtually impossible. A woman who drinks may also smoke cigarettes, drink coffee, take prescription pills and as mentioned earlier exhibit the effects of poor nutrition.

Finally, it must be understood that no two women have the same exact pregnancy and thus, there is no clear definition of a "normal" pregnancy. In essence, the unavailability of a control group. With these factors in mind, the evidence is mounting that the risks are substantial enough to encourage pregnant women to abstain from alcohol and other drugs.

Two conditions have been discovered involving fetal reactions to exposure of alcohol and drugs such as heroin. Fetal Alcohol Syndrome (FAS) and Neonatal Narcotic Abstinence Syndrome. FAS is the term used to describe a set of abnormalities associated with the use of alcohol. These abnormalities include central nervous system dysfunctions, mental retardation, microcephaly, growth deficiencies, facial anomalies (such as abnormal eyes and malproportioned faces), and variable major and minor malformations (Little et al. 1982). The term "Fetal Alcohol Effects" (FAE) has been used recently to describe less extreme examples of this syndrome. Neonatal Narcotic Abstinence Syndrome (NAS) is characterized by central nervous system hyperirritability, gastrointestinal dysfunction, respiratory distress, and vague autonomic symptoms such as yawning, sneezing, mottling, and fever.

Several researchers have studied the effects of maternal alcohol consumption on fetal development and found that there is a strong relationship between the amount of alcohol ingested and infant abnormalities. Jones et al. (Little et al. 1982) examined eight children born of mothers who drank excessively throughout the pregnancy and for two to 23 years before. These children displayed gross physical retardation. Minor ocular, facial, skeletal and other abnormalities were also observed.

Another study done in Boston by Ouellette et al. (Little et al. 1982), reported on data collected on 633 pregnant women. The first prenatal visit determined whether the woman was an abstinent (or rarely drank), moderate or heavy drinker. The infants were examined by a pediatric neurologist who had no knowledge of the mother's alcoholic intake. Of these infants, 322 were judged to be abnormal. Seventy-one per cent of these abnormal infants were the offspring of heavy drinkers. Less than half of the babies born to the moderate and rare drinkers had abnormalities. "The frequency of abnormality in all three groups is remarkably high. However, from this study it appears that an increased frequency of abnormality is not found until 45 ml of ethanol (3 beverage units) per day are exceeded" (Blake 1982, p. 159). As the intake of alcohol increased, so did the chance of producing an infant displaying abnormalities.

Hanson et al. (Blake 1982) examined the average maternal alcohol consumption per day from two months preceding the determination of pregnancy to five months into the pregnancy to study the effects of alcohol on the developing fetus. In the study, "there appeared to be a direct relationship between the frequency of abnormal offspring and the average quantity of alcohol ingested during each period" (Blake 1982, p. 160). Increased risk of perinatal mortality in children of heavy drinkers has also been reported (Little et al. 1982). A study in France "revealed a rate of stillbirth among women consuming at least 3 drinks daily that was 2-1/2 times the rate for women drinking less than this; a dose-response trend was evident" (Little et al. 1982, p.113).

The evidence is mounting that correlates the amount of alcohol ingested to the degree of abnormality in the infant. Studies show that women who drink place their infants at risk of a variety of abnormalities including the possibility of death. The more a woman drinks, the higher the chances are that her baby will be affected. The same is true for the woman who uses other drugs. Finnegan (1982) examined several studies that found the morbidity rate among infants "born to drug-dependent women was directly related to the amount of prenatal care as well as the kind of dependence (heroin or methadone)" (p.67).

Finnegan also found that "once the umbilical cord of the infant of the narcotic-dependent mother has been cut, symptoms of abstinence can be expected to follow. Symptomalogy has been reported by many investigators in hundreds of these infants" (p. 71). Neonatal narcotic abstinence syndrome because it is so visible has, in many ways advanced the medical field's premise that alcohol and other drugs negatively effect the developing fetus. Infants born of drug abusing mothers have shown far more dramatic and immediate withdrawal symptoms and abnormalities. Prematurity (and accompanying complications), low birth weight, growth retardation, behavioral problems (such as irritability, tremulousness, jerkiness of motor movement and increased muscle tone), seizures, respiratory difficulties, and sleep disturbance have all been reported by many researchers to be linked to the mother's ingestion of drugs (Finnegan 1982).

Although it may be difficult, at times, to prove that infant abnormalities have been directly caused by the ingestion of alcohol or other drugs, there is a strong enough correlation to make the following statement. These social drugs do pose harm to the developing fetus. Women should be discouraged from drinking alcohol or taking any drugs (unless advised by a doctor) while pregnant as it is difficult to determine a safe level of use. As illustrated earlier, no two pregnancies are alike and no two fetuses are effected the same way by the same drug. Though it cannot be said with certainty that drinking X amount of alcohol or taking X amount of a drug will result with consistency in a particular abnormality, the evidence is strong enough to alert the public that alcohol and other drugs effect the development of the fetus and is therefore contraindicated for pregnant women in any amount.

The Denial System of the Pregnant Alcoholic

To increase the chances of having a heathy baby, the pregnant woman must have access to good prenatal care. One aspect of this care is ensuring that the mother abstains from alcohol and drugs. For the female alcoholic, this poses an obvious conflict. The definition of alcoholism described in Chapter 1 was that social drinking crosses the line into addiction when there is a change in tolerance and a loss of control over the drinking. The woman needs more of the alcohol to feel its effect while having lost the ability to choose whether or how much to drink. It has been established that the more the woman drinks, the greater the possibility that her baby will be born with abnormalities.

The pregnancy requires that she be able to choose not to drink or at least ingest less than three drinks a day. The earlier on in the pregnancy that she makes this "choice", the better her chances are of delivering a healthy baby. Unfortunately, it is not about choice. The compulsion to drink prevents the possibility of choice. The mother caught in the grips of an addiction cannot stop drinking and using even though she may realize that it is harmful to her baby.

Unable to face the conflict between the compulsion to drink and the knowledge that alcohol can cause birth defects, the pregnant alcoholic has only two options. The first is the most popular with the public. The woman is expected to admit she has an addiction and go for treatment. From those who have little understanding of what it means to be a female alcoholic, there tends to be a great deal of criticism and disgust. Society accuses the mother who cannot abstain of not caring about her unborn child. There is difficulty perceiving the pregnant alcoholic as sick and unable to fight for what is in the best interests of her baby. Her resistance to get help is seen as further proof of the stereotype that female alcoholics are bad mothers. Most of the public misses the point that, by admitting she is an alcoholic, she is admitting that she is a bad mother anyway.

The second option is more popular with the pregnant alcoholic in dealing with this no-win situation. By convincing herself that she is not an alcoholic or that alcohol and drugs cannot harm her baby, she can avoid the pain created by the conflict. By activating her defense mechanisms she can "live with herself". This is an unconscious process outside her awareness. She has probably long ago become quite adept at denying her alcoholism. It is not a great leap to continue that denial around the harmful effects of drugs and alcohol on the developing fetus. The denial system of the pregnant alcoholic is further reinforced by the unpredictability of alcohol's effect on the infant. Because not all babies subjected to alcohol by their mother's drinking suffer ramifications of this exposure, it leads credence to the woman's belief system that her infant will not be harmed.

Sandy's Story

Sandy was 18 when she met Dave. She was already heavily involved in the drug culture when they became sexual. They used cocaine and heroin together as well as alcohol and some marijuana. One night, Dave gave Sandy some pills to go along with the cocaine they were using. After they had sex, Sandy passed out on the bed for several hours. When she came to, Dave wanted to do some more drugs. She refused and went back to sleep. When she woke up in the morning, Dave was laying beside her in bed dead from an overdose.

Several weeks later, she found out she was pregnant with his baby. She continued to use throughout the pregnancy. Dave's death from a drug overdose did little to convince her to quit. The baby was born "normal".

Three years later and pregnant again, Sandy was confronted about her drinking and using during the pregnancy. Her rational was that her first baby was conceived the night the baby's father overdosed and she used heavily throughout that pregnancy. Since the baby had been born without any problems, she insisted that drugs would not harm this baby either. There was simply no way to prove her wrong until the second baby was born.

Her denial system was supported by the "evidence" of the birth of her healthy daughter. Because her daughter had been conceived under such dramatic circumstances and had been exposed to all types of chemicals throughout the pregnancy, it was impossible for her to believe that any alcohol and drug use would harm her second baby.

Factors That Make the Difference

There are a number of factors that influence the pregnant alcoholic's ability to be abstinent during her pregnancy. They include:

> * whether it is a planned pregnancy
> * how far along she is in her alcoholism
> * what support system she has available to her
> * what kind of treatment she can get
> * what the drinking status is of her partner (whether he is an alcoholic)
> * how her partner feels about her drinking
> * how far along she is in her pregnancy by the time she knows she is pregnant
> * how the woman feels during her pregnancy
> * how the woman feels about becoming a mother (or having another child)
> * what kind of prenatal care, if any, she receives

Much depends on whether the pregnancy is planned and how far along she is in her alcoholism. If the pregnancy is planned and she is in the early stages of addiction, chances are that the woman is more committed to her baby's welfare than in practicing her disease. This commitment to delivering a healthy baby can make the difference in her ability to confront her alcoholism. Having a strong support system, access to treatment and a sober partner who wants her to abstain can also be strong factors in favor of abstaining. However, the further along she is in her alcoholism, the more difficult it is for her fight the denial system triggered by the disease.

If the pregnancy is not planned, chances are greater that the mother will experience conflict between the compulsion to drink and her desire to protect her baby. The further along she is in both the pregnancy and the alcoholism, the more difficult the conflict. As the pregnancy progresses, so does the woman's denial. "Just as the alcoholic's denial becomes harder to penetrate in the later stages of alcoholism so does some woman's denial become greater as her pregnancy progresses, perhaps due to extreme guilt and fear about the baby's welfare" (Finklestein et al. 1990, p. 281).

If it is an unplanned pregnancy, chances are that the woman has been drinking and using drugs before, during and after conception. The further along in the pregnancy she is, the more difficult it is for her to accept the diagnosis of alcoholism. The reasons are obvious. To take responsibility for exposing her baby to potential harm would label her a "monster".

The mother has to rationalize that the drugs and alcohol she has already taken during the first and second trimester have not harmed her baby. If she were to abstain in the third trimester, the female alcoholic is admitting that her earlier behavior may have hurt her baby. For most women, this is an unbearable pain to endure. Defense mechanisms are triggered to help the woman deal with her shame and guilt. The further along she is in the course of the disease, the more invested she is in convincing herself that the baby is not affected. The conflict between the need to protect her unborn child and the compulsion to continue drinking result in an even greater need to lie about the effects of alcohol on the developing fetus.

Pregnancy as a Trigger to Drink

How the woman feels physically during her pregnancy and emotionally about being pregnant can have an enormous impact on her ability to abstain from alcohol and drugs. Morning sickness, back pain, leg cramps and other normal physical consequences of being pregnant can overwhelm a newly sober alcoholic. Compounded with the pain of withdrawal, the physical discomforts of pregnancy can be perceived as unbearable. Even for female alcoholics who have been sober for years, the physical stamina needed to carry the extra workload on the woman's heart, lungs, and other body systems of sustaining a new life can trigger a craving to drink. Nine months is a long time to not feel well, especially for an alcoholic.

The emotional consequences of pregnancy can also lead to relapse or a failure to abstain. Adjustment to all of the bodily changes involved in pregnancy can be overwhelming for some women. Body image and self-esteem are serious issues for many pregnant alcoholics. Many women feel ugly and fat instead of pregnant. Undiagnosed eating disorders can flare up at a time when the woman needs to eat for two. All of these factors are exacerbated if the pregnancy is not planned or the baby not wanted.

Fears around the pregnancy and about giving birth are not acknowledged in our society. Women are often ill-prepared for what will happen to them during childbirth. Even in the smoothest cases, giving birth can be traumatic for many women. Most women are overwhelmed at the new responsibilities involved in mothering and the financial burden babies create. Finally, the woman's relationship to the baby's father can have a huge impact on her success at abstaining during the pregnancy. Women who have been abandoned or lack any kind of support system are less likely to seek treatment for their addiction. Women who do not want the baby can be resentful at being confronted about their alcoholism hurting their infant. Alone, frightened and possibly resentful at being pregnant, alcohol may be the woman's best (and perhaps) only friend.

Alcoholics use alcohol to numb out negative feelings and create the illusion of positive ones. Pregnancy can be filled with a mixture of emotions depending on the circumstances around conception, giving birth and parenting. For many pregnant alcoholics, the pregnancy is surrounded by far greater negative consequences. The largest being the fact that the mother's decision to drink alcohol and use drugs can potentially harm her unborn child. The mother's denial system can be activated in an attempt to avoid dealing with her ambivalent or negative feelings both about her pregnancy and her addiction.

Prenatal Care

Problems with prenatal care occur in two areas for the pregnant alcoholic. The first concerns women's access to services. This access may be denied because of financial reasons, lack of childcare, limited transportation, practical considerations (such as scheduling) and denial of services due to substance use. According to Lynne Wittenberg, a Health Educator who specializes in women's reproductive health and perinatal substance use issues " important gaps exist within the prenatal care delivery system. Due to liability concerns, many prenatal care providers will discontinue care to a pregnant woman if substance use is detected, often leaving her few options" (Wittenberg 1993, p.77).

Many women can not afford the cost of prenatal care, childcare during these office visits or transportation to the site. It can be an incredible hardship to overcome these financial obstacles. To be denied service because of substance use can defeat the woman and places the unborn child's chances of survival at risk. Out of fear of prosecution and the belief that help is not available, the woman may give up any attempt to receive prenatal care. For many women, there are no services offered.

Prenatal care is crucial to the health and welfare of the pregnant woman and her baby. It is during these office visits that screening for substance use can take place and education given on the effects of alcohol and drugs on the developing fetus. It is much harder for the female alcoholic not to heed the warnings of the medical staff because they are seen as experts in this field. These women have a better chance of being reached and helped during regular office visits. In one study of nearly 30,000 women, it was found that those mothers who did not receive prenatal care tested positive for alcohol two and a half times more often than women who received care. The same group of women tested positive for illicit drugs seven times more often and for smoking three times more often than those women who got such care (Wittenberg 1991).

The second area focuses on the women's fears of utilizing health care services because of the negative consequences to themselves. Wittenberg states that " problems arise when women are reluctant to reveal their history of substance abuse (especially illicit drugs) and/or seek prenatal care out of fear that they will lose child custody" (Wittenberg 1993, p.77). She insists that "a punitive climate toward perinatal substance use makes delayed prenatal care more likely" (Wittenberg 1993, p.77). If women are to get the message that they need to stay abstinent during their pregnancy, they must be encouraged to seek out prenatal care. This care must include information on the effects of alcohol and drugs on the developing fetus, screening for use and/or abuse of these chemicals and access to treatment for addiction that doesn't place the woman at risk for losing custody of her baby.

Obstacles to Treatment

Another factor contributing to triggering the woman's denial system is the drinking status of her partner (often the baby's father). As was noted earlier, women are often introduced to alcohol through a relationship and they are often pressured to drink to maintain that relationship. This presents an additional conflict between the needs of the fetus and her need to stay connected to the baby's father. Many women fear abandonment if they abstain from alcohol and their partner continues to drink. This fear is greater when the woman is vulnerable during her pregnancy and lacks any other resources or support system. The pregnant alcoholic may be depending on the man for financial and emotional support. Without him she may be unable to keep her baby.

Finally, treatment options for pregnant alcoholics are nearly non-existent. According to Lynne Wittenberg (1996), many programs are uncomfortable or ill-equipped to take on the medical needs of mother and fetus. Other programs are simply not set up to provide for the particular needs of women in general, let alone pregnant women. Although Wittenberg insists changes are being made, funding for programs addressing the needs of the pregnant alcoholic have been and continue to be limited. For those pregnant alcoholics who do find treatment centers set up to meet their needs, access is difficult. Treatment is expensive and women are even less employable during their pregnancy. Many do not have insurance or family assistance. Furthermore, many women fear being reported for child abuse because of exposing their babies to drugs and alcohol in utero.

The Pregnant Addict

While the pregnant alcoholic must deal with the conflict between her need to practice her addiction and her need to protect her baby, the pregnant alcoholic/addict faces much more. Women who use illegal drugs are exposed to an environment that presents several obstacles to delivering a healthy baby. Poverty, inadequate health care, lack of prenatal care, poor nutrition and physical illnesses are realities of the drug world. In addition, physical and sexual abuse, violence and prostitution have a huge impact on the chances of the pregnant addict carrying her baby to term. The lifestyle of the addict is a dangerous one and a huge risk to her baby.

> The risk of exposure to AIDS is increasingly becoming recognized as a danger to unborn children of alcohol or drug abusing women who constitute the largest group of women at risk. AIDS can be transmitted from mother to fetus in utero, during childbirth or possibly through breast feeding. An HIV positive woman with no symptoms may have a greater likelihood of developing AIDS during pregnancy because pregnancy compromises her immune system. If a mother tests positive for the AIDS antibody there is a 50% chance the child will be positive (Finklestein et al. 1990, p. 283).

Babies exposed to cocaine, heroin and other drugs "are more likely to die before birth or to be born prematurely. They have a lower birth rate and an increased risk of crib death as well as an increased incidence of strokes. Other physical and neurological abnormalities may produce long-term damage in the newborn showing itself in irritability, lack of responsiveness and learning difficulties" (Finklestein et al. 1990, p. 282). Many of these babies are born with abstinence withdrawal syndrome (Finklestein et al. 1990).

Women who abuse prescription drugs may have to resort to the same manipulative, deceitful and lying ways that their sisters on the streets are forced to do to obtain their drugs. However, the middle-class housewife does not necessarily experience the poverty, poor nutrition and exposure to sexually transmitted diseases that the addict does who uses illicit drugs. Nevertheless, women addicted to pain medication frequently lose access to their supply when doctors refuse to give prescriptions to them when they are pregnant or nursing.

As a result, these women learn to doctor-hop, lie about their pregnancy and find other resourceful ways to get their drugs. One addict described how she got her doctor to give her a prescription under the guise that her breasts hurt when she tried to wean her son. She proceeded to take the medication while continuing to nurse him. Her husband caught her before she got the second prescription from another doctor.

Society's Attitude Toward the Pregnant Alcoholic

Society's attitude toward a woman who drinks while she is pregnant is harsh. It fits in with the stereotype that women alcoholics are bad mothers. There is little compassion for the pregnant alcoholic as a sick woman unable to properly care for herself and her unborn infant. Understandably, public outcry is against the woman who could so easily jeopardize the life of her baby. Accusations of child abuse ring loud and threats of removing the baby once it is born sound valid.

According to Lynne Wittenberg (1991), "the tendency to view women solely in terms of their reproductive capacity, and their role as primary caregiver within the family, has historically served as the basis for judging women more harshly for their addictions, and, in particular, for their substance use during pregnancy" (p. 5). This judgement has led to a crusade to criminalize the pregnant alcoholic's behavior rather than focus on her need for treatment. As a result, few treatment centers are sensitive to the unique needs of female alcoholics or equipped to give immediate help to the pregnant woman. Many centers fear the liability involved in treating a woman who may then give birth to a baby with disabilities (Wittenberg 1991).

Other treatment providers lack the facilities and staff to provide childcare for the woman's other children, safe and sober housing, financial assistance or job training. The end result is that women fear seeking out prenatal care and addiction treatment because they are often denied services or provided inadequate care. In addition, pregnant alcoholics are forced to face the "guilt and shame for exposing their unborn to drugs and alcohol" and the potential "loss of child custody and/or criminal prosecution for their substance use" (Wittenberg 1991, p. 13) if they do ask for help.

There are no easy answers when it comes to deciding how best to help these women and their babies. One thing is certain though. If it is our desire to ensure the safety and welfare of the developing fetus then it must also be true that we ensure the safety and welfare of their mothers. To condemn one is to condemn the other. As long as women fear seeking help because;

* they will face child abuse charges,
* are confronted by society's attitudes that they are monsters as mothers rather than sick with an illness,
* are paralyzed with obstacles to treatment, and
* lack access to financial and emotional resources that would enable them to change their lives,

pregnant alcoholics will continue to drink and use drugs. They will not have the support they need (and deserve) to protect their unborn babies. As a result, they will continue to make decisions that are not in the best interest of themselves or their babies. This will only serve to perpetuate the stereotype that they are unfit mothers.

This myth will also prevent our society from recognizing its contribution to reinforcing the cycle of addiction and the denial that goes along with it. It will not stop the damage done to these babies. In reality, it will encourage the abuse to continue.

7

The Alcoholic Mother

Alcoholism as a Pervasive Illness

When I was thirteen, my father married a woman who had epilepsy, a disorder that resulted in seizures. She had suffered from the illness since childhood and was adamant that everyone in the family know what to do when she had a seizure. I was taught what medication she took, how to respond during a seizure and who to call for help.

During my adolescence, she had many attacks, many of them at work. Some seizures resulted in cuts and bruises because she fell. Other times, she came home after a seizure disoriented, shaken and exhausted. There were times when she needed to be hospitalized because the attacks would not stop. And when she began to experience heart problems, the doctors struggled to balance her heart medication with her epilepsy pills. When she had heart surgery, everyone was concerned that she would have a seizure during the operation.

My step-mother's epilepsy had a tremendous impact on my life. I lived in fear that I wouldn't know what to do, that I would do the wrong thing, or not move quickly enough to prevent injury. I was afraid something horrible would happen to her. It had such a profound effect on me that years later, I was still able to rattle off the medication and precautions to take when a client had just been diagnosed with epilepsy. Yet, I never saw my step-mother have a seizure. Not once!

Alcoholism has a similar impact on children's lives. They may never see their mother drinking but the illness pervades every aspect of their lives. Their mother may pass out, experience hangovers, become lethargic after a drinking episode, display mood swings or a loss of memory. Like epilepsy, alcoholism has a set of recognizable symptoms, a course of action that children need to take when it is present and an aftermath that reminds the family that all is not normal.

Regardless of the exact circumstances, chances are that every child with an alcoholic parent is aware on some level that there is an illness in the family. It may not have a name. It may not be talked about. It may even be denied. But the children know. Over the years of working with families in private practice, this truth has been proven over and over again. The children know something is wrong.

Society's Attitudes Toward the Alcoholic Mother

Alcoholic women coming into recovery face huge obstacles when addressing motherhood issues. Society automatically assumes female alcoholics are bad mothers. Though it is true that a mother's drinking impacts her children, this impact is different for every child. In some families, alcoholic mothers are so impaired that the children experience numerous problems. Violence, divorce, child abuse, neglect and trauma are substantial in these homes. In other families the alcoholism seems to have a less debilitating effect. A group of researchers studying alcoholic families found that many families adapted to the alcoholism remarkably well. They discovered that they were "making do".

> By 'making do,' we mean that a substantial group of families with alcoholic members seem to remain intact over their life span (no divorce; continue to live with the alcoholic member), are economically viable, avoid the more dramatic and devastating types of family violence, and suffer no higher levels of anxiety and depression than the general population. Presumably these families also lead compromised lives as a consequence of their exposure to alcoholism. But this impact, this constriction of family life, if it does occur, does so in ways far more subtle than is seen in those dramatic examples of family pathology represented by spouse abuse, incest and the like (Steinglass et al. 1987, p. 23).

Alcoholism affects children differently in each family and, in fact, differently for each child in that family. There are a number of variables that contribute to this. One is the personality, gender and birth order of that child. Older female children tend to become caregivers while younger male siblings frequently play the scapegoat. The role each child assumes in the family greatly influences the child's perceptions of what is happening in that family. Another factor is how far along the alcoholism has progressed.

A mother in the early stages of the disease may be able to maintain routines, schedules and some predictability in her children's lives. In the advanced stages of alcoholism, mothers are frequently unavailable for any semblance of parenting. In addition, the father's drinking status, the parent's relationship and the role of the extended family influence the stability of family life. Alcoholic fathers and grandparents may offer little in support or healthy parenting.

Society assumes that all alcoholic mothers are abusive, neglectful and failures. It is true that alcoholism impairs a woman's ability to parent. So does cancer, migraine headaches and mental illness. The difference is that alcoholism is not seen as a disease, especially when it comes to mothers. Mothers are trusted with the job of nurturing the next generation; fathers are not. When alcoholism impairs her ability to do that job, she is viewed as having failed to protect her children.

Furthermore, alcoholic women are frequently abandoned by their husbands and left to parent the children alone, increasing their sense of responsibility. In homes where the marriage remains intact, the father is usually an alcoholic as well. When these fathers are impaired, it is assumed that the children experience little or no effect because their mothers protect them. However, when the mother drinks, it is assumed that there is no one to protect the children and that it is the mother's fault that this is the case. In spite of the definition of alcoholism as a loss of control over drinking, women are condemned for not being in control of it.

In our society, mothers have been placed as solely responsible for their children's welfare. Therefore, alcoholic fathers seldom face society's disapproval for what their drinking has done to their children; even when faced with the evidence that it has damaged them.   Women are expected to accept sole responsibility. And they do.

Alcoholic Women as Mothers

Alcoholism creates personality, behavioral and physical changes regardless of gender. However, because women are the sole caretakers, these changes have a profound effect on the children in their care. Over the course of their disease, alcoholics turn their focus on to alcohol. Their world narrows to concerns about protecting their supply of alcohol, denying their use of alcohol, denying the consequences of that use, and coping with the symptoms of withdrawal (Evans et al. 1990). This takes up a great deal of the female alcoholic's time and energy, leaving little for others in her life, including the children.

The female alcoholic has a primary relationship with the "bottle", making it difficult for her to form an honest, intimate and dependable relationship with her children or other adults (Covington 1986). Alcohol comes first and children are quick to learn this. When the alcoholic becomes a parent, the bond with the bottle interferes with a mother's ability to bond with her children. If her children are to survive, they must learn to relate to their mother on their mother's terms; and that means on the alcohol's terms.

Alcoholics have certain behavior characteristics that are symptomatic of the disease. Many lie, make excuses, hide and sneak around to cover up their drinking.

> Lying is the most commonly known characteristic of alcoholic thinking. Most alcoholics lie in different ways at different times. They use lying to confuse, distort and take the focus off their behavior. Lying takes three forms:

coadmission- making things up that simply aren't true;
omission- saying partly what is so but leaving out major sections;
assent- making believe that one agrees with someone else or presenting or

approving others' ideas in order to look good when, in fact, the person has no intention of going along with this or does really agree (Evans et al.1990, p. 44).

Blaming others is another method alcoholics use to explain away their behavior (Evans et al. 1990). Similar to making excuses, blaming justifies the reason for drinking. It often places the people being blamed on the defensive, further encouraging the probability that they will have difficulty confronting the drinking. Often, the people being blamed shift the argument to proving that they are not at fault. The alcoholic is then free to build resentment over what has been identified as the cause of the drinking.

In order for blaming and making excuses to be an effective defense mechanism, the alcoholic must spend "a great deal of time assuming what others think, what others feel, what others are doing" (Evans et al. 1990, p. 45). Women alcoholics create a complicated fantasy life from these assumptions and use their interpretations of people's reactions to them as excuses to drink (Perez 1994).

Female alcoholics can become adept at manipulating people, situations and reactions to their drinking. They use anger and power plays to control others by

* criticizing them,
* using put-downs,
* blaming,
* keeping or telling secrets,
* being vague about commitments,
* threatening abandonment,
* withdrawing attention,
* refusing to listen,
* minimizing the other person's feelings
* maximizing or dramatizing their own feelings,
* minimizing the impact of their behavior on others,
* maximizing the impact of others' behavior on them,
* intimidating them,
* attacking them or someone important to them
* not following through on agreements (Evans et al. 1990).

Children are particularly vulnerable to these tactics as they depend on parents to define their reality and subsequently, their self-esteem. When the alcoholic mother is angry, blaming the children for her anger (and consequent drinking) and threatening abandonment, the children are more likely to try to improve their behavior than confront the mother on hers. Reality is continually denied in favor of a distortion that supports and reinforces the woman's drinking.

Living with an alcoholic can be confusing, crazy-making and chaotic. Alcoholics have mood swings, use defense mechanism and "act out" distorted thinking by intellectualizing (Perez 1994). Their relationship with alcohol is exclusive, possessive and demanding. Alcoholic mothers can appear to be loving and nice one moment then fly into a rage the next for no apparent reason. The goal however, is always the same; protecting their supply, their denial and their disease. Being nice can win trust; being angry can win cooperation. "The alcoholic often overdoes being nice to others and going out of (her) way to act interested in other people. The alcoholic's out to find out what (she) can get from other people, how (she) can manipulate them, use them, or control the situation to (her) own purpose" (Evans et al. 1990, p. 45).

Alcoholics will use whatever works to achieve these goals. They are not always consciously aware of what they are doing or why, but they can be very skillful at finding the vulnerability of others. Because of their own ability to exploit others, alcoholics perceive the world as hostile (Perez 1994). Many are convinced that others think the same way they do and do not trust them. They believe that others, including their own children, are trying to manipulate them. This is "proven" when children find ways to control their mother's drinking.

In the alcoholic home, there is little trust. The children cannot trust their mother and the mother does not trust her own children. This creates an environment of secrecy, fear and emotional distance as family members protect themselves from each other.

Finally, female alcoholics are notorious for playing the victim role (Evans et al. 1990, Perez 1994). Alcoholic mothers are in a perfect situation to play this role with their children. Children are naturally tolerant and compassionate for their mothers, alcoholics or anyone in a position of helplessness. They can relate to what that feels like. When they see that their mothers cannot cope, they assume responsibility by taking over for them.

Alcoholics can become quite skilled in whining, complaining, acting helpless and crying when they do not get what they want. Children needing to feel safe and secure are quick to respond to this behavior. They respond by trying to give the alcoholic what she wants; allowing their mother to avoid responsibility for her behavior.

Dyanna's Story of The Cycle

It was so very painful being the child of alcoholic parents. Always wondering if other people lived like you. One day of many, I remember coming home from school to find my parents lying nude in a blackout on the kitchen floor. I wondered how many other children my age lived like this. Life seemed so out of control. I recall feeling so painfully vulnerable and powerless.

I spent most of my childhood living like this. I grew up full of resentment and in fear that these two lifeless bodies were the only people in my life I had to depend upon. These two, very sick people, were all I had to protect me from the outside world. This was my reality. I decided that when I grew up and had children of my own, they would never have to live like this. My children were going to have all the things in life that were never possible for me.

I wish changing family cycles could be that simple. For as fate would have it, I became addicted to alcohol and other chemicals. My disease of addiction never reared its ugly head until my husband, my best friend in the whole world, the man on the white horse who had taken me away from all this pain and given me a warm, loving home, was killed in a work-related accident. I was a child of twenty-three, mother of two babies, alone and in extreme pain. In no time at all, my need to escape from my feelings became the one and only focus of my life. Slowly, but surely, my children were pushed away.

An alcoholic parent carries many painful memories and one in particular comes to mind. One day, when my son was in second grade, he came home from school and asked if I would take him to the movies the following afternoon. I agreed and felt so proud that he would want to spend that kind of time with me. I thought about the movie we would see and what ice cream store we would visit after the movie. We were going to have one of those family days that I never got to experience with my parents.

The next day, I decided that I would not smoke a joint or take a drink, for I wanted to be fresh and clear to spend this special moment with my son. He went off to play in the morning with some of his friends and I stayed home to do some housecleaning. At around noon, the doorbell rang and a friend of mine who had moved to Hawaii several months before, was standing on my porch with a bottle of Zambucca in her hand, some Hawaiian pot in her purse and a very big devilish grin on her face. I was so happy to see her. In no time at all, we had smoked a joint and pretty much killed the bottle.

An hour or two went by, and my son arrived home, rushing so as not to be late for our special day. He came running into the house with a big smile on his face, took one look at us and the smile drained slowly from his face. Although I didn't think of it at the time, he looked very much like me when I walked in the door to find my parents loaded. He asked, "When are we leaving for the movies, mom?" I told him that I wasn't feeling up to it, but we could go some other time. He said "all right" in his usual understanding way and ran off to play. I felt a twinge of guilt in my heart.

The next day, another friend of mine called. She seemed very upset. She told me that on her way home from the market the day before, she had seen my son sitting on a stone wall visibly upset. She stopped the car and got out to sit with him for a while to find out what had happened. He said, "My mom doesn't love me. She just wants to be with her friends. They mean more to her than me." My friend consoled him as best she could and told him that I loved him with all my heart. I don't think he ever believed her.

Today, I am in recovery and I have had an opportunity to make amends to my children for my (alcoholic) behavior. I will never, however, to my dying day, forget that incident. I hold it as a symbol of the many wonderful experiences with my children that my addiction stole from me.

Children of Alcoholic Mothers

Children, growing up in a home where the primary caretaker must use a variety of defense mechanisms to avoid detection of her alcoholism, find that their reality becomes distorted. They learn to keep quiet and to depend only on themselves because people are not trustworthy. Children of alcoholics repress, deny or distort what they think and how they feel in order to create a sense of security. Not knowing what the truth is, they have difficulty figuring out what is real and what is part of their mother's fantasy world. These children learn not to talk, feel or trust (Black 1981).

Alcoholic mothers say things they do not mean, agree to things they do not do, promise to not do things they do do and continually blame the children for their alcoholic behavior. To add to the confusion, the alcoholic denies doing any of the preceding behavior; implying instead that the children are crazy for suggesting it.

There is no validation, support or explanation for the mother's erratic personality changes. With no reference point, the children tend to believe the lies and half-truths. In order to be able to relate to their alcoholic mother, children adapt to her behavior; adopting many of the alcoholic's defense mechanisms as their own. Children of alcoholics often act like alcoholics in their attempt to maintain their relationship with the alcoholic parent. They learn to lie, blame, make up excuses and be vague in order to avoid being blamed (Perez 1986). "Such learning, militates against learning to make commitments, to share feelings, to admit errors, and to learn responsibility for one's behaviors. These, of course, are the behaviors which make for successful living. Small wonder then, that children reared in alcoholic homes grow up bewildered and feeling emotionally isolated" (Perez 1986, p. 69).

This adaption to alcoholic behavior does not necessarily mean that children know that alcoholism is at the core of their problems. Some are aware that a parent drinks but do not know what that means.   Others may never see the parent drink or deny seeing it. Many are confused between what they see and what their mothers say they see.   It is estimated that 40% of the children who grow up in alcoholic homes do not realize that their parent has an addiction (Seixas 1985). Most parents do not fit society's stereotype of a "drunk". Many of these children have no other reference point.

Adapting to alcoholic behavior means tolerating mood swings, personality changes, and mixed messages from the alcoholic (Evans et al. 1990, Perez 1986). Their mother may be happy one moment, violent the next. Confusion reigns when promises made during a blackout are adamantly denied by the mother when sober. Many children perceive their parents as crazy; others perceive themselves as the crazy ones. They know something is wrong, but are not sure what it is. Their parent(s) however, insist that everything is fine. This discrepancy between what children see is happening to their family and what they are told is going on creates self-doubt. Children of alcoholics cannot trust what they see, what they hear, what they feel or what they are told. They learn not to trust anyone, including themselves.

Alcoholic mothers lie to their children to protect themselves, the family and (they believe) the children themselves. Part of this lying comes in the form of mixed or double messages. "Double messages are those where the words spoken do not jibe with the emotional tones on which they ride or on the behavior displayed" (Perez 1986, p. 65). Lying, being vague, double messages and blaming serve to keep the focus off of the drinking. Children grow up believing that they caused the alcoholism and the problems associated with the drinking. Frequently, children spend their time and energy protecting themselves and trying to decide how to respond.

> Perhaps the most devastating effect upon children reared in double message system is that they never learn to value the truth because they never know what the truth is. Not only do they not know what the messages they get mean but just as importantly they never learn to *feel* about the messages they get. *People reared in a system of double messages frequently become alienated from their own feelings.* They don't know how they feel because they don't know what's true. Indeed truth, to them, especially in communication, becomes an irrelevancy, unimportant. *This is precisely why the children of alcoholics frequently lie when they could just as easily tell the truth.* What they learn as children is that truth is not important, or again lying doesn't really matter (Perez 1986, p. 65).

Children of alcoholics, trying to form the bond with their mother necessary for survival, adopt the communication style, distorted thinking, distrustful attitude, and other behaviors associated with alcoholism. These children learn to respond, enable and ignore alcoholic behavior. Many become so skillful at these behaviors that they look like alcoholics themselves, making them attractive to other alcoholics for friendships and relationships. This explains why a large number of daughters of alcoholics marry an alcoholic (Black 1981).

The Self-centeredness of Alcoholism

It is rare for the alcoholic member to change his or her drinking behavior to better mesh with family routines--but the reverse is quite common. Thus such behaviors as food preparation and mealtimes, social activities in the home, housekeeping, and the like are often arranged to minimize the likelihood of interference from alcoholism (or to minimally interfere with drinking behavior) (Steinglass et al. 1987, p. 73).

Adapting to the alcoholic's drinking routine, accepting blame for the drinking and associated problems, and attempting to please the alcoholic provides children with, at least, the illusion of control and security. However, this behavior provides the mother with reinforcement for her distorted thinking. It is painful for any parent to think she has harmed her children. This pain can act as a huge stumbling block for alcoholic mothers when faced with the damage alcoholism has done to their children. Believing that the children are not affected is much easier to tolerate. As a result, women perceive their children's willingness to accept the blame for the drinking as evidence that it is their fault rather than the children's attempt to have some control over their environment.

As her disease progresses, the mother becomes more focused on protecting her supply of alcohol and her time to drink it. The family's adaption to this focus on the primacy of alcohol creates an environment that continually reinforces the mother's belief that her drinking, and therefore herself, is most important to the family. As schedules, routines and behaviors are constantly made or changed to suit her needs, the alcoholic mother comes to expect this response from her family and is extremely offended if she does not get it. Claudia Alonzo, a therapist that works with children describes this phenomenon as the "me, me, me syndrome". She finds that alcoholic mothers have a very difficult time understanding that their children have needs that may be different from their own. Alcoholics Anonymous calls this self-centered thinking.

Alcoholic mothers are self-centered because their primary concern is alcohol. They are not even aware of what is happening to their children because their relationship to them is secondary. One recovering alcoholic mother insisted that her six year old son did not suffer negative consequences from her drinking. She only drank after he had gone to bed. As far as she was concerned, he never saw her drink, drunk or with a hangover. Therefore, he was not affected. However, when the boy told his version of his mother's behavior over the years, the mother was horrified.

The most devastating story was his description of waking one night to find her passed out on the couch. He thought she was dead because he could not wake her. When she did finally come around, he could not understand what she was saying to him. She was not aware that he was so shaken. She told him to go back to bed and not bother her. His mother had no recollection of the incident. Even after several months of sobriety, her son still came out at night when she was sleeping to check on her. He was afraid that she might die if he did not watch over her.

Attention is given to drinking activities or people who support the drinking. Children who enable their mother's drinking receive more attention than those who do not. They quickly learn not to talk disparagingly about her drinking or tell anyone else. If they do, punishment is inevitable. The rules are clear to the children--adapt to the mother's drinking. The results are just as clear. The drinking is never confronted or acknowledged as the problem. In addition, the mother believes that she is unique and the most important family member (Evans et al. 1990). She expects the children to continue to cater to her needs.

Guilt, Shame and Denial of the Alcoholic Mother

Alcoholic individuals are not all alike. Their behaviors, including their drinking patterns, vary widely and consequently place very different demands and constraints on the environments in which they are attempting to survive. If we read 'family' for 'environment' in this equation, then different types of alcoholism will place different demands on families. In some instances, the family will find these demands intolerable and will either force the individual to stop drinking or to get out. In other families, however, an acceptable 'fit' will be achieved. That is, in such instances, family temperament is fully compatible with the coexistence of the particular type (pattern) of alcoholism manifested by the alcoholic family member (daily drinking, binge drinking, etc.) (Steinglass et al. 1987, p.57).

In single parent families headed by an alcoholic mother, children find "an acceptable fit". They lack the power or support to force her to stop drinking. Children therefore, adapt to their mother's drinking with whatever resources are available to them. Although mothers frequently try to protect their children from their (as well as their father's) drinking as much as they can, children are obviously affected. In some cases, the effect is minimal; in others it is profound. Factors that influence how alcoholism impacts children include:

> * the family's ability to respond to the drinking,
> * how far along the mother is in her disease (early, middle or late stage),
> * what other resources the children have (sober grandparents etc.),
> * what behaviors the children adopt in their attempt to bond with their mother,
> * whether the alcoholism is denied or condoned,
> * whether the father is an alcoholic as well,
> * whether the father has remained in the home, and
> * how active a role the father plays in caring for the children.

The variables involved in determining the impact of alcoholism on the family are interrelated and complex. As a result, it is almost impossible to predict how each child will be affected by each alcoholic parent. The inability to measure with accuracy how each child will respond to the mother's alcoholism, coupled with society's stereotype that all alcoholic mothers are the same (abusive), feeds into the alcoholic's denial system. The alcoholic mother denies that she fits the picture society paints of her and she is probably right. Few families fit that worst case scenario.

Nevertheless, alcoholic mothers have a lot invested in protecting themselves from seeing how their children are harmed by their addiction. The information is painful and the woman usually feels powerless to prevent the damage. Even mothers who have remained clean and sober for years have little ego strength to face the damage done to their children. Society offers little in supporting the idea that the addiction is a disease that infects the entire family. Women continue to be blamed for their drinking and the consequences of that drinking when it comes to their children.

This is particularly true with mothers who introduce their children to alcohol and drugs by drinking with them or acting as role models for drinking behavior. One mother who drank and used turned to selling drugs as a way to support herself and her two young children after she was abandoned by her husband. She was horrified to find, twenty-five years later, that her drug-addicted son had started his career in drugs after finding her personal supply. She could not take any responsibility that he had grown up watching her, her friends and her drug buyers drink and use drugs in her home. Nor could she admit that her son's access to drugs began when he discovered her hiding place under her bed.

Although she was not responsible for his addiction, her fear, shame and guilt over how he was introduced to drugs kept her from being honest about her own addiction. She denied her problems with alcohol and drugs and insisted that, unlike him, she had been a social drinker. This woman continued her denial through several of his attempts at treatment.

Most women do not want to be bad mothers and they do not want to hurt their children. Many mothers are devastated when they realize the pain their children have suffered because of the drinking. Alcoholism damages not only the alcoholic but everyone the alcoholic touches-- especially the children. However, alcoholic mothers are no more at fault than anyone else suffering from a disease that prevents them from parenting their children. Everyone, in contact with alcoholism in any way, is harmed. Rather than persecute women, society needs to provide help to them and their family.

Alcoholic mothers feel ashamed of their addictions and, what they perceive, as their failures as parents. They fear the damage done to their babies during pregnancy and feel guilty for the inadequate care they provided for the older child. Parenting is the most difficult job for any individual, especially for those who have little education or good role models of healthy parenting. When suffering from an illness like an addiction, parenting can be an impossible task. Finally, being blamed for parenting mistakes created by alcoholism is inhumane.

Women need access to treatment for their addiction, education to parent their children, and support to deal with their guilt. The guilt most alcoholic mothers feel is made worse by each physical, emotional or learning problem her child experiences which often " lead(s) to feelings of hopelessness, helplessness and possible relapse. Therefore, it is important to help an alcoholic and drug abusing woman in treatment understand that both she and her family have been victims of alcoholism and drug abuse, not her deliberate or intentional behavior; that parenting is a learned behavior for which many adult daughters of alcoholic parents never had positive role models; and that during her period of active drinking or drug use, her options were limited" (Finklestein et al. 1990, p. 228).

8

The Alcoholic Adult Daughter
of Alcoholic(s)

Daughters of Alcoholics Becoming Alcoholics Themselves

Studies have proven that female alcoholics are more likely than their male counterparts to have grown up in alcoholic families and to describe these families as chaotic (Finklestein et al. 1990). Several studies have found that living in an alcoholic home is stressful for everyone but "especially so for women who, because of the nature of the family culture and construct, are unable to hide their vulnerability to the adverse effects of alcoholism as well as men" (Perez 1994, p. 57). Daughters of alcoholics are "at least twice as likely to becoming alcoholic as are daughters of non-alcoholic parents" (Finklestein et al. 1990, p. 189). This is particularly true for daughters of alcoholic mothers. Researchers believe that "the emotional deprivation which a little girl encounter(s) growing up with an alcoholic mother contribute(s) to her becoming alcoholic herself" (Perez 1994, p. 57).

Alcoholism is genetic and many of these daughters inherit the predisposition for alcoholism. However, environmental factors play a huge role in whether these children become alcoholics. Frequently, alcoholic mothers are unable to maintain the family structure and rituals needed to reduce the level of chaos. Families who are able to adhere to bedtime routines, scheduled mealtimes, holiday traditions, vacation plans, and religious rituals, in spite of alcoholism or alcoholic behavior are less likely to transmit alcoholism to their children (Brown 1992, Steinglass et al. 1987). In families, where structure and rituals do not center around alcohol, the denial about the alcoholic parent is minimal. When education about alcoholism is provided, children are not necessarily resigned to imitate the alcoholic behavior. Many turn to the non-alcoholic parent as a role model.

In contrast, families that are continually disrupted by the alcoholic's need to drink, are not able to provide their children with any other perspective than the importance of alcohol. For these children, alcohol is an emotional issue. They see the family identity as centered on drinking and that they must center their own lives on alcohol if they are to bond with their parents. To succeed, they adopt the beliefs and attitudes about alcohol that their parents share including the function of denial. Many daughters of alcoholics believe that they can control their own drinking in the same way their alcoholic parents believed they could control theirs. The parent-child bond supports the idea of control and the drinking patterns of alcoholism as normal. This is particularly true if both parents are alcoholics. The children have no reference point or alternative model to challenge their parents' denial system.

The parent's relationship greatly influences their children's perceptions of marriage and many find alcoholic spouses to replicate what was familiar to them as children. Many women are not aware that they are doing this and are shocked to discover that their husbands are alcoholics. The husband may have been in the early stage of the disease when the two met. He may have a different drinking pattern or act less dysfunctional than the daughter's alcoholic parent ever did, making it difficult for her to spot the alcoholism in her husband. Or, the daughters' training at denying the truth about their parents' alcoholism creates an obstacle in recognizing the pattern in a husband. Adult daughters of alcoholics have long ago stopped trusting their own perceptions, feelings or instincts.

Finally, daughters of alcoholics learn to take care of their alcoholic parent(s) by addressing the parent's needs instead of their own. Girls, in alcoholic homes, are often expected to take responsibility for the alcoholic parent and younger siblings. They become accustomed to not having their own physical and emotional needs addressed. When they become adults, daughters of alcoholics may willingly neglect their own health, nutrition, sleep needs or emotions making them very attractive to alcoholic partners. They are needed by men who do not want to take responsibility for their drinking and need someone to care for them while their energy is centered around drinking.

Adult daughters who become alcoholics can hide their own drinking behind that of their husband's. The fact that a woman chooses an alcoholic husband increases her likelihood of becoming an alcoholic herself because she is inclined to drink with him (Steinglass et al. 1987). She will act as a drinking companion to her husband and do little to confront his drinking. In return, he will invite her to drink with him, encouraging her to keep up with him.

Michelle's Story

I was an alcoholic from the first drink. When I was eight years old my mother, sister and I went to live with a man who drank wine every night with dinner. I remember talking my mother into giving me a glass, and then another, and I convinced her that she didn't need to water it down for me. By the time I was fourteen and living with my father, I had boyfriends who could supply the alcohol. Six months later, a police officer brought me home for drunk and disorderly conduct. My stepmother only comment was that she thanked God it wasn't drugs. My father told me not to tell my mother or she would take me away from him. I never told.

For the most part, drinking was a pretty normal activity at home. Everyone did it and they did it openly. We even joked about how much we could 'hold our liquor' and who was 'on the bandwagon' this week. My father's drinking was the most obvious, mainly because he did it with huge numbers of friends. His idea of spending time with his children was to buy them lunch (and then sometimes dinner too) at a bar and then ignore them while drinking with his buddies.

We never went to a park, rode a bicycle or learned how to play ball. Once or twice, my dad took us to the park before he retreated inside to a warm house and a cold beer. No one ever called him an alcoholic or said he had a problem except my sister when she was nine. She came home from school with pictures of the human body after someone smoked or drank. My dad told her he'd rather die young and happy than old and miserable. It made sense to me at the time.

My mother did say that my dad could control his drinking and eating if he just wanted to and if he had the will-power. My stepmother just sat up nights waiting for him to come home (if he did) and got mad. Occasionally, she locked him out of the house. Since he never carried a key, he would have to bang on the door until someone let him in. I was the one who got up to let him in.

When I was sixteen, I drank just like my father. I had my own 'buddies' and I found a job at a bar that gave me an unlimited supply of beer - his drink. I worked there six nights a week. I had to buy my own drinks on my night off. No one ever said anything about my drinking and because I was the only one in my family still in school, they thought I was doing just fine.

What I learned the best in my home was how not to feel, even to the point of not recognizing physical needs. I continued to be malnourished as an adult because I had long ago forgotten what it felt like to be hungry. I was a workaholic because I never could tell when I was tired. And I was unable to maintain relationships because I did not know what I was feeling or that you can have two different feelings at the same time. I assumed that if I was angry with a friend, it meant I didn't like them anymore. So I ended the friendship.

The Alcoholic Family

There is no one type of alcoholic family just as there is no one type of alcoholic. Depending on the drinking patterns, number of alcoholics in the family and the stage of the disease each alcoholic suffers, children respond to family alcoholism in many different ways. When the drinking pattern of the alcoholic is predictable, children have an easier time adapting to alcohol as part of the family dynamic (Steinglass et al. 1987). Far more frightening for children is the confusion associated with unexpected bouts of intoxication. Children tend to try to control the events that lead to drinking in an effort to develop some sense of security in the family. Unfortunately, they experience little success in controlling the drinking of an alcoholic who has lost control.

This controlling behavior is not abandoned easily, however. Adult children frequently try to protect one or both parents from the consequences of the alcoholic's drinking. Some defend the non-alcoholic spouse while others help the alcoholic one. Nevertheless, children often feel overwhelmed by their parents' needs and blame themselves for failing to stop the drinking. Many feel responsible for literally keeping the alcoholic parent alive and become extremely anxious when they are not able to control what is happening to the family.

> Denial and the loss of realty testing contribute to the development of an omnipotent belief on the part of the child that something she or he does, or does not do, will effect the drinking of the parent. Because of the tendency of the family to externalize the cause of the drinking, and of the denial of the alcoholic, the child does not learn from the repeated evidence that the drinking is independent of any family member's behavior or attempts to control it (Brown 1985, p. 238).

As the alcoholic becomes more preoccupied with alcohol, the children become more focused on taking care of the parent. Children of alcoholics know that there is no one available to meet their needs. Alcoholic parents do not recognize that children have their own feelings, perceptions and needs or they feel threatened when these needs conflict with their own. Eventually, children realize that it is not safe to need and that these needs are not going to get met. Daughters of alcoholics put their energy in meeting the needs of others, starting with their parents, and do not have expectations that their needs will be addressed.

Family Roles

The alcoholic family takes on certain characteristic roles to help each member cope with the chaos and dysfunction of the addictive environment. Claudia Black (1981) who works with children of alcoholics identified three common roles; the Super Achiever, the Adjuster and the Placating Child. Sharon Wegscheider (1981) came up with four roles; the Hero, the Scapegoat, the Lost Child and the Mascot. The role each family member plays can depend on when the individual entered the family system, their gender, which parent they resemble (the alcoholic or the spouse), and their natural born strengths and weaknesses. For example, the first born child often takes on the hero role while the second plays the scapegoat.

However, if the first born is a male who tends to rebel and the second born is a female who has been taught to be a caretaker, their roles may be reversed. Although the roles tend to become rigid, family members will pick up the roles left behind by departing siblings. For example, if the hero leaves for college, the scapegoat might adopt the newly vacant role to maintain the balance of the family. Keeping the family roles in balance is the children's attempt to stabilize the unpredictability of the disease.

The Hero or Superachiever is the good child. Heroes learn to shine as the stars. This brings their families a sense of self-worth. They are high achievers in any number of areas; at school, in sports, leadership roles, at a job or through some talent. Heroes allow the family to deny their dysfunction by representing how well they have raised their children. Often, this is the child that takes on the caretaking role for other siblings when the non-alcoholic spouse is too obsessed with taking care of the alcoholic. The hero may also become the family "counselor" listening for hours to their enabling parent complain about the alcoholic.

Heroes often feel responsible for "fixing" their families. They will work hard to improve the situation. Unfortunately, heros cannot solve their families' problems because of their powerlessness to confront the drinking. There is often too much denial surrounding the disease. These children end up focusing on the symptoms; which ultimately offers only temporary relief. This is enough for the family to continue seeing them as the hero, but, it effects little change. Not understanding the nature of alcoholism, these children blame themselves for failing to stop the progression of the disease. They struggle with seeing themselves as the scapegoat when they are unable to prevent a crisis. Every hero feels like the scapegoat at some time and works hard to avoid that role.

The Scapegoat is the bad child. Scapegoats keep the family's attention off of the alcoholic by "acting out". This helps to divert focus from the alcoholic's inappropriate behavior and convinces the family (and often teachers and counselors) that the family's difficulties are because of the child. Some of the problems the scapegoat may experience are getting pregnant, using drugs and alcohol, running away, getting into trouble with the law and/or school, or joining a gang. The scapegoat is looking for acceptance and a feeling of belonging outside the family. Their only avenue for getting attention is to be in trouble.

The Lost Child is the invisible child. Lost children learn to play quietly and require little attention. They prefer solitude and time alone rather than risk relating to the alcoholic family. No one notices these children. They function to provide relief to the family by doing what they are supposed to do without being told. In this way, their parents do not have to worry about them. It is the safest role to play in the family as this child can avoid the focus of alcoholic rages or violence as well as the burden of responsibility in trying to "fix" the family. Lost children have few friends. The only time these children get attention is when they are sick or injured.

The Mascot is the comedian of the family. Mascots are cute and fun to be around. They make the family laugh, using charm and humor to help the family survive the pain of addiction. Mascots have a hard time being serious. If they were, they would not be able to continue denying their pain of growing up in an alcoholic family. They are the life of the party, the class clown and they get attention by performing rather than by being themselves.

The Adjuster is the easy child. They do not upset the family but go along with what the family needs. Adjusters do not express feelings or create conflicts. The name says it all. These children adjust to whatever is happening to them. They follow directions, are flexible, and do not get upset with the family.

The Placating Child tries to make everyone happy. These children are particularly sensitive to what others need or want and are quick to respond. They do not express what they need. They get their needs met by taking care of others. Placating children often mediate between family members to decrease conflict and get their self-esteem from pleasing others.

The Denial System of the Alcoholic Family

To preserve the family and maintain some stability, children growing up in an alcoholic home assume responsibility for perpetuating the denial system of the alcoholic. Children adapt their thinking and behavior to fit the alcoholic's belief system out of fear of losing love or being abandoned. They are not willing to risk breaking the family up by telling the truth about the drinking. Denial is the most important defense mechanism for the alcoholic family. In some families, the fact that a parent drinks at all is denied. In other families, the drinking is acknowledged but the consequences are denied (Brown 1985).

> Children in a family in which both parents are alcoholics learn not only that alcohol is normal but that it is used to cope with many problems in life. Some parents have no relationship outside the use of alcohol. These parents drink as apart of every interaction. Children learn that alcohol is a part of the experience of love, sorrow, joy, hate, anger, and all kinds of emotions (Brown 1985, p. 248).

When they grow up, daughters of alcoholics understand the role alcohol plays in interpersonal relationships and are inclined to find alcoholic partners for themselves. In their own relationships as adults, children of alcoholics recreate the alcoholic bond. Having grown up isolated from outside experiences, the alcoholic world is frequently the only one daughters of alcoholics understand. Forced to reject information from their own perceptions (because it would conflict with their parent's interpretation of the family), adult daughters are ill-equipped for any reality other than the one the family shares; that alcoholism does not exist.

> Adult children of alcoholics often find themselves replicating their relationship with the alcoholic parent by choosing a dependent or alcoholic mate. Some avoid close relationships altogether, finding themselves more and more isolated and less and less able to trust. Those who marry and have children frequently feel that their main commitment is still to their parents (Brown 1985, p. 253).

Alcoholism within the family demands constant accommodation and the use of defenses such as denial. The heavy reliance on defense mechanism for survival prevents children from focusing on normal developmental tasks like identity formation, self-esteem and interpersonal skills. As a result, many daughters leave the alcoholic home to create one of their own, either by becoming an alcoholic or by marrying one. In doing so, they can use the skills that they have developed as children to cope with an alcoholic parent. By developing a tolerance for the alcoholic thinking, distorted perceptions and dysfunctional behavior, daughters of alcoholics are well prepared to relate to an alcoholic spouse.

Characteristics of Adult Daughters of Alcoholic(s)

The emotional climate of an alcoholic home is characterized by isolation, unpredictability and extremes in behavior and emotions. Children growing up in these homes become hypervigilant to their parents moods and constantly adapt their behavior to meet their parents' needs. It is difficult to feel loved, wanted, secure and safe under these adverse conditions (Perez 1986). As a result, children from alcoholic homes frequently have poor self-esteem. "Children of alcoholics come to negate the worth of their own love and feeling unworthy of anyone else's" (Perez 1986, p. 118). As adults, these children share a number of personality traits (Perez 1994, p. 64, Woititz 1983). Adult daughters of alcoholics:

> * experience a constant need for approval,
> * have a low ability to persevere (to follow a project through from beginning to end),
> * have an inability to trust,
> * can be unreliable,
> * have a tendency to lie a lot and often with no reason,
> * are attracted to pain,
> * have difficulty getting close to others,
> * have a tendency to become involved in relationships that are based upon pity not love,
> * are in terror of being evaluated
> * and live a frantic lifestyle.

Alcoholic parents are difficult to please, trust or depend on. Children modeling their parents' behavior learn to lie, not follow through on promises or get close to others. It is natural that adult daughters have difficulty trusting others. Their parents were not trustworthy. They were unreliable, broke promises and were frequently abusive. Consequently, women from alcoholic homes have difficulty valuing honesty, dependability, intimacy and unconditional love because they lack the experience of these characteristics in the context of a loving relationship. They are accustomed to working hard to win any approval from their parents. Most children equate the pity they felt toward their parents as love. They have little understanding of any other form of closeness.

Pain and pity become part of the parent-child relationship and the daughter's experience of love. When they grow up, women find themselves attracted to men who are abusive. By recreating the cycle of pain they experienced with their parents, adult daughters feel comfortable because it is familiar. By feeling pity for these men, daughters recreate the "love" they felt for their parents. As a result, adult daughters of alcoholics frequently choose abusive men they pity and fear as partners.

Joseph Perez (1986) believes that daughters are also attracted to pain because they feel it is punishment for all the guilt they feel. Unable to control the drinking or fix the problems associated with the drinking, children blame themselves for failing. Alcoholic parents reinforce this sense of failure by blaming the children for their drinking. The children turn to defense mechanisms such as lying to avoid this blame.

Many children from alcoholic homes learn to lie for several reasons. Lying, primarily serves as a way to avoid blame and escape abuse. Faced with punishment if they admit fault, it is easier to tell alcoholic parents what they want to hear. In addition, many children of alcoholic parents, according to Perez (1994), believe their lies.

> As children they spent much of their lives in fantasy to escape the chaotic, harsh reality of their real world. Many learn to find so much reward in their world of imagination that their fantasy lives become as important to them as the real world. For some, it becomes more important. For all of them *fantasy has become an integral defense for the harsh reality which daughters of alcoholics continue to perceive in adolescence and adulthood.* To mitigate that harshness they invariably blend their fantasies with reality. The effect of all this fantasizing is to develop a distorted perception of self, and/or of reality, and simply, of what's true. More often then not, they come to believe the reality which they perceive even though it is a blend of their own imagination (p. 67).

Furthermore, children from alcoholics lie because they have never been taught to value honesty. Unaccustomed to being told the truth by alcoholic parents, many daughters fail to see the importance of being truthful. Parents often did not mean what they said or failed to follow through on what they said they were going to do. Living in a fantasy world, lying to avoid being blamed or abused and unable to trust the people responsible for their care, children of alcoholics have difficulty forming close relationships. As adults, they lack the basic interpersonal skills necessary to be successful with a partner.

Adult daughters of alcoholics have difficulty with making decisions and solving problems that are important tools in any relationship. Unable to trust their own perceptions, to know their own feelings or needs and to respond to the world without looking for approval, daughters of alcoholics are unable to form their own identity. They are particularly sensitive to criticism or situations where they are being evaluated. Angry people and confrontations are frightening so they avoid conflict at all costs and are uncomfortable with authority figures (Woititz 1983).

Children from alcoholic homes grow up terrified of abandonment and will do anything to hang onto a relationship (Finklestein et al. 1990). They take care of others, love people they pity (Finklestein et al. 1990) and are overly responsible or overly irresponsible in relationships (Woititz 1983). Adult children of alcoholics tend to (Woititz 1983):

* guess at what normal is.
* judge themselves without mercy because they have learned there is no way that they could be good enough. As children, they were constantly criticized and often blamed for the parents drinking.
* have difficulty having fun and they take themselves very seriously because most were forced to take care of themselves.
* feel that they are different from other people.
* are extremely loyal even in the face of the evidence that loyalty is undeserved.
* are impulsive and do not think through to the consequences of their behavior.

Finally, adult daughters of alcoholics often have difficulty with feeling good about themselves, their feelings, their needs, and being intimate in relationships. They have trouble being honest about how they feel and who they are. Many have difficulty taking care of themselves and with setting boundaries because they do not trust their own instincts and perceptions of reality. Children, from alcoholic homes have a hard time letting go of the victim role, knowing how to resolve conflict, being vulnerable and letting go of control. Most of all, like their alcoholic parents, adult daughters dislike deferring gratification and tend to act like a child or parent in their relationships. They have been known to create crisis and feel bored when things are going smoothly.

Nadine's Story

Both my parents are alcoholics. I didn't know that that was the problem when I was a child. I always thought there was something wrong with me. I felt responsible for the world. My mom needed me to run the family and I did it without knowing how to. I remember trying to cook a pot of corn. I had no idea how the stove worked, but I knew I had to make something. My mom was furious with me for not doing it right. I hadn't put enough water in the pot and it cracked. I realized later she didn't seem too concerned that I could have been burned. She was just mad I couldn't do it right.

I knew I wasn't allowed to have feelings. Well, all except guilt. I felt guilty every minute of every day for as long as I can remember. I still do. When anyone gets mad or is disappointed that I won't do something, I feel guilty. I feel guilty just thinking about saying 'No' to someone.   And I feel guilty about feeling guilty. I will go to great lengths to do something for someone just to not feel guilty.

I wanted to fix my mom for as long as I can remember. She told me stories about how bad it was for her at work, living with my dad, having me and dealing with her mother. I wanted her to be happy. I would have done anything to make her happy. I felt it was my responsibility. I never saw how she helped to make her own misery. It never occurred to me that she could change her life if she didn't like it.

She blamed me for most of her unhappiness. That's probably why I felt so guilty and so responsible for fixing it.   I figured if I changed what I was doing, it would make everything better. Her biggest complaint was that her life was difficult because she had to support me. When I could, I worked to make money and helped with expenses. I went to live with my dad so that I wouldn't be such a burden to her. She just got upset that I left. Now I had abandoned her.

Eventually, I figured out that no matter what I did, it was not going to be the right thing. I was always going to be wrong. It would always be my fault. Over the years, I avoided my mother more and more until I just stopped seeing her altogether. Apparently that's all my fault too. I feel guilty about it.

9

The Female Alcoholic and Abuse

The Alcoholic Family and Abuse

The alcoholic family is characterized by denial, shame, fear, tension and the collective decision to maintain the secret about the alcoholism (Brown 1985). This atmosphere places children of alcoholics at risk for abuse. Some are neglected by the alcoholic parent who is too busy to drink; some by the nonalcoholic parent who is too focused on the alcoholic and survival to notice the children. When tempers flare, children are easy targets because they are too helpless to fight back.

> Children who grow up in alcoholic families grow up emotionally deprived. Sometimes they are reared in situations where the climate is explosive. Temper tantrums, sudden and unpredictable happen, seemingly for no reason. Here people scream, cower, and cry. Sometimes the climate is just the opposite, so undisturbed that the children learn to live in an environment which could be described as tomb-like; one where no talk, no communication occurs and where members function in isolation and keep secrets from one another (Perez 1986, p. 117).

The alcoholic home is frequently one of "chaos, inconsistency, unclear roles, unpredictability, arbitrariness, changing limits, repetitious and illogical arguments, and perhaps violence and incest" (Brown 1985, p. 239). If the children are not being abused themselves, they are often witnesses to other family members' violence and victimization. Children, from such homes, grow up believing that abuse is normal. It is considered an appropriate way of interacting with others. The ways children are hurt and abused are divided into four general areas or types of abuse; physical, emotional, and sexual abuse, and neglect.

Stephanie Covington's (1986 p.11) research on alcoholic families found that:

* 50% of alcoholic parents are child abusers;
* 67% of sexually aggressive acts against children involve alcohol use;
* 80-90% of husbands who batter use alcohol;

* 50% of incest victims are from alcoholic homes.

Covington's (1986) research on alcoholic women found that 74% had been sexually abused, 52% of them had been physically abused and 72% had been verbally abuse. "All of the cases of sexual and verbal abuse and 74% of the physically abused cases had experienced the abuse by the time they were ten years old. The alcoholic women (also) reported a greater number of perpetrators of abuse and experienced more instances of each type of abuse" (Covington 1986 p.42).   They were also abused more often by a close member of the family.

Adult children of alcoholics have a "well-developed denial system about both (their) feelings and (their) perceptions of what is happening in the home" (Black 1981, p.45). They learn not to talk about it but rather to ignore it or rationalize the drinking (Black 1981, p.33). Adults molested as children understand the unwritten family rule of "don't talk, don't feel and don't trust" as well. Children from alcoholic and abusive homes feel unlovable, unworthy and lack self-esteem (Gil 1983).

As these children reach adulthood, they often feel lonely, depressed, and unable to be intimate without really understanding why (Black 1981, p.32). As far as the abused woman is concerned, abuse is a sign of love. "If they care, they show it by having sex with you" (Gil 1983 p.40). These feelings increase their desire to either drink or become involved with someone else who does.

The woman who has been sexually abused by her drunken father, physically abused by her drunk mother, or verbally abused by both will experience difficulty forming healthy relationships with men. For this woman, her sexual needs take second place to the man's. Her identity comes from fulfilling him. Her way of feeling loved, cared for or nurtured is to be the victim; sexually, physically or verbally. She repeats the only type of relationship she knows.

Children of alcoholics are overwhelmed and fearful of feelings because they never "had the guidance to put them into perspective" (Black 1981, p.108). They have learned that "it is simply best to not trust that others will be there for them, emotionally psychologically, and possible even physically" (Black 1981, p.39). Adult daughters of alcoholics often do not perceive others as a resource. "In their home it was quite likely that the person drinking and the enabler or spouse were focused on the alcohol and the alcoholic behavior respectively rather than on the child" (Black 1981, p.46).

Physical Abuse

Physical abuse can be defined as any act by a parent or caregiver that results in a non-accidental injury to the child (Edwards et al. 1986). Discipline or physical punishment that leaves marks or scars on the body is abuse. Some of the signs of physical abuse include (Edwards et al. 1986, p. 49):

* Unexplained bruises, welts, cuts or broken bones that are in various stages of healing.
* Human bite marks, unexplained hair loss (due to hair pulling) and lacerations.
* Physical signs may also reflect the shape of the article used (belt buckle, electric cord).
* Unexplained or unusual burns - especially cigarette, cigar or rope burns.
* Unexplained abdominal injuries including swelling and localized tenderness or constant vomiting.
* A history of previous or recurring injuries that may include attempts to hide the injuries.

Children who have been physically abused display various symptoms including:

* Being afraid of adult contact, fearful, passive and too obedient.
* Extremes in behavior such as aggressiveness, withdrawal, compliance, and negativity.
* Being clingy and indiscriminate in his/her attachments.
* Being hypervigilant, nervous and avoids eye contact.
* Avoiding physical activity (because of being sore).
* Lying about the injuries
* Having a history of school problems, running away, drug or alcohol use, depression, or suicidal behavior.

Frances' Story

Frances grew up in a large family where the bigger people hit the smaller ones. It was like an assembly line starting with her father hitting her mother and both hitting the children. It was not long before the elder siblings were hitting the younger ones. It was so commonplace that explanations for the beatings became unnecessary. Family members just assumed it was a part of life.

In addition to the violence in the home, Frances always felt a great deal of sexual energy from her father. Although he never touched her, he would make sexual remarks toward her. Eventually, she and her brother began acting out sexually with each other.

Anxious to leave home, Frances moved in with a man she barely knew. At first, she thought Dan was her prince charming but over time, he became verbally and physically abusive. When he had an affair, she confronted him only to be battered for questioning his behavior. Accustomed to this type of behavior from a man, she stayed with him. Dan continued with the affair and with battering her. She stayed with him for ten years.

Emotional Abuse

Emotional abuse is the most common type of abuse. In fact, it is rare for a child to be abused physically or sexually without some form of emotional abuse involved. Signs of emotional abuse include (Edwards et al. 1986, p. 56):

   *Verbal insults or put downs.
   * Unreasonable expectations.
   * Blaming the child.
   * Parent withholding love from the child (cold and rejecting).
   * Willful cruelty or unjustifiable punishment.

Children respond to emotional abuse in a variety of ways including:

   * "acting out" and other behavior problems.
   * Becoming withdrawn and depressed.
   * Experiencing other emotional problems/turmoil.
   * Rigidly conforming with adult instructions, very compliant.
   * Making derogatory remarks about self.
   * Child attempts suicide.
   * Displaying pseudomaturity or infantile behaviors.
   * Becoming extremely aggressive or extremely passive.
   * Developing a habit disorder such as thumb sucking, nail biting, enuresis etc.
   * Showing abnormalities in motor, speech, social or intellectual development.

Demi's Story

Demi's mother was always telling her how wrong she was. Being humiliated in front of the family at the dinner table was a common occurrence. Demi had no privacy in her home. Her parents would walk in on her when she was in the bathroom or listen to her conversations when she was on the phone. Her mother frequently read her diary and then used the information to ridicule her.

When Demi grew up and got into a relationship, she found someone who also thought she was wrong all the time. He went through her letters and ridiculed her about her sexuality. She would complain that she felt like she was a child in the relationship but was afraid to leave. Most of her relationships prior to this one had been physically abusive and comparatively speaking, this one was better. Her tolerance level for emotional abuse was high after years of exposure to her mother's treatment.

Abby's Story

I would like to blame my alcoholism on one event but since I have to be honest, I can see how my life was headed in that direction anyway. I was just brought to my bottom a little sooner. The event was 'the wedding'. On the day my youngest daughter got married, I lost my relationship with my parents over a trivial matter of seating. Of course, alcohol had exaggerated the situation as well as the emotions.

Then the next day, my father-in-law blew his brains out. Some said it was due to us not inviting him to the wedding. My husband chose not to include him because of my father-in-law's alcoholism and the fear of him ruining this special day.

The guilt and sadness of both events were too overwhelming for me. I cried every day-- all day long. I felt I had no one to talk to or understand my feelings. Then it hit me; I was alone. My girls were gone (my parents, my father-in -law). The empty nest syndrome had set in. I remember looking at my life and thinking 'is that all there is?' I felt my husband and I had nothing in common. We didn't communicate, we didn't have the same interests. We were doing our own separate things in life.

Sexual Abuse

Sexual abuse or incest is defined as acts of sexual assault on a child by a parent. The sexual exploitation of minors includes genital fondling, molestation, exhibitionism, rape, pedophilia, incest, and/or forcing a child into pornography or prostitution (Edwards et al. 1986). Signs of sexual abuse include:

* Child reporting sexual activities to a trusted adult.
* Detailed and age-inappropriate understanding of sex.
* Child has genital or perineal trauma.
* Child has sexually transmitted disease.
* Child is pregnant.
* Abrupt change in a child's moods and behavior (anxiety, depression, hysteria).
* Reluctance to be with a particular person.
* Child has sleeping problems such as nightmares and afraid of falling asleep.
* Genital redness, pain or itching.
* Child has abdominal pain, appetite disturbances and corresponding weight change.
* Child is unwilling to participate in physical activities (especially ones enjoyed in the past).
* Child has attempted suicide.
* Child has a psychosomatic illness.

Child sexual abuse can include a wide range of activities. Offenses that do not use force include verbal stimulation, obscene phone calls, exposure, voyeurism, and showing a child pornographic pictures or films. Forcible offenses involve fondling, oral, vaginal or anal intercourse or attempted intercourse, and exploitation of children through prostitution and/or child pornography. "It is estimated that twenty-five million children under the age of eleven live in homes where they are sexually abused, most often by fathers or step-fathers" (Finklestein 1990, p. 243).

The oldest daughter is the most frequent victim of incest. However, other daughters are vulnerable if the oldest resists, leaves home or is simply unavailable. Alcohol and drug dependent women report a high incidence of sexual abuse including rape and incest as children and as adults (Finklestein 1990, Black 1981).

Christina's Story

Christina's father molested her over a number of years. It started when she was about four and continued until she left home in her early teens. She tried telling her mother who accused her of lying and reacted by physically abusing her. Christina tried to avoid her father by staying late at school or pretending to be asleep. She ate to gain weight so that he wouldn't be attracted to her anymore. She tried to pretend to be asleep. Nothing worked. It was a great relief when she was able to move out on her own.

When Christina got married, she told her husband about being molested. He was supportive and Christina thought she would be safe at last. However, as the marriage continued, she noticed that her husband drank a lot and when he did, he had a quick temper. Everything made him angry. Eventually, he began to physically abuse her. After the battering, he would frequently demand sex. She was not safe at all.

Tabitha's Story

Tabitha grew up in both an alcoholic and abusive home. Her mother was physically abusive to her and her father was emotional abusive. When Tabitha was fifteen, she went over to her friend Sarah's house. Both drank as they did almost every weekend. Tabitha had watched her father do the same thing with his friends. As the night grew late, Sarah's boyfriend showed up. Tabitha decided to stay longer and have a few more drinks. At some point, she passed out on the couch.

When she woke up, she felt pain between her legs and blood running down her leg. Sarah's boyfriend was getting up from lying on top of her. It took a moment for her to realize that she had been raped. She had no idea where Sarah was. Tabitha never told her what happened.

Years later, Tabitha got pregnant and married her alcoholic boyfriend. She did not finish high school or follow her dreams for a career in law enforcement. She also married a man who was verbally and physically abusive. He was also sexually demanding. When Tabitha's son was older, he told her he was fearful for her safety. He did not like the way his father treated his mother and could not understand why she tolerated the abuse. He wanted his mother to leave but she defended his father's behavior instead. She felt she did not deserve anything better.

Adult Daughters of Alcoholics and Rape

Adult daughters of alcoholics are not necessarily safe when they leave home. Many who have been abused as children grow up to be assaulted again as adults. There are several reasons for women's vulnerability to repeated abuse. In the first place, daughters of alcoholics are taught not to talk or confront dysfunctional behavior, have difficulty trusting their own perceptions and are experts in denial. Perpetrators of abuse count on these very behaviors to ensure silence from their victims. Men who are violent or sexually abusive are attracted to adult daughters of alcoholics because of their ability to tolerate boundary violations and to remain silent in the face of abuse. These women do not know how to protect themselves and make easy targets.

Second, statistics describe how daughters of alcoholics grow up to become alcoholics themselves and/or marry alcoholics. This places them in an environment where they become attached to men capable of violence. Alcoholic men are attractive to adult daughters because the men's behavior is familiar and therefore, comfortable. The woman's own alcoholism places her at an even greater risk if she is too intoxicated to make safe decisions or protect herself.

Third, children who have experienced abuse and maltreatment grow up with specific problems. Victims of childhood abuse have incredible trouble trusting anyone, including themselves. "Such mistrust fosters social isolation, an inability to express one's needs, and overcautious behaviors" (Edwards et al. 1986, p. 191). Childhood abuse coupled with parental alcoholism compounds the difficulty in building trust. As a result, relationships that require intimacy are difficult to maintain. Survivors of childhood abuse know how to keep secrets, maintain denial and avoid social contact. They do not have the skills to communicate, negotiate, set limits or healthy boundaries or be honest and develop trust; the behaviors that are required in healthy interpersonal relationships.

In addition, children who have been abused or grown up with alcoholic parents tend to have low self-esteem. "It is not uncommon for adults who were abused or neglected as children to feel unworthy of love, attention, and support, to consistently make self-deprecatory statements, and to attribute rewards they achieve to external circumstances rather than to their own efforts" (Edwards et al. 1986, p. 191). Women who do not feel good about themselves are vulnerable to becoming alcoholics and to get involved with men who do not respect them either. These women are unable to differentiate between men who feel good about themselves when they overpower others and men who have high self-esteem.

Finally, victims of childhood maltreatment learn to deny their feelings to survive the abuse. Their experiences as children teach them that they are helpless because they were not able to protect themselves. This sense of helplessness carries over to adulthood where women continue to feel unable to make decisions, assert themselves or make demands on their partners to stop the abusive treatment. They tend to recreate relationships from their childhood. "An adult who was sexually abused as a child, for example, may repeatedly involve herself in sexually abusive and exploitive relationships that maintain her role as a victim" (Edwards et al. 1986, p. 192).

Alcohol and Rape

In our society, women are considered sexually available when alcohol is involved. Studies indicate that college students believe that a woman will be sexual if she is at a bar ordering a drink (Blume 1988). The woman's chances of having intercourse increase, according to this population, if the man pays for her drink. Although a woman's decision to drink and to have a man pay for that drink does not mean she has consented to have sex, the myth states otherwise. As a result, female alcoholics are seen as sexually available rather than in the grips of a disease of addiction.

Consequently, female alcoholics are at risk for being sexually and physically abused simply because they have been drinking. In addition, alcohol impairs a woman's cognitive abilities to make safe decisions and places her in an environment where males that have been drinking experience lower inhibitions for aggressive and sexual behavior. Women are then told that they ask for sex because they are drinking and therefore, are at fault for the abuse.

Natasha's Story

When Natasha was in her first year of college, she attended a party at another dorm. She did not know very many people but felt comfortable after a few drinks. Natasha knew what alcohol was about. Her father was an alcoholic. However, it never occurred to Natasha that her own drinking was crossing over the line to addiction. By the end of the party, Natasha was too intoxicated to find her way back to her own dorm. As she was leaving, one of the men she had been talking to throughout the night offered to walk her home. He told her it was not safe to go alone in the dark because she was too drunk to protect herself if a strange man came along and tried to hurt her.

Natasha felt grateful for both the advice and the offer of assistance. It did not occur to her that she did not know this man and that he might be the one who would try to hurt her. As they walked back together, Natasha talked about school and classes. Before they reached her dorm, the man pulled her into one of the school buildings and raped her. He had been right. She was too drunk to fight him off. Afterwards, he left her there to walk the rest of the way home alone.

Years later, Natasha continued to blame herself for the rape. She believed that she drank too much at the party to get home safely. She saw that she was unable to protect herself when he did attack her and that because she had been drinking, she would be the one blamed if she told anyone what happened. Natasha never told anyone until she went into a treatment program for alcoholism.

Neglect

Parents who do not take care of their children's basic physical needs threaten their health and welfare. This is known as neglect. Signs of this type of abuse include (Edwards et al. 1986, p. 50):

* Child is always hungry or provided an inappropriate diet.
* Child is always sleepy (does not receive at least 9 hours of sleep most nights).
* Child lacks adequate medical or dental care.
* Poor supervision or parent leaves child unattended for long periods of time (not age appropriate).
* Child is left with someone who is likely to harm the child.
* Child is always dirty or lacks basic care such as teeth brushed, hair cut, nails trimmed.
* Child is inappropriately dressed for weather (does not have warm clothes for the cold).
* Child has ill-fitting clothes or shoes.
* Child does not have adequate shelter.

Some parents neglect their children because they have prioritized alcohol above the family. Alcoholic mothers are frequently unable to see that teeth are brushed or homework is done. Daughters, especially the eldest, are expected to grow up fast and take over the responsibilities belonging to their mother. Another form of neglect (rarely talked about) is when the alcoholic parent fails to protect her children from the disease of alcoholism by acting as a role model for drinking behavior. Some women even invite their children to drink with them.

Introducing Children to Alcohol and Drugs

Over the past few years, there has been dissension on how to respond when a woman exposes her baby to alcohol by drinking during her pregnancy. One camp wants to see the mother punished for abuse; the other wants to help the mother get treatment for addiction. Another controversial issue that deserves attention is the number of children introduced to alcohol and drugs each year by their parents who encourage their children to drink with them.

Children of alcoholics are exposed to alcohol and drugs as a part of the family dynamic. Sometimes this includes getting or making drinks for the parents. Eventually, it can mean getting drinks for themselves--with or without parental permission.

Some children become interested in experimenting with alcohol and drugs after witnessing their parents modeling drinking and drug use. Others are encouraged to join in with their parent(s) as a drinking companion. For children who are starving for affection from alcoholic parents, drinking may become the only way to finally get their parent's attention.

Alcoholic mothers do not see themselves as abusive or neglecting their children's welfare by including them in drinking activities. For the female alcoholic in denial, the family is involved in a mutual activity that creates the illusion of intimacy and understanding between parent and child. This denial is reinforced by the knowledge that countless non-alcoholic parents allow their adolescent children to drink in the home as a way of controlling their children's drinking rather than letting them risk experimentation outside the family. How does one decide what is abusive if a large portion of the population is doing it.

Emily's Story

Eddie showed up literally on my doorstep with a couple of changes of underwear and another T-shirt in a paper bag. He had been thrown out of his dad's house two states away (where he had lived with his stepmother, brother and two half-brothers); thrown out for smoking pot and drinking beer. He was fifteen and a half, six foot four, and ready to 'kick back and party down, Mom'.

If I had known he was coming, I might have been able to set some ground rules. But I was not about to make him feel homeless after his father had stripped him of all his possessions (including a car that he had paid for himself, his albums, stereo, clothes, mementos, and even his driver's license). In addition, he lost contact with his brother, lifelong friends and school. He put up a pretty good front but I knew he was hurting.

Although I had not smoked in front of him except for one occasion some years before (when we were visiting and someone passed a joint around the circle), I had not made a big secret of the fact that I did smoke marijuana sometimes. In fact, we had discussed that I did not think pot was a terribly harmful or awful thing. I knew he would come up against drugs and alcohol with friends eventually. I wanted to establish an open forum for discussion since I knew he would not get it at home in spite of the fact that his stepmother was a counselor for troubled teens within the school system.

I got him enrolled in school and he went. We smoked together and I helped him with homework and we talked a lot. He began to make friends and our house became the hang out. I allowed pot smoking but not cigarettes since neither Eddie nor I smoked tobacco. I hated the smell and did not feel like young kids needed any encouragement. I was not comfortable with becoming the boy's club but I could keep my eye on Eddie this way and I didn't want the kids to be in a worse place. They were well-behaved, usually playing records and talking. My small apartment didn't allow for much else.

I got home an hour or so after Eddie did and busied myself in the kitchen within earshot, joining the boy's occasionally. The pot smoking was not extreme as the kids didn't have much money to spend on it. Occasionally, I bought them small amounts of beer, but said no when Eddie asked for hard liquor or beer for a school holiday when I would be working. He tried to buy it anyway and was arrested. When I arrived home after the call, the police had him in handcuffs on the patio. Through the patio doors, I could see the other boys inside passing a joint, oblivious to the action outside. Somehow, we got through these times. Looking back, I'm not sure how.

There was a time when Eddie was determined to try LSD. I tried to dissuade him, remembering my own experience when someone gave me acid and I didn't know what I had taken. It changed my life forever and I had not done it again. When it became apparent to me that he was going to do it anyway, I finally consented in order to keep an eye on him. I had him get me a hit also with the idea I would be 'the control' as LSD came in many forms, cut with many things, and was always a risk. I was terrified but soon found I could control my experience to some degree and watch out for him too.

We moved to a small town where drugs were very available once we met the right people. We continued to smoke pot and do acid together. We both drank a little but usually with our own friends and not at home. Eddie was underage, but with a beard and his size, he was rarely questioned, although I was carded frequently. He would beg me not to come where he was (drinking) so no one would put it together how young he was. When we met by chance, we would smile and say hello and try to be cool. It was a very small town.

We bonded around alcohol and drug use. It's hard to write about as I have a lot of feelings about whether I led him to drugs that he would not have used otherwise or kept him away from some of the harder drugs like speed, cocaine, and prescription drugs that were also available. It seems like it was a constant struggle and after he moved out of my house, I know he did experiment with speed and heavier drinking.

Today, he is a minister in the same small town with a lovely wife and three outgoing, beautifully behaved children. Though we keep in touch, we are not as bonded now that we are both clean and sober. I have a hard time with his fundamentalist religion and I live far away so it's difficult to bond around the children. Perhaps the distance is natural under the circumstance. Many of his friends from those days have died, or have done time in prison, so I am grateful he has found another way. Even looking back, it is hard to say what would have been best.

Alcoholic parents have a high tolerance level for drinking behavior in their children. Like Emily, many parents see nothing wrong with their children using the drugs that they use themselves. These drugs are considered acceptable and less harmful than those not used by the parent.

Part 4:

Women, Addiction and Mental Illness

10

The Female Alcoholic and other Addictions

The Addictive Process

Female alcoholics use other compulsive behaviors for the same reasons they use alcohol. Needing to connect in relationships, repressing memories of chaotic and abusive childhoods, low self-esteem and surviving difficult situations in our society can lead many women to become addicted to other substances as well. Eating, exercising, working or spending money can become addictive when compulsion and loss of control is involved.

Not confronting the other addictions a female alcoholic suffers from places her at an increased risk for relapsing. There are several reasons for this relapse potential. First, in order to practice any addiction, the woman must continue using defense mechanisms, distorted thinking and particular behaviors that support the addict lifestyle. This reinforces behavior patterns that were used to maintain the alcoholism. As a result, the slide back into drinking is not such a great leap from the way the woman is acting in her life presently.

Second, the underlying needs being coped with by the addictive behavior, whatever the addiction, do not get addressed. Some women eat over an unhappy relationship, act out with money over their disillusionment associated with poverty or exercise compulsively because of body image problems connected to rape or abuse. These issues must be confronted to insure the woman's success with abstinence. If left to fester, the pain attributed to these unresolved issues can become so great that drinking becomes a viable option for coping.

Third, acting compulsively and feeling out of control over any type of behavior is painful. The woman's self-esteem suffers as does her self-respect and her ability to trust her own perceptions. Women tend to feel a great deal of shame over their addictions and punish themselves for them with critical self-talk. When mothers see their children suffer from the addiction as well, their pain increases. They feel horrible about themselves as mothers and alcohol can seem to be the only remedy from this pain. The thinking behind this type of relapse is that

"I'm an addict anyway. What difference does it make if I drink as well."

Finally, practicing any kind of addiction places women in bad company - other addicts. Women seeking a partner will find one that also practices an addiction. This type of relationship tends to nurture each person's addiction. A woman who is a compulsive overeater may find a man to eat with who also happens to drink. Alcoholism does not look so bad when a partner's drinking does not seem to produce negative consequences. As a result, she may forget the truth about her own drinking history and begin using alcohol again.

Addictions can be to a substance that is ingested such as nicotine, sugar or caffeine or to a process such as working, sexual activity or gambling. The more common addictions for female alcoholics are eating disorders, smoking, workaholism and spending money. Eating disorders include compulsive overeating, anorexia nervosa and bulimia. Although a complete discussion of all types of addictions is not possible, an overview of the more common ones for women follows.

Eating Disorders

There are three types of eating disorders; compulsive overeating, bulimia and anorexia. Women use food to cope with feelings, to meet emotional needs in relationships and to deal with body image issues. Eating disorders have a biological, psychological and sociocultural component. Scientists believe that there may be a malfunction in the body's feedback system (Marx 1991). Women may not recognize when they are full or what food the body needs to function because of a chemical imbalance or other problem in the hypothalamus that regulates food and water intake.

Genetic studies have also demonstrated that like alcoholism, the potential for eating disorders can be inherited. "Identical twins, who grow from a single egg and share an identical genetic blueprint, have a higher incidence of anorexia nervosa than fraternal twins, who grow from separate eggs" (Marx 1991, p. 29). Compulsive overeaters also tend to run in families. However, it is difficult to determine how much biology plays a role in behavior that can also be learned. Many overeater mothers have difficulty in determining what amount of food constitutes a normal meal for their children and may encourage overeating in them out of denial and ignorance.

As in alcoholism, family dynamics does play a part in women's vulnerability to eating disorders. According to Russel Marx (1991) in his book *IT'S NOT YOUR FAULT Overcoming Anorexia and Bulimia through Biopsychiatry*,

> Some patterns that have been identified in certain eating-disordered families include an overemphasis on appearance, social isolation, emotional rigidity, and the inability to

resolve conflicts. However, there is no such thing as a 'typical' eating-disordered family. The same dynamic that triggers an eating disorder in one person may allow another to thrive (p. 30).

Another factor that contributes to the potential in women of developing an eating disorder is the experience of a crisis or trauma. Any kind of loss or rejection, a major life transition or a blow to her self-esteem can trigger the downward cycle of addiction (Marx 1991). As noted earlier, women growing up in chaotic alcoholic homes are more likely to develop alcoholism themselves. It would seem that these women are also at risk for developing eating disorders.

Finally, our society's obsession with thinness affects women's perceptions of their own bodies and as a result, their self-esteem. Commercials, billboards and magazine advertisements portray an "ideal" body image that is unrealistic for most women -- even for the models in the ads. Unfortunately. this does not stop women from trying to achieve the perfect body weight and size. In addition, society views those outside the "ideal" as fat and fat is considered bad.

> Chubby children suffer cruel teasing by their schoolmates -- teasing that can become the trigger for an eating disorder. Fat people are the targets of jokes and whispered comments. Some find the doors to advancement closed. The cultural pressure to be thin can make feelings of insecurity, self-doubt, or unworthiness much worse (Marx 1991, p. 30).

In light of how the family and society contribute to women's vulnerability to eating disorders, it is not surprising to find that women as a group suffer from this addiction in much larger numbers than men. Furthermore, women tend to have more access to food, specifically time alone with food, as they are the ones more likely to prepare the family meals. Eating disorders could be considered the perfect addiction for women. Food can be a fairly risk-free addiction. It does not involve a dangerous drug culture, hurt anyone else but the woman practicing it, does not prevent her from functioning appropriately in her role as wife or mother, and does not require any one else's participation (such as a doctor to write a prescription).

Compulsive Overeating

A compulsive overeater consumes large amounts of food because she has lost the ability to choose how much she eats. The primary characteristics of this addiction are a preoccupation with and loss of control over food. Women with this disorder have become dependent on food as a way to cope with their life and to regulate their feelings (McFarland et al. 1985). They react to stress, anxiety, fear, or pain by eating. Women overeaters also eat to avoid feeling lonely, their own sexual desire or helpless. Women frequently use food when they feel powerless to assert themselves in a relationship or on the job.

In the same way women use alcohol and drugs to feel connected in a relationship, food is used as a way to stay connected. Many women who are unhappy in their marriages need food to repress their anger, fear and lack of sexual feelings. In this way, they can find ways to deal with the unpleasant feelings without risking a loss of the relationship.

> This is a major 'benefit' of being fat. If a woman feels she doesn't deserve to be happy, she doesn't have to worry about finding ways to improve her life. She can even talk herself out of her anger toward others by convincing herself that she has no right to be mad at anyone but herself (Stuart et al. 1987, p. 61).

Women attempt to deal with their pain over a relationship by nurturing themselves with food. Eating to deal with unmet emotional or physical needs is common for women. Unable to cope with these emotions and not knowing how to change the circumstances leading to these feelings, women cope by translating these feelings into a hunger for food. Food is always available, easily accessible and reliable. Women who are genuinely hungry for food are more likely to crave something nutritious. Those who are hungry for sweets are more likely to be hungry for affection and love.

Food works to silence the body's natural alarm system that serves to warn them when something is wrong. This something could be feeling lonely, unloved, angry or rejected sexually. If the woman is unable to respond to the warning signal, she finds a way to quiet the alarm. She learns to tune out the signal by stuffing those feelings down with food. Overeaters become numb to the pain, to the risk of being violated and to their awareness that they are not getting their needs met.   In particular, they do not have to face their fear of failure or their fear of abandonment.

Because a woman's self-esteem is frequently dependent on her success in a relationship, her unhappiness with her husband can feel like she is the failure. In addition to feeling afraid that the end of the marriage is her fault, many women experience fear of becoming independent. There is fear of being alone, fear of abandonment and fear of financially supporting themselves. There is fear around finding work outside the home for those who never developed a career. And for others, there is fear that they will never find another man.

Finally, many women have lots of fear around being sexual. It has been established that women use alcohol to cope with their fears around their sexuality. Alcohol allows women more freedom in expressing themselves sexually by lowering inhibitions and society's expectations of "lady-like" behavior. Food, on the other hand, can help by stuffing sexual desire, sexual repulsion or avoiding sexual attention by others.

> Being heavy and feeling unattractive can be as useful for keeping husbands at bay as for avoiding outside attention. Many women, consciously or not, put on weight to escape

marital sex. Weight gain usually serves a double purpose: it diminishes a husband's sexual interest, and it inhibits a woman's own sexual desire (Stuart et al. 1987, p. 56).

Husbands can play an important role in women's overeating. Many men have fears that if their wives confront their eating disorder that it will have a huge impact on their own lives by disrupting their daily routine (Stuart et al. 1987). Wives losing weight may be less willing to fix big meals, go out to fancy restaurants or bake rich desserts anymore. Men who overeat or practice another addiction also fear being confronted once their wives become successful in remaining abstinent (Stuart et al. 1987).

Some men fear that they will lose their wives because the weight loss will make them attractive to other men or that problems in the marriage blamed on the overeating will now surface as valid issues (Stuart et al. 1987). In the same way women choose to continue drinking to hang onto their marriage, many women continue eating to maintain a relationship with their husbands.

Bulimia Nervosa

Bulimics engage in recurrent episodes of binge eating where they consume a large amount of food in a short amount of time. The primary characteristics of this disorder are a lack of control over eating, a persistent concern with body shape and weight and a pattern of behavior that ensures that weight gain does not occur. This behavior can be self-induced vomiting (purging), use of laxatives or diuretics, strict dieting, fasting or vigorous exercise (Goff 1984). The cycle of binging and purging is often done in secrecy with the bulimic having to adapt their lifestyle in order to have the time, privacy, and resources to practice their addiction.

The bulimic becomes dependent on binging and purging as a way of coping with stress, emotions (especially anger), sexual abuse issues and her lack of assertiveness about her needs in her relationships. The rate of alcoholism for bulimics and family members of bulimics is much higher than the general population (Goff 1984).

Women with bulimia are subject to a number of physical problems such as stomach pain, abdominal swelling, pancreatitis, cramps, nausea, involuntary vomiting, amenorrhea (absence of menstruation) and ruptures or lesions in the stomach, throat lining and mouth (Goff 1984, Marx 1991). Malnutrition causes electrolyte imbalances, hair loss, softening or discoloration of fingernails, weakness, fatigue, dehydration and dental decay (Goff 1984, Marx 1991).

Women who induce vomiting are also at risk for fluid loss, edema, burning sensation in the mouth and esophagus, diarrhea, constipation and scars on the hand when fingers are involuntarily bitten when used to trigger vomiting (Goff 1984, Marx 1991). Chronic vomiting can lead to rupturing the stomach, creating bowel tumors, rupturing blood vessels in the face, damaging the kidneys and female organs, gastritis, bleeding, enlarged lymph and salivary glands, throat infections, and eroding enamel from teeth (Mitchell 1985).

Finally, bulimics can suffer from depression, mood changes, disturbed sleep, abnormal brain waves, muscle spasms and tingling sensations (Goff 1984, Marx 1991).

Anorexia Nervosa

While bulimics have a compulsion to eat, anorexics have a compulsion to not eat. Women who experience a weight loss of 15 percent below normal weight and refuse to gain or maintain normal body weight are classic examples of anorexia (Mitchell 1985). Anorexics can be very obsessed about gaining weight, insisting that even the most minuscule amount of food will make them fat. They can have extremely distorted body image which is demonstrated when they insist their bodies are overweight when in fact they may be emaciated. Many refuse to eat to the point of starvation even though they continue to experience huger pains. "The mortality rate is higher for anorexia nervosa than for any other psychiatric illness" (Stern 1988, p. 143).

This disorder is more often seen in middle-class, Caucasian women who are 12-25 years old. In clinical practice, it has been observed that anorexics can also be continuing this pattern of eating because they experienced it in childhood. Children who are abused or neglected by being denied food are at risk of acting out this pattern of abuse on themselves as adults.

Many of the physical problems associated with bulimia occur with anorexia such as chronic constipation, thinning hair and dry, flaky skin (Mitchell 1985). However with anorexia, the body often deteriorates faster. Extreme weight loss can cause swelling of feet and ankles, anemia, severe muscular weakness, loss of sexual desire, lowered blood pressure, body temperature, and pulse rate and heart failure (Mitchell 1985).

In addition, anorexics experience bone deterioration from malnutrition, deficiency in the female hormone estrogen, a downy growth of fuzz on the body, eyes that may appear glazed, difficulty in concentrating and often distracted, difficulty sleeping, feeling cold, and feeling uncomfortable sitting as the amount of physical padding shrink (Mitchell 1985).

The use of laxatives and diuretics can produce severe dehydration, electrolyte imbalance and decreased chloride and potassium levels. Medical aspects of this disease also include diabetes, hypertension, heart attack, hypoglycemia, gum disease (from vomiting), tearing and bleeding of the esophagus, hiatal hernia, electrolyte imbalances, dehydration, amenorrhea, osteoporosis, stomach rupture, and colon dysfunction (Mitchell 1985).

Anorexic women are also known to store food but not eat it in order to prove that they have willpower only to find themselves on food binges triggered by fighting hunger for so long. Many women cook elaborate meals for others which they do not eat, insist they're not hungry or eat only one type of food. Others sneak food or compulsively exercise. Most lie about their relationship with food.it

The following are symptoms characteristic of the disease of anorexia (Mitchell 1985):

* Intense fear of becoming fat even when underweight or normal
* Disturbance in the way in which one's body weight, size or shape is experienced.
* Compulsive exercising to lose weight and energy.
* Use of laxatives (though laxative abusers only lose 10 percent of available calories with this method and most of the weight loss is from water).
* Inordinate pride in their thinness or ability to go without food.
* Preoccupation with food and weight (may constantly weigh herself).
* Development of food rituals such as cutting up food into tiny pieces, chewing each bite slowly, picking at or playing with food without eating it or spitting it out in napkins or other hiding places.
* Limiting fluid intake as they make her stomach feel full and therefore, fat.
* Isolation from family and friends.

Abby's Story

My story begins as a child growing up in an alcoholic and food addicted family. The two were considered a reward for hard work. Alcohol and food meant family get-togethers, fun and love. As an only child this fulfilled most of my loneliness. I also felt abandonment and insecurity because I was illegitimate and came from a family where having affairs was normal. As a child, I was molested by an uncle and at fourteen I was raped on a date. Alcohol and food helped me deal with my life.

I can remember my mother constantly nagging me about my appearance and weight since this was a problem for her. I was blamed as a child and even to this day, how I had ruined her body because of her weight gain during the pregnancy. It seems ironic now, but my own doctor prescribed diet pills during both my pregnancies. I had trusted this doctor and was lead to believe that I was carrying large babies. In order to have easy deliveries, I had to maintain my weight. After the birth of my second child, I was given an on-going prescription of Ritalin. After three years, I became dependent on this drug and realized I needed to free myself.

Alcohol came into play the first year of my marriage. Due to a couple of unpleasant incidents while drinking, we both decided we couldn't handle the alcohol. There was a period of two-three years we didn't drink at all. And then it was done occasionally at social functions.

As I look back to my childhood and into adulthood, loneliness played a big role in my life. I was even lonely in my marriage because the two of us could not express our true feelings or thoughts without becoming defensive or blaming the other. Due to lack of communication skills, I closed off and stuffed my feelings. My girls became my life, my companions and confidantes. If I didn't turn to them, it would be my mother.

We eventually moved to the mountains and I became my own person. It was the first time in my life that I felt any confidence in myself. I reached out and made many friends in different circles. The down side of all this socializing came at the once a month luncheons, which became two to three times a month. Drinking was always a part of these lunches. This group of ladies became obsessed with their weight including myself. We joined aerobics, walked three times a week, shared diets, and talked about food seven days a week.

These were the beautiful people to me. They had money, were well educated, had community position and respect. I had wanted to be part of all this, I could taste it. In order to feel equal, I used anorexia and bulimia as a tool to stay thin and look good. They used acid peels, liposuction, face lifts, implants and collagen injections to look good. In order to escape reality, we drank, shared secrets and diets.

Our afternoon lunches (became more frequent and) we would usually end up in a bar. Then the lies started to cover up the afternoon outings, and then the guilt set in. My vicious cycle had begun--the sneaking, lying and cheating. My three or four glasses of wine in the afternoon had increased to a bottle. By now, my husband would make comments or insults about my drinking. There came a time when he said it had to halt and he cleaned the house of all alcohol. What a joke, as if I couldn't go buy more!

Which I did and then the 'sneak' drinking began. I had resorted to hiding the wine in a closet or any convenient place I could get a quick glass. It was at this point that I felt the pressures of control and resentment towards him. So between the guilt, shame and lies, I would comfort myself with food and wine and purge all of this in the toilet, along with my feelings. The binging and purging would sometimes take place ten to fifteen times a day.

At the peak of all this, I remember driving from one fast food restaurant to another, gobbling the food while driving home, running into the house to purge and then drinking down the wine to forget the guilt or shame. It took three and a half years and a shot gun in my mouth to finally reach my bottom. (A family intervention, treatment program and counseling followed).

My alcoholism has been a successful three and a half years in recovery but the bulimia has only been one year. I figure the reason I held onto the bulimia was for a safety net from going back out with the alcohol. Anytime there was stress, I would purge my feelings in the toilet. At the time I felt my addiction wasn't hurting anyone but myself.

(Abby's daughter was seeing a counselor to deal with her own pain around her mother's addictions.)

Smoking

Smoking is one of the hardest addictions to address because it is one condoned by society and can be practiced continuously throughout the day. Another factor that makes it difficult to treat is that the negative consequences are more difficult to identify. Because it is a slow poison, it does not disrupt a person's lifestyle with divorce, arrest, job loss, car accidents or hangovers. Often with alcoholism, the effects of years of drinking are more visible. The negative consequences of smoking however, are more subtle in the beginning and when they do become apparent, there is less time for an intervention before a life may be lost.

Another issue is secondhand smoke. Many nonsmoking women are exposed to their partner's smoking. While the smoke the smoker inhales is filtered through the cigarette, the passive smoker inhales sidestream smoke. This comes off the burning end of a cigarette and contains higher amounts of the compounds that are linked to cancer and heart disease. Although the passive smoker breathes in less smoke, these compounds occur in smaller particles and tend to settle deep in the lung tissue where it takes longer for them to enter the bloodstream and lymph tissue. The active smoker inhales both types of smoke.

Women smoke to stuff their feelings in the same way they eat. It becomes an addiction to nicotine when the woman continues to smoke in spite of negative consequences, lose control over the option to smoke and experiences physiological withdrawal symptoms when quitting. Smoking is extremely dangerous to women. It makes them vulnerable to lung disease, emphysema, all kinds of cancers, heart disease and embolisms.

Pregnant women exposing their fetuses to nicotine often give birth to babies of smaller weight and/or birth defects. Many of these babies are still births or suffer from sudden infant death syndrome. For children whose parents smoke, there is a higher incidence of bronchitis, pneumonia, wheezing, coughing, middle ear disease and the possibility of lung damage.

Many women have reported that quitting smoking is one of the hardest addictions to stop.

Even hard core heroin addicts complain that nicotine is more addictive. Smoking is often the last addiction a woman is willing to deal with and many women refuse to address it at all. There are two schools of thought in the addiction field regarding when to quit smoking and drinking. One group believes that all addictions should be dealt with at once to decrease the likelihood that smoking will lead to a relapse in drinking. The other theory suggests that a relapse is more likely when an alcoholic tries to quit everything all at once and becomes overwhelmed with feelings of being deprived.

Workaholism

Workaholism is one of the hardest addictions to diagnose because it is reinforced by today's society. Most companies want employees that make personal sacrifices, are willing to work overtime and have an emotional investment in the outcome of their work. However, for those caught up in this disease, the physical and medical consequences can be fatal. The stress and anxiety of putting in long hours at the office can lead to heart disease, ulcers, stomach problems and high blood pressure.

Women who overwork become physically worn out, have difficulty sleeping and are at increased risk for other addictions (Fassel 1990, Robinson 1989). Many of these women suffer from depression, chronic headaches, backaches, high blood pressure, ulcers, stroke, heart attacks, and other serious illnesses (Fassel 1990, Robinson 1989).

As with alcoholism, women addicted to working experience self-esteem problems and a strong denial system that supports the addiction (Fassel 1990).

> Today, the societal demands on women to be competent in multiple areas are coupled with nagging self-esteem issues arising out of the need for women to prove they are worthwhile. This is a deadly combination. It leads so inevitably to a set-up for work addiction that one wonders why all women aren't in this sinking ship (Fassel 1990, p. 62).

Researchers point out that women workaholics "frantic activity is an attempt to attain an identity through doing. And some more than just doing: doing well, doing perfectly, and in such a way that (they) please others" (Fassel 1990, p. 58). To support this addiction women workaholics become dishonest, self-centered, isolated, controlling and frequently perfectionistic (Fassel 1990). These women have a great deal of difficulty relaxing and having fun.

Major signs of a work addiction (Fassel 1990, Robinson 1989) include:

* Rushing, busyness, caring, rescuing.
* Inability to say "No" or set limits.

* Constantly thinking about work.
* Compulsive list making.
* Staying late in the job.
* No days off (working on weekends).
* Always carrying a briefcase or a book to read.
* Hours exceed 40 hours consistently.
* Rarely absent because of illness or need for a break.
* Often skips or cuts short vacation time.
* Always busy / eats fast.
* Reluctant to delegate.
* Exaggerated belief that no one else can do the job.
* Family members are expected to accommodate work schedule.
* Social life diminished or nonexistent.
* Giving up relationships and relationship obligations.
* Using work to not feel.
* Periods of staring into space.
* A high tolerance level for stress.
* Need to be in control.

Workaholics prefer their jobs to socializing with friends and family, taking vacations or even coming home. Frequently becoming overwhelmed with the amount of work they have to do, many workaholics experience "burn-out"; growing increasingly more tired, irritable, anxious, and unable to concentrate. Anyone can be a workaholic; homemaker, parent, or the professional woman. The pay off is the same. The addict gets to numb emotions and cover up for her insecurities. Work or the product made from working makes her look important and guarantees her some attention. She may receive lots of appreciation from others which she perceives as love and respect. The time spent working however, is time taken away from experiencing true intimacy.

Recovery entails education about healthy work habits, time management, social skills, boundaries, and leisure activities. Self-esteem and relationship issues need to be addressed as well as learning how to manage feelings and distorted thinking. Women often have a very difficult time letting go of long work hours unless they have other activities to occupy their time. A strong support system is needed when women face how empty their lives have become because it has revolved around work. Often group work is very effective.

With some workaholics, it is not the act of working that they are addicted to but a means to a greater end. Some work to earn money for drugs and alcohol; others work for money with which to shop. Many alcoholics and drug addicts in recovery have difficulty budgeting and managing money because their priority was to buy their drug of choice. Often, there were little funds left over to take care of the other responsibilities such as rent, food, utilities etc. This mattered less and less as their disease progressed. Most addicts became adept at making excuses and lies about why they were short on covering their monthly expenses. They frequently found others to bail them out financially.

Compulsive Spending

Compulsive spenders experience the same distorted set of priorities as the alcoholic with the exception that the money is not set aside for alcohol. The compulsion to shop becomes the focus for the spending addict and just as with the alcoholic, rent, food and other necessities take on a lower priority. Acquiring possessions seems to soothe painful feelings, low self-esteem and inadequacy. By surrounding themselves with lavish purchases, compulsive spenders can at least feel better about themselves. "People with compulsive spending habits do not buy because they like to buy. It is the only way they can feel good. It is their fix" (Kaye 1991, p. 60). As with all addictions however, the "high" is short-lived and the consequences of spending beyond their means can be devastating. Shoppers feel a high from shopping and feel deprived when they are prevented from spending.

Many women lose their credit rating, their homes, their cars etc. when they are unable to pay their bills. Others steal money from friends and family and may even embezzle from their employers. Compulsive spenders isolate or only socialize with others who spend or enable their spending. Most shoppers lie, make excuses, rationalize or explain away their spending habits.

According to Yvonne Kaye (1991) in her book *CREDIT, CASH AND CODEPENDENCY,* "pathological spenders come in two varieties: those who spend on themselves and those who spend on others" (p. 44). In both cases, these women are covering up feelings of low self-esteem, fear, and pain. In addition, Kaye found that women with a money addiction often came from families who had their own issues with money and acted these issues out by neglecting their children's needs.

> The overspending/underspending in the family of origin was extremely dysfunctional. Several people were victims of ill health because parents refused to spend money on nutritious food or visits to the physician. Some of them have major problems with their teeth because they never went to the dentist (Kaye 1991, p. 27).

Characteristics of compulsive spenders (Kaye 1991, Forward 1994) include:

* Shopping sprees that bring only limited pleasure and eventually no pleasure at all.
* Shopping is used to not feel.
* Compulsion to shop in spite of negative consequences.
* Many purchases are never used.
* Negative consequences include debt and an inability to pay bills.

* Shopping leads to feeling anxious, guilty or remorseful afterwards.
* Shopping is more important than other activities.

Compulsive spending, like workaholism is condoned by society. Advertisers cater to the addictive mentality by insisting that more is better. Commercials convey the message that their product will make you feel better about yourself. Credit card companies continually send out new cards to people who already posses cards. Our whole society is built on the idea of "buy now, pay later". An attitude that reinforces the compulsive spenders behavior to shop above their means for items they don't use, let alone need.

11

The Female Alcoholic
and
Dual Diagnosis

Psychiatric Illnesses and Alcoholism

There are a number of psychiatric illnesses that are more prevalent in alcoholic families than the general population (Pickens et al. 1985, Evans et al. 1990). Depression, anxiety disorders, eating disorders, attention deficit disorder (with or without hyperactivity), post traumatic stress disorder, and alcoholism are more commonly diagnosed in women (Pickens et al. 1985). Schizophrenia, dementia, bipolar, and borderline personality disorder are frequently seen in the female alcoholic as well. Since male alcoholics are more likely to experience antisocial personality disorder than their female counterparts, they will not be discussed in this work (Evans et al. 1990).

The combination of alcoholism and different psychiatric disorders is endless and far too extensive a topic for this chapter. However, a general review of the most common disorders will give some idea of how dual diagnosis can influence treatment issues. Female alcoholics with a coexisting psychiatric disorder complicate the process of making an accurate diagnosis.

For many women, psychiatric disorders coexist with their alcoholism. In other words, the woman is suffering from both a mental illness and an addiction and treatment is necessary for both. Although the disorders may be independent of each other, female alcoholics with psychiatric disorders often cannot separate the two illnesses. Consequently, treatment for either the addiction or psychiatric illness without addressing both can result in relapse.

The interplay between the disorders can be complicated. For example, a woman alcoholic seeking treatment for major depression may receive antidepressants that do little to help her if her alcoholism goes undiagnosed. The prescription she receives may even harm her if the medication is taken with alcohol. Similarly, if she becomes abstinent and her depression is not treated, she may relapse or begin using other chemicals to self-medicate her psychiatric symptoms.

When the mental illness precipitates the alcoholism, women may become addicted to the substance used to self-medicate the symptoms of their psychiatric illness. In this example, women experience alcoholism as part of their depression. These women become addicted to the alcohol and other chemicals being used to mitigate psychiatric symptoms. By the time they seek treatment, it can be difficult to determine which illness occurred first. Nevertheless, treatment for the depression is crucial to prevent further addictive use as a coping mechanism for the psychiatric disorder.

In other cases, female alcoholics experience depression as part of their alcoholism. The losses associated with an addiction, the lifestyle, the effects of withdrawal, and the consequences that occur when abusing alcohol can be depressing. In other words, the depression is caused by the alcoholism. This type of depression disappears with abstinence and treatment for the addiction. Finally, some psychiatric disorders occur during acute intoxication or during withdrawal. Hallucinations, psychotic episodes and other psychiatric symptoms have been observed during detoxification from alcohol and other drugs (Evans et al. 1990).

Unfortunately, it is not always possible to determine if the psychiatric symptoms are indicative of a mental illness or caused by the ingestion or withdrawal of a chemical. Mood swings and anxiety associated with withdrawal mimics the symptoms of bipolar and anxiety disorders. Drug-induced psychosis can look like schizophrenia. Cocaine use produces weight loss, abnormal sleep patterns and suicidal thoughts similar to a major depression.

It is therefore important to evaluate for a psychiatric illness thirty days after abstinence has been established (Evans et al. 1990). After thirty days, alcohol and other chemicals are no longer detected in the body. However, an ongoing evaluation (sometimes for months) is important to carry on for women suffering from depression or an anxiety disorder. Their illness may be the result of an abusive relationship or an undiagnosed prescription drug addiction.

Depression

Depression is the most common psychiatric illness in female alcoholics (Evans et al. 1990). Symptoms of depression (Shimberg 1991, p. 39-40) include:

* a lack of interest in previously enjoyed activities,
* feeling low or irritable,
* showing signs of hopelessness,
* loss or increase in appetite (weight loss or gain)
* change in sleep patterns (insomnia, sleeping longer periods or waking up earlier),
* decrease in sex drive,
* psychomotor agitation or motor retardation,

* loss of energy,
* feelings of worthlessness, inadequacy, or excessive (and inappropriate guilt),
* reduced concentration or indecisiveness,
* suicidal ideation (thoughts of death or actual suicide attempts).

Some women eat more when depressed while others lose interest in eating at all. Similarly, some depressed women sleep for longer periods while others have difficulty sleeping. The most important determinant for a diagnosis of depression is that it interferes with the woman's daily functioning, extends over a period of time and is not caused by a specific event such as a divorce or loss of a loved one.

Female alcoholics frequently enter treatment with depression because they have experienced a number of negative consequences from their drinking. Many women have been abandoned by partners, parents and their children. Most women become depressed at the prospect of admitting that they are alcoholics. Female alcoholics that have experienced parental alcoholism, incest, physical abuse, rape or are in a battering relationship will most likely be depressed. However, their depression is situational and improves as the issues associated with the alcoholism and traumas are resolved.

For women, whose depression existed before the onset of alcoholism, treatment for their addiction does nothing to improve their depression. Depressed people are often very isolated and need encouragement to become involved with activities and other people (Daley et al. 1987). They also need help in confronting their depressive thoughts that dominate their moods. Taking action, substituting positive thoughts for negative ones and socializing with others help women in combating their depression (Daley et al. 1987). Medication is sometimes warranted.

Another type of depression, known as dysthymic disorder, is similar to major depression. The woman experiences a loss of interest or pleasure in activities, but her ability to function is much higher. Unlike major depression, dysthymia occurs for greater than two years and becomes part of the way the woman views the world (Daley et al. 1987). Medication is rarely given for dysthymia. Women with dysthymia appear to be unmotivated, passive and hopeless about life (Daley et al. 1987). Treatment involves confronting the woman's sense of powerlessness, low self-esteem and negative view of life. Group work can be effective in modeling other options and offering encouragement to women who are afraid of taking risks.

Maria's Story

Maria began using alcohol and marijuana in her late twenties. She had experienced a childhood of physical abuse by her father, a marriage with a verbally abusive man who had raped her and had lost her children to her husband when they were young. She was very depressed and she described feeling that way most of her life. She believed that nothing good would ever come her way and daily functioning was about surviving each crisis that she was confronted with.

Alcohol and drugs helped her feel better. She began drinking with a boyfriend and was eventually introduced to marijuana. Twenty years later, she found herself even more depressed but now it was brought on by her addiction. Maria entered treatment for her depression. The doctor recognized the symptoms of alcoholism and insisted that she get help for both illnesses. Although she been abstinent now for years, she still struggles with depression occasionally.

Bipolar Disorder

Bipolar disorder or manic depressive illness is a cyclical mood disorder with alternating episodes of mania and major depression. The manic phase is characterized by (Daley et al.1987):

> * a euphoric sense of well being,
> * grandiosity,
> * erratic or irrational behavior,
> * irritability, especially at the hint of setting limits on this behavior,
> * hyperactivity or unusual restlessness, usually disorganized illogical and even bizarre,
> * pressured speech that may be difficult to follow and unrelated to the topic of conversation,
> * flight of ideas with rapid shift between topics and an inability to focus on any issue or task,
> * sleep disruption including staying awake for days at a time and
> * involvement in activities that carry painful consequences such as credit card over runs, buying sprees, sexual entanglements or affairs, drug or alcohol binges, reckless driving, unwise investments, and so on with no apparent recognition of potential risk.

Depression often follows the manic phase. Studies have documented that women frequently use alcohol during the manic phase of their illness as a way to feel calmer (Daley et al. 1987). However, female alcoholics do drink during both the manic and depressive phases of the bipolar cycle.

Attention Deficit Disorder with or without Hyperactivity

Attention deficit disorder (ADD) occurs more often in children from alcoholic families than those who do not have alcoholic parents (Barkley 1990). In addition, children with ADD, usually have one or more relatives with attention deficit disorder (Barkley 1990). ADD was once considered a childhood disorder, but studies have concluded that children do not necessarily outgrow the condition (Evans et al. 1990, Weiss et al. 1993).

According to Katie Evans and J. Michael Sullivan (1990):

> Children with attention-deficit with or without hyperactivity disorder (ADD-H; ADD) show inappropriate inattention, impulsiveness, and rates of motor behavior that interfere with their ability to tolerate situations requiring controlled behavior for successful academic or interpersonal outcomes. In addition to their cognitive failures, which often result in depression, acting-out behavior, and membership in socially deviant groups, many of these persons will continue to show symptoms of attention deficit disorder and hyperactivity into adulthood and not outgrow the syndrome as formally thought. These individuals, in our experience, appear to be at high risk for substance abuse (p.89).

The characteristics of attention deficit disorder are distractibility, impulsivity and with ADD-H, hyperactivity (Weiss 1992). Individuals with ADD have difficulty sitting still for an extended period, are talkative, disorganized and have difficulty concentrating. They make impulsive decisions by failing to plan ahead or examining the consequences of their behavior (Hartmann 1993).

Academically, ADD children tend to fall behind in school. They frequently shift their attention from one task to another before completing any of them and have difficulty following instructions (Hallowell et al. 1994). Their work is disorganized, frequently lost, forgotten or incomplete, and difficult for teachers to interpret (Hartmann 1993). In the workplace, ADD adults have similar problems in completing tasks and organizing work.

ADD children and adults lack basic social skills (Hartmann 1993). Many are excessive talkers who have difficulty sustaining a conversation with others because of their inability to pay attention to what is being said (Weiss 1992). They frequently interrupt, blurt out responses, have difficulty waiting for a turn, and disclose inappropriate information.

ADD adults have a low tolerance level for frustration, get bored easily and have difficulty paying attention to others. Ironically, people with ADD can stay focused on something that interests them or is highly stimulating for a long period which serves to lead others to believe it is a disciplinary issue (Hallowell et al. 1994). It can also prevent proper diagnosis, especially in women.

ADD in women is consistently undiagnosed and untreated. Women tend to be daydreamers and less likely to manifest the hyperactivity with ADD (Hallowell et al. 1994). As a result, their behavior is less disruptive in the classroom and workplace. They show less aggression, violent outbursts, and extreme mood swings in response to frustration.

In addition, ADD women seem to suffer from depression, shame, and guilt to a much greater degree than ADD men. Often the source of these feelings is their interpersonal relationships. Women tend to hold themselves accountable for the smooth functioning of relationships. This makes ADD women particularly vulnerable to feelings of failure, as the consistently inconsistent nature of ADD-ers' ways of relating to others often produces turmoil. The shame and guilt generated by not being able to live up to role expectations takes a heavy toll on ADD women. The shame stems partly from their inability to be the gatekeeper in relationships, and partly from their chronic disorganization, which prevents them from being the supermoms or wonder women they think they should be (Hallowell et al. 1994, p. 131).

The stresses of living with ADD includes experiencing constant failures, disappointments, frustrations, rejection by others and low self-esteem. Women with ADD are at risk for eating disorders (Hallowell et al. 1994), alcohol and drug abuse (Evans et al. 1990), compulsive spending and workaholism (Weiss 1992). One female alcoholic with ADD-H described how cocaine made her feel normal. Another explained that cocaine made it possible for her to focus. Many alcoholics diagnosed with ADD-H talked about alcohol and marijuana as the only way to be able to relax.

ADD also makes women vulnerable to developing relationships with partners who have ADD and/or addictions. The characteristics of ADD-H are similar to those experienced by alcoholics including (Hallowell et al. 1994):

   * deficits in attention and effort,
   * impulsivity,
   * problems in regulating one's level of arousal, and
   * the need for immediate reinforcement.

It is easy for women with ADD, especially if they are alcoholics as well, to relate to male alcoholics. The drug world is very accepting of the behavioral characteristics of ADD and may explain why the disorders are found together so often in families. Couples come together in a shared reality. Alcohol and drugs used to medicate the symptoms of ADD become the focus of both partners with ADD and alcoholism.

One of the most controversial issues surrounding the treatment of attention deficit disorder is the use of stimulant medication such as Ritalin or Cylert (Evans et al. 1990). By the time they are diagnosed with ADD, female alcoholics have frequently become addicted to stimulants. This presents obvious problems with the possibility of prescribing medication. Katie Evans and J. Michael Sullivan (1990), two therapists who work extensively with alcoholics who have ADD, recommend behavioral interventions rather than a reliance on medication.

Debbie's Story

I always thought something was wrong with me. At least my mom said there was. She was always screaming at me to think before I acted or talked. I was always banging into walls because I moved faster than I could watch where I was going. My dad was always yelling at me to stop swinging my legs when I sat on the couch. I was always being sent out into the hall at school because I couldn't sit still or quit talking. My mom hated my talking. She would scream, hit me, punish me - just to shut me up. You'd think I would learn to stop talking. I never did.

People still get mad at me for interrupting them or doing all the talking. They say I don't listen to them. But the problem is that my mind wanders unless I say something to keep me focused. And if I don't answer the question immediately, I forget what I was going to say. Sometimes, I just prefer to be alone. I get tired being around people. Trying to listen to them, take turns, sit still and remember what to say back. It's a lot of work.

I found friends with people who drank. Alcohol relaxed me. I would get a kick every time one of the guys on speed thought I was high before I took anything. I would have to explain that I wasn't on speed. This was normal for me. I would tell them that I used drugs to calm myself down not to hype myself up. I didn't know any other way to feel better. Until drinking became a problem.

Anxiety Disorders

Women suffering from an anxiety disorder frequently self-medicate with alcohol placing them at risk for a potential addiction (Evans et al. 1990). Studies have found that 10 to 20% of phobic women meet the criteria for alcoholism, making it the second most common dual diagnosis (Daley et al. 1987). Studies have also indicated that 27% of women with agoraphobia and 20% with social phobias grew up in alcoholic homes (Daley et al. 1987). The more generalized the anxiety, the more impairment for the woman, and the more likely she will abuse alcohol and other drugs for relief from her symptoms. Anxiety disorders include (Evans et al.):

* panic disorder with or without agoraphobia,
* agoraphobia,
* social phobia,
* simple phobia,
* obsessive compulsive disorder,
* post traumatic stress disorder, and
* generalized anxiety disorder.

Panic attacks are the main characteristic of a panic disorder. These attacks are unpredictable, last for a few minutes and seem unrelated to any specific stimuli. Nevertheless, a common response to a panic attack is to avoid whatever was happening when the attack occurred. Panic attacks are extremely uncomfortable, involving feelings of intense fear, shortness of breath, heart palpitations or racing pulse, dizziness, shaking, sweating and fear of insanity or death.

Agoraphobia is a fear of being in public places and is often a result (though not always) of having panic attacks outside the home. The most common fears are of crowds, theaters, offices, tunnels, traffic, bridges and elevators. Many women with agoraphobia are completely isolated in their homes and will only venture out with a family member (Daley et al. 1987).

Phobias are more specific fears such as a fear of snakes, bugs, water, or sharks. Social phobias include public speaking, using public lavatories, eating with others or writing in front of someone. Women suffering from an obsessive-compulsive disorder experience persistent intrusive thoughts about something unpleasant or frightening such as an accident, an attack, a disease or germ contamination. Women with this psychiatric disorder frequently perform rituals to ensure cleanliness and personal security (Daley et al. 1987).

Many female alcoholics who grew up with parental alcoholism suffer from post traumatic stress disorder (PTSD) (Daley et al. 1987). This disorder can result from being a victim of rape, assault, childhood abuse or violence. Women with PTSD re-experience the stressful event through intrusive thoughts, nightmares, or memories and withdraw from the outside world. Psychiatric symptoms of PTSD include an exaggerated startle response, hypervigilence and sleep disturbances (Daley et al. 1987).

Finally, the symptoms of generalized anxiety disorder include shakiness, jumpiness, trembling, sweating, palpitations, clammy hands, high resting pulse and rapid breathing, tingling in hands or feet and other signs of activation of the nervous system. Women with this disorder are apprehensive and fearful that something bad will happen to them but have no idea what specifically to be afraid of. As a result, women are anxious about being anxious and have difficulty concentrating and sleeping.

Alcohol and other drugs can mimic the psychiatric symptoms of the anxiety disorders, especially during withdrawal. Cocaine addicts often experience anxiety around the lifestyle associated with drug use as well as the chemical's reaction during use. Alcohol is frequently used to self-medicate the symptoms. Eventually, many women become addicted in addition to suffering from a psychiatric disorder. Others, experience a decrease in symptoms of an anxiety disorder once alcohol and other chemicals are removed from the body. Many times, panic attacks are found to be associated with withdrawal as opposed to a separate disorder. The rule of thumb of waiting thirty days to re-evaluate for a dual diagnosis applies equally to anxiety disorders.

Borderline Personality Disorder

A personality disorder involves a long-term pattern of relating that becomes rigid and fixed and leads to impaired functioning (Evans et al. 1990). Out of the eight criteria for borderline personality disorder, five must be present for the diagnosis (Kreisman et al. 1989):

* unstable and intense interpersonal relationships,
* impulsiveness and potentially self damaging behavior such as substance abuse, sex, shop-lifting, reckless driving, or binge eating,
* severe mood shifts,
* frequent and inappropriate displays of anger,
* recurrent suicidal threats or gestures or self mutilating behaviors,
* lack of clear sense of identity,
* chronic feelings of emptiness or boredom,
* frantic efforts to avoid real or imagined abandonment.

Studies show that women with borderline personality disorder outnumber men and that alcohol abuse among women borderlines is high (Kreisman et al. 1989). In fact, substance abuse is one of the defining characteristics of this disorder. Alcohol use is frequently in response to the unpredictable mood swings, uncontrollable rage, chronic emptiness, and the lack of an identity associated with the disorder. According to Jerold J. Kreisman and Hal Straus (1989), authors of *I Hate you - don't leave me Understanding the Borderline Personality:*

> Mood changes come swiftly, explosively, carrying the borderline from the heights of joy to the   depths of depression. Filled with anger one hour, calm the next, (s)he often has little inkling about why (s)he was driven to such wrath. Afterward, the inability to understand the origins of the episode brings on more self-hate and depression (p. 8).

Borderlines are known for their chameleon-like behavior in adapting to their environment, situation or relationships. One female alcoholic with a borderline personality disorder was able to become part of a religious group, a separate twelve-step group, and a woman's group by pretending to be who she thought these groups wanted her to be. She did not know if she believed in anything that any of the groups stood for and she definitely did not feel she belonged in any of them. She was convinced that she was at risk of being dropped by all three groups. However, her group members thought highly of her and assumed she was content with her membership in their groups.

Alcohol and drugs can be used as a way to feel a sense of belonging to a group, to cope with the emptiness and loneliness experienced by borderlines or to provide the illusion of an identity. Borderline women also use alcohol as a way to feel something or to punish themselves for their angry outbursts. Suicide and self-mutilation are used in much the same way (Kreisman et al. 1989).

Women with borderline personality disorder frequently come from extremely emotionally deprived and abusive families marked by alcoholism and depression (Kreisman et al. 1989).

"One study reported that a history of verbal, physical and/or sexual abuse, or of prolonged separation or neglect by primary caregivers was the most important factor in distinguishing borderline patients from those with other disorders. Other studies have found a history of severe psychological, physical or sexual abuse in 20 to 70% of borderline patients" (Kreisman et al. 1989, p. 9).

A final characteristic of the borderline woman is her inability to see the good and bad qualities of an individual as part of that person's personality. Others are either seen as heroes or villains. "At any particular moment one is either 'good' or 'evil'; there is no in-between, no gray area" (Kreisman et al. 1989, p. 10). This defense mechanism is known as "splitting" and describes how a borderline woman can admire someone one day and then totally despise him or her the next. While she admired that person, the individual was seen as all good. However, the moment she hated the person, the good qualities no longer, if they ever did, exist. Consequently, relationships are difficult to maintain.

In addition, borderlines have trouble finding a balance with intimacy and independence. "Too much closeness threatens the borderline with suffocation. Keeping one's distance or leaving the borderline alone--even for brief periods--recalls the sense of abandonment (s)he felt as a child. In either case, the borderline reacts intensely" (Kreisman et al. 1989, p. 12).

The mood swings, the vacillation between the need for closeness and space, the chameleon behavior, and the rage attacks make it difficult for borderlines to establish intimate relationships. For women, who need this connection, alcohol and other drugs (and the world and people that accompany that lifestyle) become an attractive way to achieve this sense of belonging. Understandably, it also places the borderline woman at risk for developing an addiction to alcohol.

Treatment Issues

Female alcoholics with a coexisting psychiatric disorder need treatment for both illnesses and at the same time. If the alcoholism is treated exclusively, the newly sober woman is at risk of relapsing when psychiatric symptoms interfere with her ability to function. As a coping mechanism or a way to manage her illness, the woman will return to alcohol use to self-medicate.

If the psychiatric illness is treated exclusively, there may be little progress made. It will be difficult to determine if her symptoms are due to the mental illness or the addiction. Many women are misdiagnosed by the mental health field when alcoholism is not considered a possibility. The woman's disturbances are attributed to a psychiatric diagnosis when if fact, she is suffering from an addiction (see chapter 3). As a result, she may be prescribed medication that will interact with the alcohol she drinks placing her at risk for becoming addicted to prescription drugs.

Part 5:

Women
and
Treatment

12

The Female Alcoholic
and Treatment

Treatment Centers

The field of addiction counseling has undergone a number of changes over the years as clinicians have experimented with how best to serve their alcoholic clients. Other than 12-step programs, two forms of treatment currently in existence today are the medical or social model treatment centers and independent counselors. Although no one approach works for everyone, both have their strengths and weaknesses. The field seems to be facing another re-structuring however, as both treatment centers and counselors in private practice come under attack from insurance companies trying to find the most cost-effective form of treatment.

For years, 28-day in-patient centers have been the treatment of choice. Their popularity stemming from the concept that by removing alcoholics from their environment to a safe haven, they could be inundated with the information required to make major lifestyle changes. These centers provided counseling, often around the clock, and eliminated distractions and temptations that place most women at risk for relapse. For battered women, an in-patient program also provides relief from the abuse in their homes.

Many treatment centers incorporated the 12-step philosophy of Alcoholics Anonymous and the peer pressure of community living to reinforce the commitment to recovery. In addition, group counseling provided a sense of belonging and continual support that helped reinforce clients commitment to sobriety. In response to criticisms that 28 days is not enough time to change lifelong behavior patterns, agencies provided year long group work known as aftercare while long-term residential care and recovery homes sprang up to accommodate those that needed even more intensive help.

The most successful aspect of treatment centers is their educational component both for the addicts as well as their families. Women alcoholics need information on how to live clean and sober. They must learn about their sexuality, relationship skills, boundaries, how to communicate and when to assert themselves. Many lack the skills to deal with abuse issues, to parent, find a job, pursue a career or get an education. According to Frank Salvatini (1994), "the true nature of the process that occur(s) in treatment is learning" and treatment centers have developed entire programs to meet this need. Their biggest contribution to their clients therefore is educating them in how to develop a healthy lifestyle in order to maintain their sobriety.

Treatment centers however, have recently come under attack from clients, professionals in private practice and insurance companies. In spite of revisions made to lengthening care, critics continue to cite the unrealistic expectation that people could change their entire lives in less than 30 days as well as continue with those changes once they leave the center. In addition, most chemically dependent clients find it is almost impossible to get a month off of work to attend a treatment program. For many women, in particular, time off has been out of the question. Often trapped in low paying jobs, women lack the flexibility to take 28 days to enter a program, have the insurance coverage to pay for treatment or have the additional financial resources to cover their loss of pay during their absence.

Treatment centers have also been slow to provide child care, forcing many women to choose between abandoning their children or their own treatment needs. Women often lack the financial resources to find safe and appropriate child care placing them at risk for losing their children if they did seek help. Men often leave the children with their mothers when they go into treatment. Male alcoholics can focus their entire attention on recovery knowing that the children are safe, their jobs are secure and their families are supportive.

Female alcoholics, on the other hand, frequently enter a treatment program divorced, with the custody of their children and little financial support from their ex-husbands. Leaving these children with their fathers make many women vulnerable to losing custody on the grounds that they are unfit mothers. Women diagnosed with alcoholism face the stigma of "abusive mother" and abandoning their children to pursue treatment can confirm that this label in the eyes of the court system. Foster care and other relatives often poses the same problems. Women do not enter treatment secure in the knowledge that their children and jobs are safe. They also lack the financial and emotional support that tends to be more available to their male counterpart.

Another deterrent is that most centers have been geared toward helping the male alcoholic. Women, gays, lesbians, adolescents, the homeless, those with dual diagnosis, the elderly, minorities, the disabled and those infected with the HIV virus are just some of the diverse population that require help with their alcoholism. Historically, treatment centers have lumped everyone together under the guise that everyone is alike and suffer the same disease. This is changing in many programs and more effort is being made to design an individual treatment plan for each patient. However, many centers are slow in realizing that women face issues specific to them.

Women drink for different reasons, under different conditions and get sick at a different rates than men (Sandmaier 1992). They come into treatment facing different obstacles and experience a different recovery process. Female alcoholics must deal with abuse issues, violence, rape and wife battering in early recovery (Covington 1991). The majority of recovering women alcoholics need job training. Treatment centers often do not recognize this need in women in the same way it does for men. Yet women who are unable to financial support themselves and their children are at risk of turning back to alcohol for relief.

In addition, treatment centers have a structured environment that insists everyone attend meetings, groups and educational lectures that may be completely inappropriate for some clients. The regulations set up in agencies to protect patients from romantic entanglements can seem ludicrous to some and rob others of their dignity and adult status. Rules about socializing with the opposite sex, make-up, how to dress, when to get up, how to care for personal items and compulsory attendance at all groups regardless of individual needs have been set up to help the agency run smoothly but not necessarily done with the client's best interests in mind.

One of the most common criticisms has been the treatment center's utilization of the 12 steps. The marriage of treatment centers and the 12-step program has many angered over having to pay for something that is otherwise free and voluntary to others. Most clients can not "graduate" from their treatment program unless they have attended so many meetings and done at least the first five steps. This goes against the spirit of Alcoholics Anonymous which states that it is "a program of attraction", its free, that the steps are recommended not compulsory and that they are to be done at the individual's own pace. A good treatment center makes 12-step meetings available but not mandatory as part of its program.

The biggest obstacle to the success of treatment centers however, is the expense of such programs. Costing thousands of dollars for a bed, meals and counseling, few are able to afford such care. This has limited the number of patients who are eligible to those who have insurance coverage for drug and alcohol treatment. Relying on insurance reimbursements has caused enormous economic stress for most centers, forcing them to shift their focus from treatment issues to the task of keeping beds filled in order to stay afloat. The first question many programs ask when a prospective patient calls is what insurance coverage they have. Many have had to change screening requirements as the level of anxiety to keep the programs filled has escalated.

Recently, the biggest blow to treatment centers has come with insurance companies and managed care's growing resistance to cover long-term or in-patient care anymore. Treatment centers have been able to offer few guarantees that their approach will work and with clients returning sometimes three or four times, the insurance industry is looking for more successful, if not, cost effective ways to treat the problem. Hence, the introduction of the addiction counselor in private practice. This is not the first time a private practitioner has been sought for help.

Before the advent of agencies and treatment centers, private counseling was one of the few options other than hospitals, mental institutions and jails. However, this is the first time that professionals have been clinically trained in alcohol and drug abuse issues. In previous years, most had little awareness of the disease process let alone how to address it. Today's professional is getting specialized training to broaden their scope of practice or even more recently, to practice in the field of addiction as a specialty of its own.

Addiction Counselors

Individual counseling from a private practitioner (ie. LMFCC, LCSW, CAADAC/NAADAC addiction counselor) or agency is cheaper, less intrusive in the alcoholic's life and more flexible.

The client is not required to follow a prescribed treatment plan designed exactly the same for everyone. Individualized care ensures that specific issues unique to each client will be addressed. There are no rules about make-up, dress code or the care of personal items. There is no concern about co-ed issues and romantic entanglements that have been the nemesis of many a center. There are no rules for community living to follow or the risk of losing one's kids, family, or job. Confidentiality is preserved.

There are many diverging theories among clinicians as to what is effective with alcoholics giving clients a variety to choose from. Some counselors approach the disease of addiction from a spiritual perspective, relying heavily on the 12-step philosophy. Some on the behavioral and/or physiological symptoms of the disease (Cusak 1984, Gorski 1989). Others argue for a more cognitive approach (Ellis 1992) while still others for an educational one (Salvatini 1994). From this standpoint, it looks ideal. And in many ways, it is. However, private practice lacks some of the strengths that treatment centers had been keen to develop.

Individual counseling does not have the same structured environment that treatment centers promote to help bring stability into many a recovering alcoholic's life. There is rarely a well-defined educational component to individual counseling and there is the loss of a peer support group to help deal with early recovery issues on a daily basis. Women in particular have lost the connection to others critical for their success to maintain sobriety. In addition, it is confusing for clients to ascertain who has the qualifications to help them.

Many licensed therapists lack the special training involved in working with addictions or to help those who require information on sober living, social and relationship skills. Conventional psychoanalytical therapy is fairly ineffective with female clients in heavy denial about their addiction or how it has affected them. On the other hand, addiction counselors whose training is strictly focused on addictions lack the education and degrees to enable them to deal with the abuse, marital and parenting issues that so often get addressed in recovery.

In addition, alcoholics and drug addicts are notorious for not following through on treatment. This poses problems for any venue but some particular difficult ones for the private clinician. Clients who don't show up for appointments mean loss of revenue. No one else can take that appointment. In a treatment center, there is another candidate down the hall. Alcoholic clients are unreliable when it comes to money. They fail to pay for appointments, bounce checks or simply can't afford the counselor's fees. Some lie about their ability to pay giving the gullible counselor a hard luck story only to discover later that the client may be better off financially than the counselor.

The drop-out rate with addicts is high, forcing many practitioners to screen out a number of prospective clients before one shows promise of following through on treatment. It also makes them vulnerable to work with clients they are not qualified to treat. Furthermore, the same complaints directed at treatment centers about using the 12-steps places private practitioners under attack. Clients do not want to pay for treatment that is available to the general public for free. Most clients are desperate for help and making the first phone call is scary enough without having to fear that this counselor has a theoretical orientation not suited to their specific needs.

What needs to happen in the addiction field is to blend the strengths of the treatment center with those of private practice while minimizing their weaknesses. Recovering alcoholics need the structure, guidance, educational component and continual support system 28-day programs provide. In addition, clients need the individualized treatment plan, freedom to carry on daily living, reduced costs, long-term treatment options and the flexibility to meet a number of different needs that private practice counselors address.

Treatment centers are certainly valuable to those clients who work best with a structured and intensive program or for those who require a safe environment until they have developed their own inner strength to maintain sobriety. Addiction counselors in private practice or working in an agency offer alcoholics a viable alternative. Individual counseling is more accessible, cheaper, can be more individualized to meet specific needs and provides a longer-term and more personal recovery program. In private practice, there is more room for developing treatment plans that take into account differences among the alcoholic population. Incorporating education, skill building and group work expands the scope of individual counseling.

It is imperative that treatment include an educational component, group work to provide continuing support and programs to work with the families. These are the elements that have proven so successful in treatment centers and can help insure the best of both worlds in private practice. It seems clear that the future of addiction treatment lies in a diversity of options including addiction counselors in private practice or agencies who adopt some of the characteristics of the treatment center.

Kay's Story

Sobriety came to me early in my forty-ninth year. I didn't mean to get clean and sober though, much less stay that way! I thought I'd be smokin' dope and drinking Mad Dog from a rocking chair (or wheel chair, or whatever). But somehow I ended up in a "hospital" in a condition of severe depression. There the staff informed me that it was their opinion that I also had a drug and alcohol problem. Well, certainly I didn't believe them but I was past caring what happened to me so I didn't object when they put me in the drug rehab program.

After several days, I began to hear people talking to me and somehow explained to me how I was attempting to medicate my depression with a substance. How when the substance wore off I was at a lower level than before, and therefore required more substance, which in turn dropped me lower....till I was deep in a pit of despair. Somehow it made sense in my scrambled brain and I began to look at sobriety as a possible option.

Next was the problem of this "higher power" in the AA program. Though I had found some kindred ideas in Taoism and Eastern philosophy that I had been reading for some thirty years, I still considered myself a card-carrying atheist when it came to a Western type deity. Clearly, this program would never work for me. Then someone told me about SOS.

Secular Organizations for Sobriety probably saved my life, or at least my sober life, at this point. Here I found sober people who did not necessarily believe in a "higher power". Here I could speak freely. Much to the dismay of my house mother at the half-way house I was now living in, I became active in SOS.

I still went to AA and NA meetings though, as this was a house requirement. I was doing two meetings on SOS days. The program was creeping into my life. But only creeping. I hung on to the old, well-known ways. At forty-nine years old, my mind was pretty set. About this time (my counselor) came into my life. I wasn't really against seeing her as I knew no one was really going to change me anyhow. She told me I wasn't going to stay sober the way I was doing it so I had to stay clean just to show her my way was fine. She told me about boundaries and helped me find mine and encouraged me through the process of setting them. She helped me through letting go of my family. She insisted that I eat regularly. She encouraged me to get some medical care.

She gave me affirmations to say and soothed my fractured ego through many job rejections. She watched me cry a lifetime of tears. I felt she was in my corner when no one else was. It was still a mystery to me how she was able to crack through the wall I had been building for more years than she had been alive. I cannot say where the turning point was when I let go of "I can't" and took the first baby steps. No one had ever gotten through to me before.

Today I have a sort of "higher power". I have a job. I still have depression but I am able to see it starting and control it. I am working on some pretty overwhelming physical problems without giving up on life. I have friends, and my family have become my friends. I have four years and four months of sobriety. I want to live.

Addiction Counseling and 12-Step Programs

There has been a marriage of sorts between addiction counseling and 12-step programs such as Alcoholics Anonymous (AA). This has come about as a result of the reported success of anonymous programs with helping members maintain sobriety. The success attracted a lot of attention and convinced those in the alcoholism counseling profession to take 12-step programs seriously.

Psychotherapists, on their part, experienced repeated failure in helping alcoholics remain abstinent though therapists did prove helpful with other psychological issues faced by the newly recovering person. In an effort to combine the strengths of both approaches, many treatment centers and addiction specialists have blended the two modalities into their programs. Hence, the appearance of 12-step meetings in treatment centers and step work as part of individual and group counseling.

Although treatment centers have gained a great deal of publicity for including 12-step programs as part of their curriculum, addiction counseling and anonymous programs work best when the client puts them together, not the professionals. Counselors are wise to recommend AA for providing "the emotional support necessary for some alcoholics to resist the strong internal and external pressures to drink" (Sauser et al. 1989, p. 135). However, 12-step work has no place in the counselor's office.

There are differences between counseling and 12-step programs. These differences should be respected and kept separate. By doing so, it offers those that suffer from alcoholism alternative approaches for help. It also maintains the integrity of both counselors being paid for their work and the nature of anonymous programs as self-help groups that are free and accessible to everyone.

At first, the blending of the 12-step approach and counseling seemed to be a welcomed addition to treatment centers and has continued to be used as a marketing tool to attract clients. Upon entering many inpatient programs, clients are given "workbooks" to do their step work in. Questions related to the steps have been developed in order to include them as part of counseling. Rules about finishing the first five steps before graduation as well as attendance requirements to AA meetings were created as a measuring stick of the client's progress. In addition, it was often assumed that the treatment center was qualified just by its recognition and inclusion of the anonymous program. It was an assumption based on the belief that AA was an important means in helping alcoholics and drug addicts remain abstinent.

This assumption, however, was never scientifically studied and so far there has been no evidence that AA is any more effective than other approaches. Although useful to some people as a source of continuing support, it has been found to be just as ineffective for others (Sauser et al., 1989). The belief in AA's success however, continues today as the popularity of 12-step programs grows. It also continues to provide inpatient programs with a resourceful marketing tool for little additional cost. "The majority of treatment centers are still offering 30-day Alcoholics Anonymous based inpatient treatment" (Sauser et al. 1989, p.153). And many of these programs advertise their 12-step philosophy as a way of attracting potential clients.

Alcoholics Anonymous

In the psychoanalytical field, Alcoholics Anonymous is seen as a charismatic therapy (Sauser et al. 1989). It is described "as a unique organization: it has no organizational hierarchy: it has no officers; it owns no property; it espouses no political doctrine" (Sauser et al. 1989, p. 133). Tradition Three of AA points out that "the only requirement for AA membership is a desire to stop drinking" (*Alcoholics Anonymous* 1976, p. 364). There are no fees to be paid and only first names are used to protect confidentiality. Characteristic of AA is that it "insists upon total abstinence as the treatment goal for all its members, yet emphasizes that an alcoholic is always recovering but never recovered. The AA member is viewed always as a potential drinker, no matter how long sobriety has been maintained" (Sauser et al. 1989, p. 134).

Alcoholics Anonymous is a spiritual program. (Critics believe that because the program uses language and prayer from a Christian perspective, it is in fact, a religion. However, members of

AA see it as a spiritual program.)   According to Bill Wilson, the co-founder of AA, alcoholics have lost the power over drinking and only a power greater than themselves can help them prevent picking up the next drink (*Alcoholics Anonymous* 1976). He notes:

> The great fact is just this, and nothing less: That we have had a deep and effective spiritual experiences which have revolutionized our whole attitude toward life, toward our fellows and toward God's universe. The central fact of our lives today is the absolute certainty that our Creator has entered our hearts and lives in a way which is indeed miraculous. He has commenced to accomplish those things for us which we could never do ourselves. (p.25)

In order to tap into this higher power, alcoholics are encouraged to attend "open meetings at which members share their stories, develop new interpersonal relationships, establish role models, identify sponsors and reinforce other members' efforts to maintain sobriety" (Sauser et al. 1989, p. 134). The alcoholic is thereby creating a support system established on a spiritual foundation that members believe unite them in helping each other stay sober. No one is supposed to tell another how to "work their program". Attendance at meetings, choosing a sponsor and working the steps is voluntary. No one makes a diagnosis or develops a treatment plan.

The book Alcoholics Anonymous (1976) assures that "we do not pronounce any individual as alcoholic, but you can quickly diagnose yourself" (p. 31). The only thing AA emphasizes other than abstinence is described in Step 12: "Having had a spiritual awakening as the result of these steps, we tried to carry this message to alcoholics, and to practice these principles in all our affairs" (p. 60). It is emphasized again in Tradition Five "Each group has but one primary purpose -- to carry its message to the alcoholic who still suffers" (p. 564). AA therefore, is a spiritual program with the primary purpose being the self-sacrificing nature of one alcoholic helping another in order to ensure their own sobriety. In AA language this is referred to as "12th-stepping".

Counseling in contrast, is structured by professionals who have been trained and educated to make a diagnosis and develop treatment goals. Unlike AA members, counselors are paid a fee, are educated in psychological matters and are expected to follow a code of ethics. While a member of AA may share their "experience, strength and hope" (*Alcoholic Anonymous* 1976) to a fellow alcoholic in crises, a counselor will confront denial and other defense mechanisms, prescribe a treatment plan, educate about the disease and teach sober living skills.

To become a certified Alcohol and Drug Abuse Counselor in the State of California, one needs 315 hours of basic alcohol and drug education, a 255 hour practicum, 6,000 hours of a clinically supervised internship, as well as passing a written and oral exam administered by the board. A licensed Marriage, Family and Child Counselor or licensed Clinical Social Worker needs to obtain further education in the form of a M.A. or PH.D, do 3,000 hours of a clinically supervised internship and pass both a written and oral exam.

To become a sponsor in AA, one must have more sobriety than the sponsee. Since it is an individual decision, requirements beyond sobriety differ with each sponsee. Many want sponsors that have attended AA meetings on a regular basis for at least a year, have a sponsor of their own and have worked all the steps. (Working the steps means they have done some writing and sharing with a sponsor on each one of the 12 steps.)

Oldtimers encourage members to sponsor their own gender but even this is not strictly adhered to. Although it may be beneficial to clients to have a counselor who is also a member of AA, it is not a requirement. Counselors help their clients get sober as part of their job not to ensure their own sobriety by "carrying the message". Counselors are trained to do a job and they get paid to do this job. AA membership is voluntary and members choose when and whom to help.

The most significant difference between counseling and 12-step programs however, is the way each approach deals with the problem of maintaining sobriety. Alcoholics in AA believe that by sharing their story on what worked for them, their fellow alcoholics can "take what they like and leave the rest behind" deciding for themselves what will help them stay sober. The spiritual component of the program promotes the idea that alcoholics will help each other without repayment as a way to ensure their own sobriety.

This sharing with another is encouraged because it keeps fresh in the alcoholic's mind, the exact nature of their own disease. Remembering "what it was like, how they got to AA, and what it is like now," keeps the recovering alcoholic's motivation to stay sober alive. The recipients of this sharing benefit both by feeling less unique as well as feeling inspired that sobriety is indeed, possible. They have living proof of someone who has been there and yet, gotten sober successfully.

Counselors, on the other hand, are trained in many theoretical perspectives to help a wide variety of people in a number of different ways. Some do approach recovery from a spiritual perspective but there are also a number of clinicians who work from the behavioral and/or physiological symptoms of the disease (Cusak 1984, Gorski 1989), a cognitive approach (Ellis 1992) or an educational perspective (Salvatini 1994). According to addiction counselors, not every approach works with every alcoholic.

Most counselors agree that working with the entire family is beneficial to the alcoholic because it has been observed that the family plays a significant part in the alcoholic's ability to remain abstinent. "Family counseling is focused on reducing marital disharmony and stress; dealing with the emotional, social, and economic impact the alcoholic's behavior has on the family; and developing and integrating more adaptive coping behaviors by which the family can help the recovering alcoholic maintain sobriety" (Sauser et al. 1989, p. 135). This is especially true for women.

In addition, counselors recognize that there are different populations affected by alcoholism; minorities, homosexuals, those with dual diagnosis, a chronic medical problem, men, women, adolescents, the elderly, and the disabled, just to name a few. These differences affect the kind of help each group of alcoholics will need and counselors must adapt their treatment goals accordingly. Critics of AA have been quick to point out that the 12-step program has limitations in helping any population of alcoholics other than the white, middle-class men the program was designed for. After all, this was the original group of alcoholics who were responsible for creating AA's structure and format in the first place. Women, in particular, have trouble with a program that was created by men for men and led by a male god. This feeling can be compounded if the treatment center makes attending meetings a requirement for graduation.

While AA's primary purpose is to achieve and maintain sobriety, counselors address a wide variety of problems faced by the recovering client. Many female alcoholics need help with marital conflicts, violence and abuse, family of origin issues, sexual dysfunctions, unemployment, HIV infection and parenting difficulties. Although the steps, sponsors and meetings focus on sobriety, counselors often address these other issues during their work on the client's relapse prevention plan. Even the book of Alcoholics Anonymous recognizes that drinking is merely a symptom of an underlying problem (1976).

Working the steps cleans up the alcoholic's past but it does not address psychological or psychiatric issues. Bill Wilson, repeatedly recommended that alcoholics seek outside professional help with doctors and therapists for treatment beyond the scope of AA and he did so himself when he suffered a ten year long depression (*Pass It On* 1984).

When Alcoholics Anonymous was first formed, Bill Wilson faced controversy over what was paid work and what was 12-step work. At a time in his life when he desperately needed money, Bill was offered employment to work with alcoholics. The hospital where he and Dr. Bob had been helping alcoholics for free was now willing to have Bill continue this work as a full-time paid employee. Although Bill wanted to do it, the other alcoholics in AA were adamant that it was inappropriate for him to be paid to do 12-step work (*Pass It On* 1984, p. 175). Reluctantly, Bill agreed and he turned down the job to continue his work in AA, thereby setting a precedent that the two were separate.

With this decision, the 12-step program was born, and Bill W. spent the rest of his life developing the steps and traditions that would guarantee, AA's independence as a self-help group. If Bill had accepted the offer, he might have become the first paid addiction counselor and AA may never have grown from a handful of alcoholics to the huge 12-step movement it has become. However, Bill Wilson saw the distinction between addiction counseling and Alcoholics Anonymous. In order to protect the future of AA, he dutifully wrote several traditions describing this separation between the two.

One of the most important traditions that Bill wrote -- tradition Six states "An A.A. group ought never to endorse, finance or lend the A.A. name to any related facility or outside enterprise, lest problems of money, property and prestige divert us from our primary purpose" (*Alcoholics Anonymous* 1976, p. 564). Bill Wilson goes on to explain in the long form of this tradition that,

> Secondary aids to A.A., such as clubs or hospitals which require much property or administration, ought to be incorporated and so set apart that, if necessary, they can be freely discarded by the groups. Hence such facilities ought not to use the A.A. name" (*Alcoholics Anonymous* 1976, p. 566).

Although Bill was primarily concerned about the AA group as a whole becoming blind to the financial appeal of recovery, the tradition can also apply to individuals or organizations who use AA as a marketing tool. According to the cofounder of Alcoholics Anonymous, "hospitals, as well as other places of recuperation, ought to be well outside A.A. - and medically supervised. While an A.A. group may cooperate with anyone, such cooperation ought never go so far as affiliation or endorsement, actual or implied" (*Alcoholics Anonymous* 1976, p.566).

In an effort to emphasize the differences between AA and addiction counseling, Bill added another tradition that AA should be "forever non professional" and he defined "professionalism as the occupation of counseling alcoholics for fees or hire"(*Alcoholics Anonymous* 1976, p.566). At this point, Bill is quite clear that addiction counselors getting paid to help alcoholics do so outside the scope of AA. According to the co-founder of Alcoholics Anonymous, the differences between addiction counseling and AA is that " our usual A.A. "12th step" work is never to be paid for" (*Alcoholics Anonymous* 1976, p.567).

A final point is made in Tradition Eleven to further demonstrate the differences between AA and addiction counseling. It states that AA's "public relations policy is based on attraction rather than promotion" (*Alcoholics Anonymous* 1976, p.564). The recent trend of treatment centers to advertise their 12-step philosophy as a marketing ploy to attract clients violates the foundation of this spiritual program. By marketing for their own treatment program, these centers, albeit inadvertently, also market for membership to Alcoholics Anonymous. In addition, by mandating meetings as part of treatment it further confuses the boundary between the paid addiction counselor and the member of Alcoholics Anonymous 12-stepping another alcoholic.

Unfortunately, the differences between addiction counseling and 12-step programs have often been blurred, at least by counselors and treatment staff in many inpatient programs. This has not been true of insurance companies, licensed professionals outside the addiction field and the clients themselves. During interviews, many recovering alcoholics talked about feeling resentful about paying for treatment that included a component which is essentially free to the general public.

It is imperative that AA (or any other 12-step) meetings are not mandatory, are not paid for as part of the package deal of the treatment plan and are not used as a marketing tool. If addiction counselors want to be taken seriously as experts in the field by other professionals, insurance companies and potential clients, then these "experts" must stand on their own by maintaining a distinction from anonymous programs.

13

The Female Alcoholic and AA

Alcoholics Anonymous (AA)

Alcoholics Anonymous (AA) was founded on June 10, 1935 by Bill Wilson and Dr. Bob Smith. Its premise of "one alcoholic helping another to stay sober" began when Bill met with Dr. Bob in order to maintain his own sobriety. Their success at helping each other and countless others that followed became the foundation of a twelve step, self-help program that has saved thousands of lives. It was a program created by men, for men, and based on a male Higher Power. It took time before women were even admitted to the meetings, but their numbers have grown over the years and the program has proven helpful to female alcoholics as well.

AA's purpose is to carry the message that sobriety is possible to alcoholics who are struggling with their drinking. The program has developed twelve steps outlining the way to maintain sobriety and a book, on which the program is named, describing the process. Meetings, where members share their stories on how they remain abstinent, provide a social means for getting more information on how the program works. The primary focus of Alcoholics Anonymous is to help other fellow sufferers to not pick up the first drink. It is believed that once the drinking begins, loss of control prevents it from stopping. Therefore, every effort is made to develop a support system that members can call upon when the compulsion to drink becomes overwhelming.

This support system involves slogans to remember, telephone lists of members to call and a relationship with a sponsor who will provide guidance. A sponsor is someone who has knowledge of the program and a history of sobriety. Sponsors are chosen based on compatibility, similar drinking histories, a shared value system or because the newcomer admires the older member's present sober lifestyle. The idea behind sponsoring newcomers developed in the early days of Alcoholics Anonymous (*Living Sober* 1985). At that time, a few hospitals began admitting patients under the diagnosis of alcoholism when an AA member with some sobriety was willing to 'sponsor' the sick person.

> The sponsor took the patient to the hospital, visited him or her regularly, was present when the patient was discharged, and took the patient home and then to AA meetings.

At the meetings the sponsor introduced the newcomer to other happily non-drinking alcoholics. All through the early months of recovery the sponsor stood by, ready to answer questions or to listen whenever needed. Sponsorship turned out to be such a good way to help people get established in AA that it had become a custom followed throughout the AA world even when hospitalization is not necessary" (Living Sober 1985, p. 26).

The unique relationship that developed between a sponsor and a newcomer during this process was found to be a strength in helping the beginner become established in the program. A sponsor could help a new member find meetings, meet other alcoholics, be available for phone calls during a craving to drink and introduce them to the twelve steps and the book of Alcoholics Anonymous (or commonly referred to as "The Big Book" by AA members). As a result, the idea of finding a sponsor upon entering the AA program became popular and continues today with Alcoholics Anonymous members around the world.

The only requirement of a sponsor is to "share their experience, strength and hope" and offer guidelines in how to follow the steps of the program. They do not get paid for this service. The process of helping another strengthens the helper's resolve to stay sober. Newcomers are not required to follow the helper's advice and the AA program strongly encourages same sex sponsoring. The idea behind sponsoring is the same one behind going to meetings; that one alcoholic is helping another.

AA is responsible for popularizing the disease concept of alcoholism based on the findings of Dr. Silkworth and others in the medical profession. It does nothing however, to encourage research on alcoholism or other treatment options for recovery (Bufe 1991). Nor does it provide any other services other than helping members to stay sober. "The only requirement for A.A. membership is a desire to stop drinking" *(Alcoholics Anonymous* 1976, p. 564).

The program promotes the understanding that alcoholism is a fatal, progressive illness that requires some form of action for recovery. "Working on the steps" in the form of writing, talking and reading about them gives alcoholics something to do instead of drinking. All of the steps require some decision or action to be completed. These steps are the foundation of the program and teach alcoholics how to maintain a sober lifestyle.

The Twelve Steps of Alcoholics Anonymous

Bill and Dr. Bob continued the success they had with each other by continuing to help other suffering alcoholics. They went to hospitals to talk to patients, recruited members through friends and created meetings where members could talk to one another in a group setting. As their efforts improved, they slowly created a "formula" that clearly worked -- over and over again. In 1938,

Bill wrote the first book to describe this recovery program. It was called *Alcoholics Anonymous* and it set forth what has become known as the twelve steps of the program *(Living Sober* 1985, p.408).

1. We admitted we were powerless over alcohol - that our lives had become unmanageable.

2. Came to believe that a Power greater than ourselves could restore us to sanity.

3. Made a decision to turn our will and our lives over to the care of God *as we understood Him.*

4. Made a searching and fearless moral inventory of ourselves.

5. Admitted to God, to ourselves, and to another human being the exact nature of our wrongs.

6. Were entirely ready to have God remove all these defects of character.

7. Humbly asked Him to remove our shortcomings.

8. Made a list of all persons we had harmed, and became willing to make amends to them all.

9. Made direct amends to such people wherever possible, except when to do so would injure them or others.

10. Continued to take personal inventory and when we were wrong promptly admitted it.

11. Sought through prayer and meditation to improve our conscious contact with God *as we understood Him*, praying only for knowledge of His will for us and the power to carry that out.

12. Having had a spiritual awakening as the result of these steps, we tried to carry this message to alcoholics and to practice these principles in all our affairs.

AA as a Spiritual Program or a Religion

Critics of Alcoholics Anonymous point to the references to God in the twelve steps and at meetings as evidence that it is a religion (Bufe 1991). They insist that AA members "zealously promote the 12 Steps" because "of religious belief, not the result of logical thinking" (Bufe 1991, p. 63). Charles Bufe (1991), in his book *"Alcoholics Anonymous: Cult or Cure?"* goes on to describe how "fully half of the 12 Steps explicitly mention 'God,' 'a Power greater than ourselves,' or 'Him.' Most religious A.A. members have little or no problem with this terminology. It fits their belief system" (p. 63).   However, Bufe believes that many nonreligious alcoholics have difficulty with the religious overtones or embrace them out of desperation for help.

Alcoholics Anonymous touts itself as a spiritual program, insisting that members' vision of a Higher Power can be anything including their own religious or nonreligious beliefs. "A.A. is not a religious cult. It is not an evangelical movement. Some members are religious, and some are agnostics or atheists. Many members choose to believe that their 'higher power' is their A.A. group" (Robertson 1988).   Others simply believe in the power of two alcoholics helping each other with the common purpose to not drink.

Bill Wilson and Dr. Bob were both members of the evangelical Christian Oxford Groups and were influenced by the religious nature of that program (Bufe 1991, *Pass It On* 1984). In the early days, these men prayed with strangers, talked about God and believed that religion was the only way to maintain sobriety (Robertson 1988). As more members with divergent religious beliefs joined the ranks of AA, the concept of a higher power derived from the member's own imagination took hold.   These newer members insisted on changing some of the wording of the steps to reflect their beliefs and Bill did so as a "concession to those of little or no faith" (*Pass It On* 1984, p.199). As far as Bill was concerned, adding in *as we understood Him* was "the great contribution of our atheists and agnostics. They had widened our gateway so that all who suffer might pass through, regardless of their belief or *lack of belief*" (*Pass It On* 1984, p. 199).

The history of Alcoholics Anonymous provides the best answer to whether AA is a spiritual or religious program. It began as a religious one established on the principals of the Oxford Group and the belief systems of the two men who left that group to develop the A.A. program. Both Bill and Dr. Bob believed in a Christian God and believed that this faith in a higher power kept them sober (*Pass It On* 1984). Bill, in particular, spoke of a spiritual awakening. He felt the presence of God was a catalyst for his sobriety and he recommended that friends join a church (*Pass It On* 1984).

However, AA eventually evolved into a spiritual program in response to the concerns of its nonreligious members and members of other religious faiths. From the beginning, there have been AA members who rejected the religious nature of the program and pushed to have it removed. Some members broke from Alcoholics Anonymous in much the same way that Bill and Dr. Bob did from the Oxford Group to form other twelve step programs (such as Secular Organizations for Sobriety, Rational Recovery, Women for Sobriety and Men for Sobriety) that reflected a more nonreligious approach. Other members put their energy into making AA a spiritual rather than religious experience. One of AA's strongest statements is to "take what you like and leave the rest behind" suggesting its own limitations in being everything to everyone.

Nevertheless, this controversy over the spiritual or religious nature of the program rages on, not only outside of AA but among its members as well. As noted earlier, nearly half the steps reference God and many meetings still end by saying the Lord's Prayer. Members often argue among themselves and nonbelievers are encouraged to pray for enlightenment (Bufe 1991). It is also true that nonreligious members are given little chance to talk about their views. In contrast, they are exposed to other members' talk about God and are subjected to the dogma that not believing in the concept of a Higher Power will lead back to drinking (Bufe 1991).

Charles Bufe (1991) takes a further stand that "many nonreligious alcoholics do drink themselves to death after investigating A.A. and rejecting it because of its religiosity. In all too many cases that appears to be the result of their acceptance of the A.A. myth that alcoholics who reject A.A. are doomed to an alcoholic hell. This belief frequently becomes a self-fulfilling prophesy" (p. 64).

Contradicting this stance are the number of nonreligious alcoholics who have joined the ranks of AA and not embraced the religious overtones of the program. Even in the early days of AA, there were members who fought for a more individual approach to the belief or non-belief in a higher power. Today, members continue to join the program while choosing to rewrite their "Big Book" and the twelve steps to reflect their own beliefs. "The degree of discomfort that a doubter or nonbeliever in God may experience in A.A. meetings depends greatly on the group. How much members talk about God and religion varies enormously" (Robertson 1988, p. 131).

Ironically, the fact that AA has such a diverse membership and that other twelve step programs with no religious or spiritual themes have sprouted from its example, suggest that the major influence of Alcoholics Anonymous does not lie solely in its belief of a Higher Power. The power of the twelve step program may never have been its spiritual nature but rather its more practical approach of one alcoholic helping another. "Slowly, Bill had come to believe that alcoholics needed to work with their own kind, that staying sober while achieving balance and peace in one's life was the only goal that counted" (Robertson 1988, p.52). For Bill, that balance and peace took the form of believing in God. Other alcoholics have found that their balance and peace may be something else. What the members did agree on, and still do today, is that alcoholics need to help each other.

Alcoholics Anonymous, at its core, is a group of people with a personal understanding of the devastation associated with alcoholism; who have come together for the common good of staying alive. "A.A.'s know alcoholism is a life-and-death affair. They know from experience that it ruins not just their health but everything in their lives that matters" (Robertson 1988, p. 98). Therapists have found this power of a common understanding and a singular goal when developing groups for clients to overcome a variety of problems besides addictions. The group process is an effective milieu to confront the cognitive distortions and denial system that are symptoms of the disease of alcoholism.

The twelve steps and the AA slogans attack the alcoholic's denial and distorted thinking. It does this by creating a plan that requires members to take responsibility, accept the consequences of their behavior and confront their own thinking. Taking inventories, making amends and the self-examination involved in Steps 6 and 7 require members to take some kind of action for their own behavior. AA members are taught to write, make gratitude lists, clean up their own side of the street and focus their energy on themselves. Slogans such as "first things first," "think it all the way through" (usually referring to taking a drink), "just for today" and "easy does it" teach alcoholics how to set priorities, see the big picture, focus on the present and understand the ramifications of their behavior on others.

AA members learn to "not judge their own insides by someone else's outsides," preventing negative comparisons so popular to the prelude of a drinking episode. They learn to tolerate other people's behavior with the slogan "live and let live" and not use others as an excuse to drink. By encouraging members to become active in the running of meetings, making phone calls and in sponsorship, alcoholics learn social skills, develop sober friendships and find role models living a sober lifestyle.

Getting active in AA teaches members to become more active in their own lives. Many must learn how to eat properly, exercise, do chores, enjoy leisure time without drinking, and develop non-drinking hobbies. Most need to recognize the environmental cues that trigger a craving to drink and develop new routines.

Alcoholics are taught the acronym HALT to use as a reminder to not get too hungry, angry, lonely, or tired. It is a useful tool in encouraging members to take care of their physical needs as well as confronting the often unreasonable resentments alcoholics create as an excuse to drink. Meetings are frequently seen as an opportunity to meet with others to ward off the loneliness that goes with the transition to a sober lifestyle and friends. Meetings also serve as an opportunity to make sober friends and confront the denial system associated with addictions.

AA members spend an enormous amount of time talking about the last drunk. When asked to chair a meeting, members share their stories. The storyteller follows the basic formula of "what happened, how they got there (to AA) and what it's like now". It serves to remind members that they are alcoholics and confront their denial that they were only social drinkers. The stories also provide an opportunity for AA members to feel grateful about their recovery.

In early sobriety, there can be a number of losses and negative consequences from the drinking. The devastating effects of alcoholism can mean loss of job, marriage, children, family and friends. Most people coming to AA feel lonely, frustrated, hopeless, despair and pain from all their losses. Listening to how life improves from older members can be inspiring.

A common saying in AA,"poor me, poor me, pour me a drink" suggests avoiding self-pity and focusing on the inspiration of others who have succeeded in changing their lives for the better.

Women and AA

AA is particularly good at confronting the denial and distorted thinking of the alcoholic because of the power that surrounds the group mentality. It is hard to maintain a different belief about yourself (such as "I'm a normal drinker") if everyone around you believes something different. This strength explains the need behind defining whether AA is religious or spiritual. Because members need to agree, they fight for their interpretation as the only right one. It is a charged issue that has not died down over the years. The power of the group has also had a profound impact on women's experiences of Alcoholics Anonymous.

When Alcoholics Anonymous began in 1935, its co-founders were subjected to the same stereotypes of alcoholics, female ones in particular, which are prominent in today's society. Bill and Dr. Bob were in the later stages of alcoholism by the time they found each other and the members that followed were considered similar "low-bottom drunks" (*Pass It On* 1984). It was difficult to believe that the program could work with anyone other than those whose drinking histories matched their own.

Bill and Dr. Bob had only their own experiences to work from. If someone "was still married, with wife and children living at home, and if he did not have money problems, he was considered probably not desperate enough to be helped" (Robertson 1988, p. 49). Both founders of AA and subsequent members had been desperate enough to embrace anything that might have increased their chances of recovery. It was this desperation that made it possible to open their minds to new ideas and to take risks.

In a similar vein, the young were not seen as likely prospects. "The feeling was they had not suffered enough, had not lived enough years and lost enough to have 'hit bottom.' Women alcoholics were not welcome either. Dr. Bob and many early members held to the Victorian ideas that 'nice' women weren't drunks" (Robertson 1988, p. 49). Nevertheless, women alcoholics came. What they found was a program that was created by men, for men and dominated by a male God. The group mentality that women face upon joining the ranks of AA is male. This poses some obvious problems for female alcoholics.

New female AA members are encouraged to read the literature, attend meetings regularly and follow the principles of the twelve steps as a way of life. Women hear the slogan "keep coming back" at the end of meetings and horror stories about other alcoholics who relapse after they stopped attending meetings. However, meetings are not always a safe place for women. Since there is no leadership or regulatory system to monitor who is a member of AA, women are often exposed to men who lack boundaries, are violent, have a criminal background or suffer from a mental illness. Frequently, women are not prepared to protect themselves because the program carries the illusion of intimacy created out of sharing a common experience. Dealing with the life-and-death issues surrounding alcoholism lends itself to developing a trust of perfect strangers.

This can be dangerous for the unsuspecting woman.

Women are also vulnerable to the group mentality when it comes to making other decisions about their lives. Although it is clear in the twelve traditions of Alcoholics Anonymous that AA "should remain forever nonprofessional" (*Pass It On* 1984, p.409), many members insist that they know the way to true recovery. Since newcomers become accustomed to following advice about reading literature, attending meetings and how to interpret the steps, it is easy to fall victim to taking instructions on other things as well. This can include decisions about where to live, whom to socialize with, whom to have as a sponsor, whether to go for counseling and whether to take medication.

Many women experience conflict about the appropriateness of taking antidepressants when confronted by a group mentality that insists on "not taking anything, no matter what." However, depression is experienced by a large number of women and the need for counseling and/or medication can become a critical issue. Both Bill and Dr. Bob believed in seeking help from professionals. Bill saw physicians, clergymen and a psychiatrist while suffering a ten-year long depression. AA is clear that it does not provide medical, clothing, housing, legal or financial assistance to its members. Tradition five clearly says that "each group has but one primary purpose -- to carry its message to the alcoholic who still suffers" (*Pass It On* 1984, p. 409). Nevertheless, this does not stop individual members from expressing their own ideas of what makes a good AA member.

The positive side of the group mentality is that women feel accepted by other women. In a society that shames women alcoholics for being bad instead of sick, AA's insistence that alcoholism is a gender-blind disease is a relief. Female alcoholics find other women who have been where they are now and understand the stigma involved. The love at these meetings is unconditional and women support each other's courage in confronting the stereotypes.

One female AA member, named Jewel describes this level of acceptance as having saved her life. "I feel relief that I can finally be the person I want to be. The AA program, the women and the support I've gotten have totally saved my life. My life has changed so much. I have gotten so many gifts in my life from working the program. I am really proud to say that I am a clean and sober recovering woman."

Women, in the AA program help each other deal with their shame and isolation associated with alcoholism. By the later stages of the disease, women have frequently been abandoned by most of the people in their lives who were important to them. Alone and frightened, AA provides these women with a group of people just like themselves who understand alcoholism in a society hostile to female alcoholics.

A.P.'s Story

It was a great relief for me to come to AA and find people like me. For so long, I felt alone in my shame and pain. I found it extremely hard (particularly in early recovery) to go to mixed meetings and share with men in the room. I usually ended up not sharing -- even if I was in a lot of pain -- and many times ended up isolating and sinking deeper into my pain. I very often found myself at risk of using again or feeling suicidal.

I began going only to women's meetings and found a few meetings where I felt safe. I found women who shared the same pain and whose programs inspired hope in me. I found women who loved me until I could love myself. I found women who changed my life and saved my life.

Recovering Alcoholic Women and Relationships

In early sobriety women are particularly vulnerable to falling in love and this is not surprising. It has been established that women derive self-esteem from their connections with others, specifically their partners and children. Unfortunately, this need to feel connected is sorely tested for female alcoholics who have experienced many losses because of abandonment from family members and partners. This makes them extremely vulnerable to making hasty decisions about the men they meet in AA meetings and placing their chances of recovery at risk.

Women often tie their sobriety to someone they are emotionally involved with. This can be disastrous for the women if her partner should relapse, abandon her or distract her from making the transitions to a sober lifestyle. If her partner begins drinking again, the woman is much more likely to relapse as well. As noted in the chapter on relationships, women are heavily influenced by their partners' drinking patterns. Women are frequently introduced to alcohol through male partners and imitate their partners' drinking styles. It is therefore not surprising that women will return to drinking if their main love interest does.

The woman is also at risk if the relationship should end or occupy so much of her time that she does not attend meetings or develop other sober relationships. If her only connection to sobriety is the partner who has just abandoned her, she will lack the sober support system necessary to cope with this loss without drinking. Furthermore, love affairs take up time and energy, both of which is needed to maintain sobriety. Even if the relationship continues successfully, the woman may have little interest in developing a sober lifestyle. This disinterest can lead to a shaky foundation and she may relapse regardless of her partner's drinking status.

Although it is discouraged in AA to begin a relationship in the first year of sobriety, there is no regulatory system to prevent it. As a result it is difficult to enforce and most AA members follow the belief of "live and let live." This is done, in spite of the fact that it is common knowledge among oldtimers that a woman's sobriety is at risk when she gets involved in a relationship before she has established her own recovery program.

To be fair, members of AA know that women's relationship needs are strong and even the best advice will sometimes be ignored in favor of meeting those needs. In addition, there are always exceptions to the rule; of women who develop relationships in recovery that encourage them not to drink. The influence of a male partner can be as equally powerful in keeping a woman from drinking as it can be in encouraging her to drink. It is impossible to know what the effects of that influence will be.

One woman in AA who had been sober for twelve years frequently told her story at meetings of how she had met her husband. They had both been sober for six months and were warned by sponsors, other members and friends that their relationship was not a good idea. However, both their marriage and their sobriety survived. She did admit that she continues to warn the women she sponsors of the dangers of forming relationships too early after witnessing first hand other women with negative experiences.

Thirteen Stepping

The one step Bill Wilson did not write or endorse is nevertheless well known in Alcoholics Anonymous. It is called the thirteenth step. Female AA members with time in the program are aware of its connotations. Though rarely acknowledged openly, women warn each other at meetings about men who use AA to find sexual partners. Thirteen stepping describes how men take advantage of newly sober women who are alone, frightened and vulnerable. These men attend meetings with the express purpose of finding newcomers who do not know them or their reputation.

Because of the illusion of intimacy that sharing on such a deep level entails, women often trust the men and women at meetings simply on the basis of membership. However, anyone can go to an AA meeting including violent, abusive criminals. There is no screening process and no means to reject someone other than by being negative toward the inappropriate person. Unfortunately, new members are not always clear about this open door policy and what that means in terms of the type of people who enter the program.

In addition, alcoholism does not discriminate. The mentally ill, criminals and sex offenders can be alcoholics as well as grandmothers, family men and school teachers. A popular story in AA to illustrate this point is the one about an alcoholic horse thief. Take away the alcoholism and you still have the horse thief. AA does not pretend to cure all of society's ills. Its purpose is to help alcoholics stop drinking.

Megan's Story

I had mixed feelings when I first came to AA. I didn't want to be an alcoholic but at the same time I was really relieved to find others who didn't judge me so harshly. I liked listening to people's stories and meeting afterwards for coffee. I really used the telephone lists a lot in the beginning. Everyone I talked to really tried to give me the time I needed.

What I didn't like was all that talk about a male God. At one of the women's meetings, I saw a woman with her big book (referring to the book of *Alcoholics Anonymous*) all marked up. When I got a closer look, I saw she had crossed out every male pronoun and written in a female one. I went home and changed my book too. I did the same thing with my other books. She also taught me a female prayer that I could say at the end of the meeting instead of the Lord's Prayer.

This woman also helped me in knowing what to say when some of the guys insisted on giving me hugs. In AA, you're supposed to be safe and trust everyone because we're all the same. But some of these guys were just after the hugs and whatever else they could get. This women made it okay for me to say "No" to the guys and "Yes" to the program.

Its Strengths are its Weaknesses

AA's strength lies in its ability to confront the alcoholic's denial system and to change the distorted thinking that is part of the alcoholism. It does this through the power of the group mentality at meetings, the intimacy of the sponsor relationship and the ideas taught through the twelve steps and twelve traditions. These ideas are passed on through literature, other members and catchy slogans that are easy to learn and remember.

In AA, members find compassion, acceptance and understanding from sharing a common experience. Members feel loved in the program after frequently facing hostility and blame from family members and society as a whole. Women, in particular, find relief from society's stereotypes and the burden of being stigmatized as sexually inappropriate or failures as mothers. Alcoholics Anonymous sees alcoholism as a disease. Alcoholics are not blamed, but learn to be responsible for their illness by following the principles of the program. These principles are clearly spelled out in the twelve steps and provide relief to many who feel ashamed and humiliated about their drinking.

AA is viewed as a spiritual program that enables alcoholics to get in touch with a power greater than themselves and their compulsion to drink. This belief in a higher power unites the group and encourages members to take the focus off themselves in order to help others. The spiritual aspect of the program provides sustenance to members who are lonely, frightened and in pain. A sense of purpose is experienced when most are at the worst point in their lives.

However, AA's strength is also its weakness. The single-mindedness of maintaining sobriety through spiritual growth may protect the program from contamination of other motives, but it also narrows its influence. Critics point to the many references to God as making Alcoholics Anonymous a religion and insist that many potential members have not returned because they felt the subtle pressure to believe in a Christian, male God.

The group mentality is only as good as its healthiest member. A group can provide a safe and accepting place to talk honestly about drinking. However, women in particular can be victimized by men who use meetings to find newcomers to exploit sexually.   The illusion of intimacy, created by sharing painful stories, can fool women into trusting anyone present at the meeting simply on the basis of their attendance and ability to listen. This can be dangerous as there is no regulatory system or screening process in place. Anyone can come to an AA meeting. Anyone.

Though this open door policy can make the most intimidated alcoholic comfortable and feel welcomed, it can also invite the most dangerous members of society. Violent, abusive and sexually inappropriate men are just as welcomed if they are fellow alcoholics (or at least, say they are) as anyone else. No one monitors members honesty. Lying about sobriety is common. AA can be a breeding ground for female exploitation or a safe haven for help with alcoholism.

The slogans, the relationship with a sponsor and the adherence to the twelve steps can provide a spiritual foundation for sobriety. Or it can create a psychological crisis for those suffering from mental illness, past abuse issues or relationship conflicts. AA acknowledges its limitations in the way that it helps its members. The program does not help with depression, suicidal ideation, past physical and sexual child abuse issues, rape survivor issues or couples counseling. Many recovering alcoholics do not seek additional help because of the belief that AA is all that is needed and sobriety is all that is important.

Furthermore, marriages have ended, not because of one partner's addiction to alcohol but to the new addiction to AA meetings. Some recovering alcoholics take the message to put sobriety first to mean that everything else can be forgotten. This only serves to make the alcoholic just as self-centered as she was when she was drinking. Family members are often ignored and abandoned for their lack of interest or understanding of the twelve step program. Children continue to be the losers when meetings become just as important to the alcoholic as the alcohol once was.

For female alcoholics to be successful in AA, it is critical that they find women's meetings, connect with female sponsors and discriminate when it comes to choosing whom to trust. Membership in AA does not automatically confer instant kinship. It is important not to give out personal information to just anyone. Telephone numbers, where one lives, the name of one's children, where they go to school or anything about one's sexuality should remain confidential until a level of trust can be established. Although the meeting may be filled with fellow alcoholics, these people are still strangers.

14

Recovery Issues of the Female Alcoholic

The Female Alcoholic Recovery Plan

Recovery from alcoholism is a process. It involves more than staying abstinent. The woman must create an entirely new lifestyle that includes forming healthy sober relationships, learning to be a more responsible parent and developing basic fundamental self care skills. One of the most important treatment issues for the woman is the need to develop a positive self-image (Perez 1994). Several studies have found that the craving to drink decreases in relationship to how much self-esteem the woman feels (Perez 1994). The other major treatment issue is that relationships are significant to women. A woman's ability to remain abstinent is strengthened when her partner has the same goals for her. In addition, the recovering alcoholic woman must have a treatment plan that includes the following:

* Early Recovery Issues (Intervention and Early Sobriety)
* Grief and Loss
* Dealing with the Stigma of Being a Female Alcoholic/Addict
* Self-Esteem and Developing a Sense of Self and Self-Respect
* Personal Power -- Taking responsibility for oneself
* Identifying and Appropriately Expressing Feelings
* Healthy Thinking
* Relationship Issues
* Healthy Sexuality
* Enabling Prevention Plan
* Communication and Listening Skills
* Boundaries/Assertiveness
* Parenting/Mothering Issues
* Healing from Family of Origin Issues
* Healing from Abuse Issues (Creating a safe environment)
* Other Addictions (including eating disorders)
* Developing a Healthy Lifestyle
* Treating another diagnosis (such as depression)

* Creating a Life Plan (Work/Career Plans)
* Relapse Prevention Plan (Developing a Support System)

Many of the issues listed above have been addressed throughout this book. Relationships, family of origin, abuse issues, other addictions and diagnosis of concurrent illnesses influence the woman's chances of recovery from alcoholism. A woman who is suffering from untreated depression, been abandoned by a partner who preferred she was drinking, dealing with repressed memories of childhood abuse, is unemployed and has children who are acting out has little support to stay sober. However the more resources the woman has in dealing with these issues, the more successful her chances are in adopting a clean and sober lifestyle.

It is important to note that every recovering female alcoholic has their own recovery process. Some women are ready to deal with abuse issues the moment they are sober, while others do not want to address these issues until several years into recovery. Family of origin work is another example of individual choice. There are daughters who know immediately that they come from an alcoholic family while others are not ready to face the idea of an alcoholic parent until other treatment issues are addressed.

Each woman must have a different treatment plan set at their own individual pace. What is significant is that most recovery plans address the issues listed above at some point or another. Although it is outside the scope of this writing to examine the entire process, the following are some highlights of the work that needs to be done.

Early Recovery Issues

In early recovery, women need information on what "triggers" the craving to drink. Psychological triggers include environmental cues, stress, physical illness or emotional upset. Physical cues are any reintroduction of alcohol into the body system. Even small doses of alcohol in medications, food cooked in alcohol, or drugs with a similar pharmacology can trigger a relapse. The body's craving for the drug is reactivated with any kind of exposure to that drug even if it enters the bloodstream "legally" through a doctor's prescription.

Newly sober women must learn to read all medication labels and notify their physicians that they are recovering from an addiction. Women admitted to the hospital for any reason other than for addiction treatment must also inform the medical staff. Doctors who have not been warned of a patient's potential for cross-addiction or relapse may inadvertently prescribe medicine containing alcohol.

Other physical or environmental cues can be an illness, lack of sleep, inadequate food intake or a negative emotional response such as anger, loneliness, tension, anxiety or stress.   The woman's menstrual cycle can also influence the emotional state of the recovering alcoholic and increase the craving to drink (Kinney et al. 1991). Charting the menstrual cycle can provide important information for the recovering alcoholic about how best to prevent relapse (Casey 1984). Sober women must learn to appropriately express feelings, develop a support system and learn basic self-care skills to build their immunity against stressful periods.

Grief and Loss

For the female alcoholic, "the bottle" became the best friend, relationship, companion and often the significant other. There is a great sense of loss in having to become abstinent (Kellerman 1977). This loss manifests itself in giving up a lifestyle that was developed to adapt to the drinking. Friends, employment, family, social activities, her marriage and identity are frequently associated with the alcohol.   The alcoholic may have to give up favorite hobbies or activities that were created as drinking events. She probably has to give up familiar places that encourage drinking such as bars, friend's homes and family gatherings. Even the holidays and day-to-day routines may need to change if they revolved around alcohol.

Women in recovery experience more than five times the rate of depression as their alcoholic male counterparts (Finklestein et al. 1990). This depression is part of the recovering woman's grieving process and can last for years. Although male alcoholics have much to grieve for when they stop drinking, female alcoholics grieve for more than the loss of the alcohol. They often have to face the stigma of being an alcoholic which damages their self-esteem, self-identity and their self-image. Many women must grieve for lost partners, loss of custody of their children, loss of missed opportunities, and feelings associated with past sexual abuse.

As part of the grieving process, women must learn how to express their feeling appropriately. Recovering alcoholics need to work on self-esteem to ensure success with abstinence. Assertiveness training, increasing personal power, learning about boundaries and creating a safe and abuse-free home also increases the likelihood of staying sober.

Change The Way The Alcoholic Thinks

One of the hardest steps for women in recovery is becoming responsible for themselves. While drinking and using, many women became quite adept at blaming others and taking a very passive stance toward life. This fits in nicely with the roles society expects women to play as well as serving the alcoholic's needs to distract attention from the addiction. Alcoholics need to have excuses and reasons to continue drinking (in order to avoid the truth about being addicted to the alcohol). They also need to blame others for the drinking and to explain away the negative consequences of that drinking.

In order to accomplish this, the alcoholic must come up with some very distorted belief systems (Ellis 1992). Some of these beliefs include a desire to avoid all responsibilities and conflicts. Avoidance becomes the alcoholic's motto. Women are further encouraged to be dependent on others and to need someone stronger than them upon whom to rely on. It is easier to blame someone else when dependent on others to make decisions. Becoming responsible is a crucial step in recovery and it begins with being responsible for not picking up the first drink. To be responsible women must develop a positive attitude, be assertive, set up boundaries, accept the consequences of their own actions and stop blaming others for what happens.

For newly recovering alcoholics and addicts there is often a lot of stress dealing with the everyday aspect of living. Relationships may be in disarray and families in crisis over divorce or child custody agreements. Financial insecurity, child care (especially for single parents), parenting issues, job or career problems and living arrangements may be in flux. It can be difficult to focus on recovery, get to meetings or counseling and establish a sober support system. Although it is not always possible to change the situation, it is possible to change the way it is perceived. For many alcoholics at the beginning of recovery, it is necessary to learn how to perceive the world differently. While drinking and using drugs, it was useful for the alcoholic to feel bad about herself, her situation and her life. It gave her the excuses she needed to continue drinking.

Alcoholics tend to have very predictable ways of perceiving the world that create more tension and anxiety in their lives. This serves their disease in two ways. One, the added stress makes it possible to rationalize the need for a drink to relax. In fact, female alcoholics can come up with elaborate ways to set up negative experiences, in order to enjoy a "legitimate" excuse to drink.

The second way their distorted perceptions help them is to reinforce the ultimate belief that they are powerless and therefore incapable of taking action to change anything in their life including the motivation needed to stay sober. In this way, they can continue to play the perpetual victim looking for others to rescue them. If they actually don't return to drinking, they can at least continue other addictive behavior. The addiction helps to avoid dealing with painful issues or having to look at themselves in any really constructive way to create change.

Some of the ways alcoholics perceive the world around them that helps to increase their stress level and therefore their desire to drink include:

Jumping to conclusions: Alcoholics believe they have all the facts without really checking out reality. The "facts" however, are often faulty and influenced by distorted beliefs.

Making mountains out of molehills: By keeping things that bother them inside instead of communicating and saying how they feel, alcoholics tend to become overwhelmed and blow up over some small issue that they would otherwise be able to cope with.

Telescopic vision: Many alcoholics have selective vision and memory that either disregards an important life situation or alters it in some form in order for it to be negative. Perez (1994) found in his study that female alcoholics have a rich fantasy life supported by the belief that they are being rejected. They then act in ways that encourage rejection. This belief is carried out in real life through their telescopic vision. This vision can also support a false positive that the alcoholic insists is true because she wants it to be. For example, a female alcoholic's can insist that her partner who batters her has only good qualities.

Black and white thinking: Instead of seeing the limitless possibilities in a given situation, female alcoholics often see things in a limited way as one extreme or another. It is either this way or it is that.

There is only one way to do things: Most people can only understand the world the way they see things, perceptions, based on belief systems passed on to them by their parents. They don't question these beliefs and are quick to judge others who do not believe what they do. Alcoholics frequently make another person's beliefs wrong as a way of making their's right. It is difficult for them to see that both could be right. It goes against their black and white thinking.

Relationship Issues

One of the most damaging aspects of the disease of alcoholism is the negative consequence it has on the alcoholic's ability to maintain a relationship with anything other than the alcohol. Relationships in recovery are far more complex and have a very different set of rules of what was expected when relating in the alcoholic or drug culture. Healthy relationships require a balance of power, respect, responsibility and needs. Unfortunately, most alcoholics and addicts have little information on how to achieve this balance and even fewer role models on how to relate without the presence of alcohol. Many alcoholic marriages revolve around the alcoholic's behavior. The rules are clear. Protect the addiction. It is the priority and all decisions about the relationship are based on how it will affect the alcoholic's access to drinking.

Once in recovery, newly sober alcoholics are often horrified to discover that their marriages are in trouble. There is little help for women regarding relationship issues in the 12-step programs and in many treatment centers. These programs advocate the need to focus on staying clean and sober. Women are instructed that sobriety is the priority now and that the relationship will work itself out. The recovering female alcoholic is expected to neglect her marriage in order to give all of her attention to meetings, counseling and work meant to keep her abstinent.

The alcoholic marriage that once revolved around the alcohol now looks the same revolving around recovery. Nothing has changed for the spouse of the alcoholic. Over time, these relationships often crumble. The alcoholic's sobriety can be shaken by such a loss. The ending of such relationships, especially for women, often results in a relapse. In addition, many female alcoholics are abandoned by partners who prefer that they drink. This abandonment can create conflict and accompanying ambivalent feelings about the value of sobriety.

Single women entering recovery face the same struggles with adjusting to the new rules of the clean and sober culture. It is not long before they realize that the illusion of instant intimacy that was present with alcohol is not present in the "real" world. Women who used alcohol to feel sexual or obtain an orgasm find themselves lacking desire. Recovering women frequently find that they are lonely and inadequately prepared to negotiate a relationship in recovery.

In the alcoholic world, relationships develop around the familiar set of rules found in most alcoholic families. Don't talk about the addiction or about feelings. Intimacy is often achieved when drinking and distance remains the norm when sober. Couples know very little about themselves, let alone each other. The focus is often on surviving a crisis, hiding the truth and maintaining the denial in order to survive. Relationships in recovery require a much larger repertoire of skills.

Healthy relationships involve people who have developed communication, negotiation and confrontational skills. Each person has usually achieved an individual identity accompanied with self-esteem and healthy boundaries before becoming a couple. This information has often been handed down by example while watching parents role model these skills in their own relationship. Intimacy, independence, respect, power, getting needs met, who takes responsibility for what, and sex roles are all negotiated in the woman's family of origin.

Children growing up in this "relationship classroom" called a family move on to develop their own relationships based on what they learned from their parents. Healthy families launch children who know how to screen a potential mate, set up appropriate boundaries, negotiate for what they need and communicate through conflicts. The alcoholic family, on the other hand, teach dysfunctional patterns of relating to their children who then repeat what they know and are comfortable doing in their own marriage. Women from alcoholic homes are ill-equipped to manage healthy relationships and desperately need information on how to do it.

Healthy Sexuality

It is not uncommon for newly recovering women to have a lot of issues around sex and their sexuality. These must be addressed, not only to protect the woman from unwanted pregnancies but from sexually transmitted diseases including AIDS (Covington 1991). It is imperative that every woman takes responsibility for protecting herself from an unplanned pregnancy. Many women alcoholics are ill-informed about the number of birth control options or have strong reservations about adopting one out of fear of not being able to follow through during the sexual encounter. For example, many women are afraid to ask their male partners to wear a condom and so remain silent without exploring other options.

Other women feel extremely uncomfortable seeing themselves as sexually active. They avoid taking the initiative of planning ahead because they do not want the man to perceive them as wanting sex. It is easier to look like they have been seduced if birth control is not discussed. For these women, guilt and shame about sex may have been the initial reason for beginning use of alcohol. Now that the alcohol is no longer available, the woman's fears surface again without resolution.

AIDS and other sexually transmitted diseases are a major area of concern for recovering women. Female alcoholics who were IV drug users or had sexual partners (or sexual partners who had partners) who were IV drug users are at particular risk. It is imperative to be tested and to become informed on the best methods of protection. Condoms are not 100% effective but provide the best protection next to abstaining from sex or sexual activity that exposes partners to each other's bodily fluids.

The most important factor in condom effectiveness is that they are used and used properly.

It is also important to use condoms during oral sex as well as during intercourse in case there are lesions in the mouth from flossing teeth. It only takes one exposure to place a woman at risk of contracting the disease. Women are more vulnerable to contracting AIDS and other sexually transmitted diseases because the virus remains in the vagina for hours.

The Alcoholic Woman As Enabler

Enabling or rescuing is the process of taking responsibility for someone else's problems or behavior that they should theoretically be capable of taking care of on their own (if it were not due to their own actions) (Miller 1988). In the addiction field, enabling is defined as taking care of problems caused by the chemical use so that the alcoholic does not suffer the consequences of her disease. However, rescuing can go beyond just problems associated with drinking or using. When a parent, friend, boss or spouse solves the woman's problems for her, they set up a parent/child or victim/rescuer relationship. Some of the ways female alcoholics are able to get loved ones to enable them include:

* spending rent money on drugs and then needing rent to be paid for her
* using others' emotions (especially anger) as an excuse to drink
* needing others to take care of children when too drunk to do it herself
* blaming others for misfortune ("Cop gave ticket cause he had it in for me")
* needing fines, medical care, living expenses and debts paid for
* making excuses for behavior to others
* needing others to take on her responsibilities in the household
* needing others to take care of physical needs (cleaning up vomit, being fed)
* needing a drive when drunk

Female alcoholics in early recovery must learn to set up boundaries for those around them that want to continue to play the rescuer role. Part of recovery for women is learning to take responsibility for themselves. Rescuers often take care of others to feel important, needed and, in short, loved. Unfortunately, this conflicts with the needs of the sober alcoholic to make her own decisions and take care of herself.

Furthermore, recovering female alcoholics have to stop enabling the other alcoholics in their lives. Women are often divorced or abandoned by the time they enter treatment. For those who are still in relationships, the tendency is to be involved with another alcoholic. This poses serious threat to the woman's sobriety both in her fear of being abandoned if she gets sober and her fear that he will reject her if she confronts his drinking. Unfortunately, enabling her partner to drink places the woman at risk for talking herself back into drinking again. This is evident when the woman, trying to control her partner's drinking, goes out with him thinking he will drink less or not at all because she is present. These drinking events however, reinforce her old drinking behavior and the thinking that follows.

Finally, by protecting her partner from the negative consequences of his drinking, she can convince herself that alcoholism is not a problem for either one of them. She may see it as unfair that "he gets to drink" when she is not supposed to. The alcoholic mind is capable of distorting reality in amazing ways (addressed further in this chapter) that allow the woman to deny her own alcoholism.

Boundaries

In early recovery, women must be educated in what boundaries look like and how to assert them (Lerner 1988). Boundaries act like a safety net and help women to set healthy limits in their relationships. These boundaries serve to protect women from being abused or violated. People are not born with boundaries. They must be learned by interacting with others who have them. Boundaries provide a structure to the relationship by allowing both participants to have separate identities. Each person has their own needs and wants in the relationship. Boundaries work to separate where one person ends and the other begins. Parents teach their children about boundaries by protecting them from being abused and confronting their children when they act abusively. Over time, children begin to recognize their own internal warning system that tells them their boundaries are being violated. A person must have their own boundaries to understand that they exist in others.

There are five types of boundaries -- physical, sexual, emotional, intellectual and spiritual (Mellody et al. 1989). Healthy relationships exist between people who are clear what their boundaries look like and can appreciate and respect the differences their partner may have with their boundaries (Katherine 1991). Dysfunctional relationships usually indicate faulty learning in the area of boundaries either in that they don't exist at all or are in some way damaged. People with damaged or nonexistent boundaries are easy targets for people who violate or abuse others. They become "victims" to these "offenders". The rules of the relationship say that one person can use the other person at that person's expense. In some cases, people have boundaries in one area but not others. That means they can protect themselves at work but are unable to do it in a relationship. This is common for many women.

Women often lack information on boundaries and the experience of fighting for the right to have them. Our society has little tolerance for assertive women and does not provide the necessary education on how women can protect themselves from being violated. Women compensate for this loss in several ways. Some use alcohol, drugs, food, smoking and sex to numb the feelings created by their internal warning system when they feel helpless to stop the abuse. Others frequently use a wall of emotions or talking to keep people away. Anger and fear are common feelings that help to create artificial boundaries.

Anger is a popular way to create the illusion of boundaries. Both men and women use it. However, the cycles can be very different. An angry person sends a message to others to stay away. The receiver of the message often complies to avoid triggering a confrontation. Women often use this defense when everything else has failed. It is part of the "Rage Cycle". This cycle begins when the woman, following her proscribed role as wife and mother, constantly defers to every one else's needs while neglecting her own. She is unable to say "No" without feeling guilty until she reaches a point of exhaustion in her relationship.

She displays no boundaries or limits on their requests and continues to give long after she is on empty. The woman makes no requests of her own to get her emotional needs met or if she does, her requests are ignored. Finally, in desperation to stop the requests from coming, she creates the illusion of an emotional boundary by raging. Blowing up, throwing things and screaming, she sends a message to her partner and family to leave her alone. Family members quickly retreat in the face of such bizarre behavior and for, at least that moment, the woman experiences relief from constant demands. Unfortunately, the true underlying reasons for her behavior are never addressed and she is blamed for responding so inappropriately. She feels remorseful and guilty and in response, begins to overdo again to make up for her outrageous behavior. This sets up the rage cycle to continue once more.

People who use walls to substitute as a boundary can find themselves isolated and lonely for intimacy. This can set them up to go to the other extreme of dropping the walls and having no boundaries just to be able to connect with others. This can be confusing in relationships where sometimes anything goes and other times nothing is tolerated. This describes the essence of the rage cycle.

Assertiveness

Learning how to be assertive is a way out of the "rage cycle". Women in recovery learn that they have boundaries and the right to protect these boundaries. Many female alcoholics have experienced abuse, violence and exploitation during their drinking days. It takes time to develop the skills and the belief system that women have a right to be treated with respect and dignity. Recovering women are often resistant to learning how to be assertive because they are afraid of:

* abandonment
* rejection
* abuse
* anger (someone else's as well as their own)
* ridicule
* being wrong
* being bad ("the bad guy")
* rocking the boat / change
* getting hurt

Unfortunately, not asserting their rights does not necessarily protect women. Frequently, the end result of passive behavior is what was feared would happen if the woman had asserted her rights. She is abandoned, rejected or hurt.

Recovering Alcoholic Mothers

Children need clear rules and consistent structure to feel safe. This means setting up routines for bedtime, meals, morning rituals and homework times. In the home with an alcoholic mother, these routines are often nonexistent. Recovering alcoholic mothers experience enormous guilt, shame and remorse for not being able to provide adequately for their children. Children often use this guilt to manipulate their mothers into giving them what they want both during the drinking days as well as when the drinking has stopped. In recovery, it can become a vicious cycle where the child demands and the mother complies in order to make up for the past. This only serves to perpetuate the alcoholic family system.

Women in recovery need a great deal of support and information on how best to parent their children. Recovering alcoholics need help in forgiving themselves for what they were not able to do for their children when they were so sick in their addiction. Women are merciless in blaming themselves for the harm their children experienced when they were drinking. However, the only way for the family to recover together is to view the addiction as an illness and not to blame the mother. In this way, resources can be used in educating the woman on parenting her children in sobriety and healing from the damage of the past.

Younger children generally adapt more quickly to change than older ones. Children often have lots of fears and feelings about their mother's drinking and how it has impacted their lives. They need someone to talk to and it is often better for everyone involved if the children can talk to someone else other than the mother. Children don't want to betray or hurt their mothers so they might hold back unless they can talk to someone who isn't involved. In addition, it can be painful for the mother to learn how her children suffered when she was in the grips of her addiction.

It is important for the mother to tell children the truth about the disease of alcoholism. Children are sometimes terrified to trust that sobriety will remain a reality. Their mother may have made promises in the past that were not kept. They may have felt betrayed at past attempts to become sober. Both mother and her children need time, support and information to heal as a family.

Adolescents sometimes have a harder time being interested in the recovery process. They have reached a developmental stage where they are supposed to be detaching from the family and may rebel if feeling forced to participate. Their rebellion is in defense of their need to grow apart rather than bond together to help their mother get sober. For the older child, recovery needs to look attractive and their part in it must be initiated by them.

Vocational Training

Lots of women coming into recovery have little or no training in fields that provide financial support. Many found jobs that supported their alcohol and drug intake such as waitressing, bartending and prostitution. Others were supported by husbands or men who have abandoned them either for their drinking or because they're getting sober. Some have lost good positions because of their alcoholism (such as nurses who have lost their licensing due to drug use). Whatever the situation, most women will spend some time evaluating their careers during the first year of recovery.

Recovering female alcoholics often need education, skill building, on the job training and experience to place them in competition for well paying jobs and sober careers. Lack of financial assistance, child care responsibilities and limited educational opportunities prevents many women from pursuing their goals. However, for women to be successful in recovery, they must be capable of supporting themselves and their children.

15

Relapse Issues of the
Female Alcoholic

The Relapse Process

Relapse among alcoholics is common. Many, if not most, return to the use of alcohol at least once after making an honest commitment to sobriety and to pursuing a structured recovery program. About 40% of all alcoholics who initiate treatment that involves both AA and professional counseling will find themselves hopelessly and inevitably drawn into the ranks of chronic recidivism. This will occur in spite of their best conscious efforts at sobriety (Gorski et al. 1982, p. 17).

It has been established that female alcoholics are introduced to alcohol, become alcoholics and experience alcoholism differently than their male counterparts. The process of recovery, including relapse prevention, is different for women as well. Relapse is a process and begins long before drinking is reinstated. It occurs when the reasons behind the alcohol and drug use are not addressed and intensifies to an overwhelming need to drink as the familiar coping mechanism. Relapse rarely happens suddenly. "The symptoms build, grow, and progress. There are many subtle warning signs and many changes in thought process, emotional process, and personality that occur before loss of control" (Gorski et al. 1982, p. 19).

Women are particularly vulnerable to the relapse process because they enter recovery facing a multitude of issues and obstacles. Socioeconomic status, marital and family cohesion, employment status and residential stability affect women's success in remaining abstinent. Women with better jobs, higher income, adequate housing and happy, abuse-free relationships have a higher rate of abstinence than unemployed, homeless, battered women. Treatment centers that offer support and education increase the likelihood that the women will be able to achieve abstinence.

In the same light, women who lack a support system, use other addictions or have untreated medical or mental illness fare poorly. Every female alcoholic in treatment must have a thorough physical and psychiatric exam. According to Katie Evans and J. Michael Sullivan (1990), "individuals with a psychiatric disorder are at increased risk for having a substance abuse disorder" (p. 2). Unless the underlying psychopathology is addressed, women are tempted to self-medicate their psychiatric symptoms.

Self-medication can also play a role in women's management of chronic pain due to some medical disorders. Female alcoholics, forced to endure pain, are likely candidates for prescription drug abuse and sliding back into using alcohol to relieve their symptoms. Many feel unable to cope without drugs. Fear of being denied help if they admit that they are a recovering alcoholic, sends women into doctors' offices lying about their addiction. Women start lying to medical staff and eventually, end up lying to themselves about their disease.

Some of the major issues that can trigger a relapse include:

* a lack of understanding of early recovery and what to expect,
* unresolved grief and loss,
* dealing with the stigma of being a female alcoholic,
* low self-esteem,
* loss or nonexistence of a primary relationship,
* problems in relationship (including sexual),
* shame and guilt about parenting,
* problems with the children,
* unresolved incest or abuse issues,
* unresolved "adult children of alcoholic" issues,
* a return to alcoholic or drug addict lifestyle,
* homelessness,
* unemployment, poverty, lack of job skills,
* stress,
* chronic physical pain,
* woman's menstrual cycle or pregnancy,
* facing discrimination because of a disability, sexual orientation or ethnicity,
* current involvement in a battering or abusive relationship,
* partner continues to drink or wants her to continue drinking,
* not learning how to manage emotions or thinking in sobriety,
* multiple addictions,
* untreated coexisting psychiatric disorder,
* biological risk factors such as a chemical imbalance, and
* psychological risk factors such as responding to cues to drink and positive expectations of what alcohol can do.

Many of these issues have been addressed previously. However, additional information will be provided describing how these problems can lead back to a compulsion to drink.

Early Recovery as a Relapse Trigger

In early recovery, the woman's body begins the healing process. Damage from alcohol abuse and the lifestyle that goes with the addiction takes its toll physically and emotionally on women. Insomnia, frequent awakenings followed by difficulty returning to sleep, mood swings, forgetfulness, residual tremors and anxiety are common in the first few months of sobriety. These symptoms indicate that the body is trying to stabilize itself once the alcohol has been removed. Unfortunately, most women are unprepared for these changes and return to alcohol as their only mechanism for coping.

When the woman's blood alcohol level is lowered, withdrawal symptoms occur. Immediately following the lower levels of alcohol in the body, the woman may experience an increase in symptoms. Typical symptoms are: physical stress, an elevation in blood pressure, pulse and respiration, a marked increase in agitation, hostility, anxiety and discomfort. More severe forms of withdrawal include: tremors, hallucinations, delirium and convulsive seizures (Gorski et al. 1982).

Post acute withdrawal syndrome begins around seven to fourteen days into sobriety and can last for up to two years. The most difficult time for women is between three and six months of abstinence. "The major symptoms of post acute withdrawal are thought process impairments, emotional process impairments, short-term memory impairments, stress sensitivity, and overreaction to stress" (Gorski et al. 1982, p. 31). Alcoholics, in this stage of withdrawal, have trouble with abstract thinking, concentration and a lower tolerance level for stress.

Many early recovering women discover that, in sobriety, they have developed food and other allergies. Most are also susceptible to colds and infections because of a weakened immune system. As the body adapts to the loss of alcohol, food cravings and rapid weight gain or loss are not unusual. Foods, high in sugar, fat or caffeine may trigger an addictive response (Gorski 1989). Terence Gorski, an expert in relapse prevention warns that nicotine (and other addictions) are not only damaging for the physical well-being of the newly recovering women but can also be a trigger for a drinking episode. Smoking can be a cue to drink if the female alcoholic used to do both together.

The woman's primary focus on obtaining alcohol and the privacy to drink, has frequently left her neglecting other important aspects of her life. Learning how to eat nutritiously, exercise properly and get enough sleep become a crucial aspect of the woman's recovery program. "Making ongoing self-care a priority enhances the quality of life in sobriety and helps prevent relapse" (Finklestein et al. 1990, p. 607). This is particularly true for women with additional medical problems.

Female alcoholics have grown accustomed to using alcohol, exclusively, as a coping mechanism. Physical and emotional pain have been medicated for years by drinking. Many women are vulnerable to abusing pain medication in the belief that something is wrong with them because their body aches more than it did when drinking. Menstrual cramps come as a shock for many early recovering women who were previously too drunk to notice they were even having their period. A woman's menstrual cycle has often adapted to the presence of alcohol. In early sobriety, physical changes can occur which can be unsettling for the woman. Many, in sobriety, begin experiencing premenstrual symptoms for the first time.

It is not uncommon for other medical problems to surface after the alcohol has left the woman's system. Liver disease, diabetes, tooth decay, back pain, arthritis, stomach problems and gastrointestinal difficulties become more obvious to the woman once her anesthesia (alcohol) has been removed. Early recovering women frequently need medical care because of the damage done by the alcohol or for an illness that went undiagnosed in favor of drinking.

Psychiatric disorders also become more apparent once the alcohol has been removed. For some women, alcoholism was a result of self-medicating psychiatric symptoms. For others, mental illness is a coexisting condition. Many women may display psychiatric symptoms in response to the withdrawal syndrome associated with early sobriety. These symptoms are frightening and professional help is imperative.

The potential for cross-addiction is higher for women who suffer from a medical or mental illness. Sometimes the disorder is caused by the alcoholism and sometimes it is a coexisting condition. Relapse can occur when the second disorder goes undiagnosed or is left untreated. In many cases, recovering alcoholics are vulnerable to relapse because of treatment for the medical or mental health problem. Pain medication used to relieve physical discomfort can create dependency. Withdrawal symptoms brought on by a cessation of medication can be perceived as a return of the medical problem. Most alcoholics have difficulty distinguishing pain from the medical disorder and pain from addiction. Their threshold for pain is lowered during withdrawal and the two often exacerbate each other.

Lifestyle as a Relapse Trigger

The female alcoholic must develop an entirely new "way of life" that supports sobriety. Making new sober friendships, finding new sources of recreation and leisure, creating a sober role in the family and learning healthy relationship skills; such as how to communicate, are some of the changes women face. A lifestyle that was structured around alcohol means that family members adapted mealtimes, bedtimes, holiday and vacation activities, leisure activities, traditions, and routines to fit the woman's drinking pattern. Now that the woman is sober, she must reorganize her life to reduce stress and involvement in activities that prioritized drinking behavior.

These changes are difficult to make. Women are frequently lonely until they develop a sober support system. It is painful to lose old friends or to give up favorite activities. Many women are unsuccessful at adopting a new lifestyle and find themselves being drawn back into the alcoholic world. One woman described her belief that she could frequent the bar she had socialized at for years only to find herself pressured by friends to drink. Another woman had a hard time with her family of origin reunions. Her parents were accustomed to seeing her drink and her refusal threatened how they perceived their own drinking. They kept insisting that she was not an alcoholic because she drank less than they did.

Female alcoholics are vulnerable to relapse when their environment cues them to drink. Lighting up a cigarette, walking past a bar, the time of day or certain people can remind the alcoholic that drinking is associated with these activities. Her body experiences craving because of "cue reactivity". Researchers have found that alcoholics experience increased pupillary dilation, physiological arousal and salivation when exposed to alcohol cues (Chiauzzi 1991). Consequently, female alcoholics are forced to change their entire lifestyle to avoid drinking cues.

Another factor supporting the likelihood that the alcoholic will respond to drinking cues comes from the woman's expectations that alcohol works. As noted in Chapter one, female alcoholics develop a relationship with alcohol. A level of trust is created when the alcoholic learns to depend on alcohol to cope with stress and alter feelings. These positive feelings about alcohol are triggered when cues to drink are present and when the woman is faced with stress.

Female alcoholics who experience homelessness, unemployment, low-paying jobs, lack of medical care, single parenting, violence and discrimination because of a disability, sexual orientation or ethnicity have a higher rate of relapse. This kind of lifestyle is stressful and offers little support in maintaining abstinence. All of the woman's energy is directed at survival.

> Families headed by women have a poverty rate six times that of male-headed families. When race is taken into account the poverty rate also increases, so that minority families supported by women have even higher rates. More than half of families of color live in poverty and 40 percent of all black children are poor. Women who work continue to be found in the lowest paid occupations. Cuts in social welfare programs including education, training, and public assistance have had the greatest impact on single parent families, 80 percent of which are headed by women (Finklestein et al. 1990, p. 537).

Homeless women and their children confront violence while living on the street. Many women are raped and beaten. Their children are hungry, cold and without medical assistance. Without resources, homeless women are not able to focus their attention on sobriety. They are concentrating on keeping themselves and their children alive. Single mothers, whether they are homeless or not, experience the highest risk for mental health problems (Finklestein et al. 1990, p. 587). It is difficult to change a lifestyle even if that lifestyle has been proven to encourage a return to alcohol and drug use.

Stigma of Being the Alcoholic Woman as a Relapse Trigger

Most women experience guilt and shame over their addiction and their behavior while drinking or using other drugs (Cusak 1984). Society, family members, and friends have frequently spent years blaming the woman for her drinking. It is difficult to understand the disease concept after only a few weeks. Women entering into treatment have low self-esteem and receive less support than male alcoholics. Female alcoholics are automatically labeled abusive mothers and promiscuous women. These labels are hard to shed in sobriety; especially if they are true.

According to Suzanne Boylston Cusak (1984):

> Even if and when a woman manages to accept and deal with her addiction and forgive herself, she often runs into the problem of her family's lack of acceptance. They are ready to let her assume the guilt and remind her of her unacceptable behavior. Her family has a hard time seeing her as a sick person with an addiction who can change and get well. I find this far more true with the female of any age than with the male. Men usually find that parents, spouses, girlfriends, boyfriends, or children forgive them once they show remorse (p. 9).

The stigma is greater for women with disabilities, minorities and lesbians. Women are held responsible for their alcoholism and blamed for the symptoms of the disease. Battered women, incest survivors, homeless women and women struggling with unemployment are offered little assistance because it is assumed that they are to blame for their plight, especially if they are alcoholics. These women feel ashamed, abandoned and frightened.

Family members frequently rally around the male alcoholic when he enters treatment (Cusak 1984). Parents, spouses and children attend family counseling. Wives care for the children and parents offer financial support. Women, on the other hand, tend to lose their children to ex-husbands and receive nothing from their parents. Alone, they are faced with the task of remaining abstinent. When relapse occurs, the stigma increases.

Many women feel incredible shame and guilt as mothers. When the children are experiencing problems, this guilt is exacerbated. One woman nearly relapsed after being told by school officials that she had hurt her seven years old daughter's ability to concentrate because she drank when she was pregnant. Her attitude was that the damage was done and there was nothing for her to do about it now, including staying sober. She had to be reminded that her sobriety for the past six years had done more for her daughter than her drinking during the pregnancy.

Relationships as a Relapse Trigger

Women's financial and emotional dependency on men make them vulnerable to relapse (Cusak 1984). It has been established that women often begin their drinking careers in a relationship and their drinking patterns are frequently influenced by their male partners. As a result her decision to stop drinking can have a profound impact on her marriage. Husbands who drink may be threatened by the woman's abstinence or experience grief over the loss of a drinking companion. The couple may find that the delicate balance centered around alcohol crumbles in the face of the woman's sobriety. Men who do not drink or, at least not alcoholically, may not like the changes in power, sexual access or dependency that occur when the female alcoholic becomes abstinent.

Problems in the relationship, battering, and sexual dysfunction can also place the woman at risk for relapse. Living with violence is exhausting and terrifying for women. It is all but impossible for women to concentrate on anything else but staying alive. Treatment for the couple's conflicts and sexual problems is a necessity in recovery. Many women begin using alcohol to cope with being sexual. If these problems are not resolved, the woman may return to alcohol as the only acceptable way of being sexual. Women in abuse-free, happy relationships have a greater success rate in recovery.

Sexual partners however, are not the only relationships affected by the woman's alcoholism. Children and parents may have a great deal invested in the woman's drinking. Many times, women have not been available to be a parent so their children have been free to exercise a great deal of power in their homes. Parents of female alcoholics may have drinking problems of their own that they fear will surface if their daughter pursues recovery. Many women report being abandoned by alcoholic parents for introducing the idea of alcoholism in the family, even if it was associated with the daughter's drinking and not the parents'.

Because it is important to women to be in relationships, it can create a huge conflict when sobriety threatens any of these connections. Women frequently continue drinking to maintain relationships with parents, children, partners, employers and friends. Making changes in any of these areas can be seen as far too great an obstacle and too painful a loss.

Emotions and their Cause as a Relapse Trigger

Emotions, for the alcoholic have been managed or controlled with alcohol. Sometimes drinking released inhibitions for women to be sexual or admit feeling angry - emotions women are not usually permitted to have. Other times, alcohol was used to cope with negative feelings such as loss, pain, fear, grief and shame. Many alcoholics drank to enhance positive feelings and as a reward for doing something they dreaded. Alcohol can also be used in an attempt to self-medicate a psychiatric disorder like depression, anxiety or attention deficit disorder.

In recovery, women must learn to manage feelings without alcohol and drugs. They need to learn to identify high risk situations that trigger negative emotional responses. Cognitive distortions that lead to emotional responses must be examined. Defense mechanisms, thinking disorders and emotional reactivity are common during drinking. They are symptoms of the disease and need to be treated. Learning to identify cognitive distortions can reduce the number of negative emotional reactions (Chiauzzi 1993).

The alcoholic woman's feelings about abstinence plays an important role in her recovery. Many women enter into treatment to avoid the negative consequences of their drinking. Fears about losing a job, custody of her children or a husband to divorce can initially motivate a woman to agree to anything. However, her intentions to remain sober were never sincere. She is simply trying to control and manipulate those around her so she can continue drinking. However, the woman increases her chances of maintaining abstinence if she feels good about her sobriety.

Menstrual Cycle as a Relapse Trigger

Women tend to relapse most often during the premenstrual phase of the menstrual cycle. Hormonal changes, psychological stress, and physical discomfort, no doubt play an important part in women's vulnerability at this time. Many women learned to use alcohol to self-medicate menstrual symptoms (Casey 1984). In addition, estrogen-progesterone control the metabolism of carbohydrates and during this time in their cycle, women experience the lowest blood sugar levels. When this imbalance occurs, women experience tension, fatigue, headaches, dysphoria, and cravings for food, sugar or alcohol. Researchers have found that 96 percent of alcoholics suffer from low blood sugar level as a direct result of their disease and that this is further exacerbated during the menstrual cycle (Evans et al. 1991).

As their blood sugar drops, women suffer from headaches, shakiness, loss of memory, disruption in concentration, irritability and depression. Their brain is not getting enough fuel to function and cravings for sugar and alcohol is the body's way of trying to obtain more fuel. Diet, exercise and vitamins work to reduce cravings. Education about the premenstrual syndrome (PMS) can also prepare women alcoholics to deal with the depression, irritability, and other symptoms of PMS in ways other than drinking.

Cross-Addiction or Multiple Addictions as a Relapse Trigger

Many women enter treatment for alcoholism with other addictions. Smoking, eating disorders, and the abuse of other drugs are extremely common. Undiagnosed and untreated, other addictions reinforce the denial system, cognitive distortions and over-reaction to emotions characteristic of alcoholism. Needless to say, supporting the woman's denial system around any addiction means supporting it for a relapse to alcoholism.

The woman frequently participates in supporting this denial system by actively accepting that she is an alcoholic because the negative consequences for her drinking were high but deny that other drugs were a problem. If she also used marijuana or cocaine, but only occasionally, she can convince herself that the negative consequences she is facing are exclusive to alcohol. The focus of treatment becomes how not to drink and little attention is given to the other drugs she may have used.

When they leave treatment, many women are inclined to substitute other drugs for alcohol. They believe that they will not fall prey to another addiction because they have learned from their alcoholism. This thinking lends itself to experimentation of other substances in search of the positive experiences once felt with alcohol. However, cross addiction makes it possible for the alcoholic to become addicted to drugs with a similar composition to alcohol despite the woman's attempts to control the drug's affect.

Warning Signs of Relapse

Terence Gorski (1989) and his associates have been able to identify thirty-seven warning signs and a progressive pattern to the process of relapse. Although an enormous study to detail for the purposes of this work, a general understanding of the pattern can be helpful. Some warning signs proven to signal a potential for relapse (Finklestein et al. 1990, Gorski 1989) include:

* difficulty in thinking clearly,
* difficulty in managing feelings and emotions,
* difficulty in managing stress,
* return of denial and other defense mechanisms,
* defensive and argumentative,
* compulsive and impulsive behavior,
* use of tunnel vision,
* depression,
* daydreaming and wishful thinking,
* feelings that nothing can be solved,
* immature wish to be happy (magical thinking),
* periods of confusion,
* irritation with friends,
* easily angered,
* irregular sleeping, eating or daily structure patterns,
* dishonesty,
* impatience,

* low tolerance level for frustration,
* self pity,
* blaming others,
* believing it cannot happen to me,
* open rejection of help,
* "I don't care" attitude.

Many of these warning signs are familiar to women alcoholics as they describe behavior patterns developed during the drinking phase of their disease. It makes sense to many women that these symptoms would surface as part of the relapse process. Relapse takes time and involves a cluster of symptoms to show up consistently. The alcoholic in relapse exhibits behavioral changes, over-reactions to emotions and cognitive distortions. A return to drinking will be the end result if intervention does not occur.

A Relapse Prevention Plan

As part of the recovery process, every female alcoholic needs a relapse prevention plan. Many women resist talking about relapse because they fear that suggesting its potential will make it happen. Some women believe that talking about it means that the counselor lacks faith in their own ability to remain abstinent. However, alcoholism is a disease and relapse is a part of the illness. Most alcoholics are faced with the possibility of relapse at some point in their recovery. Relapse prevention is required as a part of the recovery process.

A good relapse plan needs to provide information on the changes expected to take place in early recovery and on Gorski's warning signs. Women with an understanding of what is happening to them are better prepared to cope when problems arise. Community services like battered women's shelters, housing, medical assistance, child care, psychiatric services and vocational training must be provided.

Every alcoholic woman needs a strong support system to fulfill her need to feel connected to others. Considering the importance of relationships to women, every attempt must be made to include the woman's family in her recovery. At the very least, women need respect for the choices they make around partners, children and parents.

Women need support to deal with the stigma associated with alcoholism and discrimination due to disabilities, ethnicity, sexual orientation and the status of women in society. Family of origin issues, including childhood abuse, incest, rape or a current battering relationship need to be addressed.

Alcoholism involves more than picking up a drink. Recovery involves more than putting the drink down.

Conclusion

Most of the women who have told their stories throughout these pages have been abstinent for years. Some relapsed several times before achieving sobriety. A few of the women continued to drink in spite of their efforts to get treatment. Their goal for sharing what it has been like for them as female alcoholics was to demonstrate the difference between alcoholism in men and women. They have shown how women are introduced to alcohol, how their drinking progressed and the ways alcoholism impacted their lives. They have described their experiences to many treatment approaches and what recovery and relapse prevention plan was needed for success. Finally, they have disclosed what alcoholism means to them in order to reach another woman suffering from the disease. I thank them for their contribution to this piece of work.

References

Ackerman, Hal. *The War Against Children,* Center City: Hazelden Foundation, 1987.

------, *The War Against Women: Overcoming Female Abuse,* Center City: Hazelden Foundation, 1985.

Ackerman, Robert J., Ph.D. *Perfect Daughters,* Deerfield Beach: Health Communications, Inc., 1989.

Adams, Kenneth M., Ph.D. *Silently Seduced - Understanding Covert Incest,* Deerfield Beach: Health Communications, Inc., 1991.

Alcoholics Anonymous, New York City: Alcoholics Anonymous World Services, Inc. 1976.

Alonzo, Claudia Bourne, M.A., L.M.F.C.C. 32705, Personal Interview. September 17, 1996.

American Psychiatric Association, *Diagnostic and Statistical Manual of Mental Disorders,* Fourth Edition. Washington D.C.: American Psychiatric Association, 1994.

Baer, Jean. *How to be an Assertive (Not Aggressive) Woman in Life, in Love, and on the Job*, New York: Penguin Books USA Inc., 1976.

Barbach, Lonnie, Ph.D. *For Each Other: Sharing Sexual Intimacy,* New York: Penguin Books USA Inc. 1982.

Barkley, Russell A. *Attention-Deficit Hyperactivity Disorder A Handbook for Diagnosis and Treatment,* New York: The Guilford Press, 1990.

Bass, Ellen and Laura Davis. *The Courage to Heal,* New York: Harper & Row, Publishers, 1988.

Bean, Reynold, Ed.M. *How To Be A Slightly Better Parent,* Los Angeles: Price Stern Sloan, Inc. 1991.

Beattie, Melody. *Codependent No More,* New York: Harper & Row, Publishers, Inc., 1987.

------. *Denial,* Center City: Hazeldon Foundation, 1986.

Bepko, Claudia. *Feminism and Addiction,* Binghamton: The Haworth Press, Inc., 1991.

Black, Claudia. *It Will Never Happen to Me,* Denver: MAC Printing and Publications Division, 1981.

Blake, David A., *"Risks of Alcohol in Pregnancy"*, *Drug Use in Pregnancy*, Philadelphia: Lea & Febiger, 1982.

Blume, Sheila B., M.D. *Alcohol/Drug-Dependent Women: New Insights into Their Special Problems, Treatment, Recovery,* Minneapolis: Johnson Institute, Inc., 1988.

Bradshaw, John. *Bradshaw on: The Family,* Deerfield Beach: Health Communications, Inc., 1988.

Briggs, Dorothy Corkille. *Your Child's Self-Esteem: The Key to Life,* Garden City: Doubleday & Company, Inc., 1970.

Brown, Stephanie. *Safe Passages Recovery For Adult Children of Alcoholics,* New York: John Wiley & Sons, Inc., 1992.

------ *Treating the Alcoholic: A Developmental Model of Recover*y, New York: John Wiley & Sons, Inc., 1985.

Bufe, Charles. *Alcoholics Anonymous: Cult or Cure?,* San Francisco: See Sharp Press, 1991.

Caignon, Denise and Gail Groves. *Her Wits About Her,* New York: Harper & Row Publishers, 1987.

Caruso, Beverly. *The Impact of Incest,* Center City: Hazelden Foundation, 1987.

Casey, Therese, M.A. *PMS and Alcoholism,* Center City: Hazelden Foundation, 1984.

Chiauzzi, Emil J., *Preventing Relapse in the Addictions A Biopsychosocial Approach,* New York: Pergamon Press, Inc., 1991.

Chiauzzi, Emil. *Reducing Risk of Relapse in Addiction,* New York: The Hatherleigh Co., Ltd. Directions in Substance Abuse Counseling, Vol. 1 Lesson 6.

Coleman, Eli. "Chemical Dependency and Intimacy Dysfunction: Inextricably Bound", Eli Coleman. ed. *Chemical Dependency and Intimacy,* New York: Haworth Press Inc., 1988.

Covington, Stephanie S., Ph.D. *Awakening Your Sexuality: A Guide for Recovering Women,* New York: HarperCollins Publishers, 1991.

Covington, Stephanie S. *Facing the clinical challenges of women alcoholics physical, emotional and sexual abuse.* Focus on Family. May/June 1986.

Cusack, Suzanne Boylston, C.A.C. *Women and Relapse,* Center City: Hazelden Foundation, 1984.

Daley, Dennis C., M.S.W., Howard Moss M.D. and Francis Campbell, M.S.N. *Dual Disorders: Counseling Clients with Chemical Dependency and Mental Illness,* Center City: Hazelden Foundation, 1987.

Dealing With Denial, Center City: Hazelden Foundation, 1975.

Diamond, Jed, L.C.S.W. *Looking for Love in All the Wrong Places,* New York: G.P. Putnam's Sons, 1988.

Drews, Toby Rice. *Getting Them Sober: Volume 1,* South Plainfield: Bridge Publishing, Inc., 1983.

------. *Getting Them Sober: Volume 2,* South Plainfield: Bridge Publishing, Inc., 1983.

------. *Getting Them Sober: Volume 3,* South Plainfield: Bridge Publishing, Inc., 1986.

------. *Getting Them Sober, Volume 4: Separations and Healings,* Baltimore: Recovery Communications, Inc., 1992.

Eating Disorders, Center City: Hazelden Foundation, 1985.

Edwards, Dayan L., M.A. and Eliana M. Gil, Ph.D. *Breaking the Cycle,* Los Angeles: Association for Advanced Training in the Behavioral Sciences, 1986.

Ehrenreich, Barbara and Deirdre English. *For Her Own Good,* Garden City: Anchor Press/Doubleday, 1978.

Engel, Beverly, M.F.C.C. *Divorcing a Parent,* New York: Balantine Books, 1990.

Ellis, Albert, Ph.D. and Emmett Velten, Ph.D. *When AA Doesn't Work for You: Rational Steps to Quiting Alcohol,* Fort Lee: Barricade Books, Inc., 1992.

Enough is a Feast, Center City: Hazelden Foundation, 1987.

Evans, Katie & J. Michael Sullivan. *Dual Diagnosis Counseling the Mentally Ill Substance Abuser,* New York: The Guilford Press, 1990.

Evans, Patricia. *Verbal Abuse Survivors Speak Out,* Massachusetts: Bob Adams Inc., 1993.

Farmer, Steven, M.A., M.F.C.C. *Adult Children of Abusive Parents,* New York: Balantine Books, 1989.

------. *Adult Children as Husbands, Wives, and Lovers: Solutions for Creating Healthy Intimacy,* New York: Balantine Books, 1990.

Fassel, Diane, Ph.D. *Working Ourselves to Death,* New York: HarperCollins, Publishers, Inc., 1990.

Finklestein, Norma, Ph.D., M.S.W., Sally Anne Duncan, M.S.W., Laura Derman, M.P.H., M.S.W. and Janet Smeltz, M.Ed., C.A.C. *Getting Sober, Getting Well: A Treatment Guide for Caregivers Who Work with Women,* Cambridge: The Women's Alcoholism Program of Casper, 1990.

Finnegan, Loretta P. *"Outcome of Children Born to Women Dependent Upon Narcotics"* Stimmel, Barry ed. *The Effects of Maternal Alcohol and Drug Abuse on the Newborn.* Advances in Alcohol & Substance Abuse Volume 1, Numbers 3/4, New York: The Haworth Press 1982.

Forward, Susan & Craig Buck. *MONEY DEMONS Keep Them From Sabotaging Your Relationships-and Your Life,* New York: Bantam Books 1994.

Frankel, Lois P., Ph.D. *Women, Anger & Depression: Strategies for Self-empowerment,* Deerfield Beach: Health Communications, Inc., 1992.

Gil, Eliana M., Ph.D. *Outgrowing the Pain,* Walnut Creek: Launch Press, 1983.

-----. *Outgrowing the Pain Together,* New York: Dell Publishing, 1992.

Goff, Gretchen M. *Bukimia: Binge-Eating and Purging Syndrome,* Center City: Hazelden Foundation, 1984.

Gordon, Thomas, Dr. *P.E.T. Parent Effectiveness Training: The Tested New Way To Raise Responsible Children,* New York: Peter H. Wyden, Inc., 1970.

Gorski, Terence T. *Passages Through Recovery,* Center City: Hazelden Foundation, 1989.

------. *The Relapse/Recovery Grid,* Center City: Hazelden Foundation, 1989.

Gorski, Terence T. and Merlene Miller. *Counseling for Relapse Prevention,* Independence: Herald House-Independence Press, 1982.

------. *The Phases and Warning Signs of Relapse,* Independence: Herald House-Independence Press, 1984.

------. *Staying Sober,* Independence: Herald House/Independence Press, 1986.

------. *Mistaken Beliefs About Relapse,* Independence: Herald House/Independence Press, 1988.

Grafton, D.M., C.C.D.C. "Enabling in Early Recovery." *The Professional Counselor,* (April 1992) 21-25.

Griffitt, William, & Hatfield, Elaine. (1985) "Autosexual Behavior". *Human Sexual Behavior.* (pp.215-219). USA: Scott, Foresman and Company.

Hallowell, Edward M. M.D. and John J. Ratey, M.D., *Driven to Distraction,* New York: Touchstone, 1994.

------. *Answers to Distraction,* New York: Pantheon Books 1994.

Hartmann, Thom. *Attention Deficit Disorder: A Different Perception,* California: Underwood Books, 1993.

Hollis, Judi, Ph.D. *I'm Not Ready Yet,* Center City: Hazelden Foundation, 1986.

------. *Humility vs. Humiliation,* Center City: Hazelden Foundation, 1986.

Jensen, Soren Buus.: "Sexual dysfunction in male diabetics and alcoholics : A Comparative Study". *Sexuality and disability.* 4(4), 215-219

Johnson, Vernon E. *I'll Quit Tomorrow,* New York: Harper and Row, 1973.

Jones, Ann. *Next Time She'll be Dead Battering & How to Stop It,* Massachusetts: Beacon Press Books, 1994.

Kasl, Charlotte Davis, Ph.D. *Many Roads, One Journey: Moving Beyond the 12 Steps,* New York:

HarperCollins, 1992.

Katherine, Anne, M.A. *Boundaries: Where You End and I Begin,* Park Ridge: Parkside Publishing Corporation, 1991.

Katz, Dr. Stan J. and Aimee E. Liu. *The Codependency Conspiracy,* New York: Warner Books, Inc., 1991.

Kaye, Yvonne, Ph.D. *Credit, Cash and Co-Dependency,* Deerfield Beach: Health Communications, Inc., 1991.

Kellermann, Joseph L. *Alcoholism: A Merry-Go-Round Named Denial,* Center City: Hazelden Foundation, 1980.

Kellermann, Joseph L. *Grief: A Basic Reaction to Alcoholism,* Center City: Hazelden Foundation, 1977.

Kellogg, Terry. *Broken Toys Broken Dreams,* Amherst: BRAT Publishing Corporation, 1990.

Kempe, Ruth S. and C. Henry Kempe. *Child Abuse,* Cambridge: Harvard University Press, 1978.

Ketcham, Katherine and L. Ann Mueller, M.D. *Eating Right to Live Sober,* New York: Madrona Publishers, Inc., 1983.

Kinney, Jean, M.S.W. and Gwen Leaton. *Loosening the Grip: A Handbook of Alcoholic Information,* 4th ed. St. Louis: Mosby Year Book, 1991.

Kreek, Mary Jeanne *"Opioid Disposition and Effects During Chronic Exposure in the Perinatal Period in Man"* Stimmel, Barry ed. *The Effects of Maternal Alcohol and Drug Abuse on the Newborn.* Advances in Alcohol & Substance Abuse Volume 1, Numbers 3/4, New York: The Haworth Press 1982.

Kreisman, Jerold J. & Hal Straus, *" I Hate You - don't leave me UNDERSTANDING THE BORDERLINE PERSONALITY",* New York: Avon Books 1989.

Kunzman, Kristin A. *Healing From Childhood: A Recovering Woman's Guide,* Center City: Hazelden Foundation, 1989.

------. *The Healing Way,* San Francisco: Harper & Row, Publishers, 1990.

Larsen, Earnie. *Stage II Recovery: Life Beyond Addiction,* San Francisco: Harper & Row

Publishers, 1985.

Lerner, Harriet Goldhor, Ph.D. *Women in Therapy,* New York: Harper & Row, Publishers, Inc. 1988.

Lerner, Rokelle. *Boundaries for Codependents,* Center City: Hazelden Foundation, 1988.

Levine, Baruch and Virginia Gallogly. *Group Therapy with Alcoholics: Outpatient and Inpatient Approaches,* Beverly Hills: SAGE Publications, Inc., 1985.

Little, Ruth E., Graham, John M., and Samson, Herman H., *"Fetal Alcohol Effects in Humans and Animals"* Stimmel, Barry ed. *The Effects of Maternal Alcohol and Drug Abuse on the Newborn.* Advances in Alcohol & Substance Abuse Volume 1, Numbers 3/4, New York: The Haworth Press 1982.

Living Sober, New York: Alcoholics Anonymous World Services, Inc., 1975.

Love, Patricia and Jo Robinson. *The Emotional Incest Syndrome,* New York: Bantam Books, 1990.

Marlin, Emily. *Genograms,* Chicago: Contemporary Books, Inc., 1989.

Marone, Nicky, *WHAT'S STOPPING YOU? Overcome Learned Helplessness and Do What You Never Dreamed Possible,* New York: Fireside, 1992.

Marx, Russell, M.D. *It's Not Your Fault,* New York: Penguin Group, 1991.

McDonald, Peter C., M.Div. *Grieving: A Healing Process,* Center City: Hazelden Foundation, 1985.

McFarland, Barbara, Ed.D. *Sexuality and Recovery,* Center City: Hazelden Foundation, 1984.

------. *Women in Treatment: Creating a New Self-Image,* Center City: Hazelden Foundation, 1984.

McFarland, Barbara, Ed.D and Tyeis Baker-Baumann, M.S. *Feeding the Empty Heart: Adult Children and Compulsive Eating,* Center City: Hazelden Foundation, 1988.

------. *Sexuality and Compulsive Eating,* Center City: Hazelden Foundation, 1987.

McFarland, Barbara, Ed.D. and Rodney Susong, M.D. *Killing Ourselves with Kindness: Consequences of Eating Disorders,* Center City: Hazelden Foundation, 1985.

Mellody, Pia., Andrea Wells Miller & J. Keith Miller. *Facing Codependence: What is it, Where It Comes From and How It Sabotages Your Life,* San Francisco, CA: HarperSanFrancisco, 1989.

Milam, James R., Ph.D. and Katherine Ketcham. *Under the Influence: A Guide to Myths and Realities of Alcoholism,* New York: Bantam Books, Inc., 1981.

Miller, Angelyn. *The Enabler: When Helping Harms the Ones You Love,* Claremont: Hunter House Inc., 1988.

Miller, Joy. *Addictive Relationships,* Deerfield Beach: Health Communications, 1989.

Miller, Merlene and Terence T. Gorski. *Family Recovery,* Independence: Independence Press, 1982.

Mitchell, Jann. *Anorexia,* Center City: Hazelden Foundation, 1985

Mueller, L. Ann, M.D. and Katherine Ketcham. *Recovering: How to Get and Stay Sober,* New York: Bantam Books, Inc., 1987.

Nakken, Craig. *The Addictive Personality,* SanFRancisco: Harper & Row, Publishers, Inc., 1988.

National Council on Alcoholism, Inc. *What is Co-Dependency.*

Nelson, Jane, Ed.D. *Positive Discipline,* Fair Oaks: Sunrise Press, 1981.

Niebyl, Jennifer R., *Drug Use in Pregnancy.* Philadelphia: Lea & Febiger 1982.

Ogden, Gina, Ph.D. *Sexual Recovery,* Deerfield Beach: Health Communications, Inc., 1990.

Orenberg, Cynthia Laitman, *DES: The Complete Story,* New York: St. Martin's Press 1981.

'Pass It On' The Story of Bill Wilson and how the A.A. message reached the world, New York City: Alcoholics Anonymous World Services , Inc., 1984.

Perez, Joseph F. *Coping Within The Alcoholic Family,* Indiana: Accelerated Development Inc., 1986.

------ *Counseling The Alcoholic Woman,* Indiana: Accelerated Development Inc., 1994.

Pickens, Roy W., Ph.D. *Children of Alcoholics,* Center City: Hazelden Foundation, 1984.

------ & Dace S Suikis. *Alcoholic Family Disorders More Than Statistics*, Center City: Hazelden Foundation, 1985.

Powell, Elizabeth, M.S., M.A. *Talking Back to Sexual Pressure,* Minneapolis: CompCare Publishers, 1991.

Preston, John, Psy.D. *You Can Beat Depression: A Guide To Recovery,* San Luis Obispo: Impact Publishers, 1989.

Robertson, Nan. *Getting Better: Inside Alcoholics Anonymous,* New York: Ballantine Books, 1988.

Robinson, Bryan E., Ph.D. *Work Addiction*, Deerfield Beach: Health Communications, Inc., 1989.

Robinson, Rita. *The Friendship Book: The Art of Making and Keeping Friends,* North Hollywood: Newcastle Publishing Co., Inc., 1992.

Roche, Helena. *The Addiction Process,* Deerfield Beach: Health Communications, Inc., 1990.

Rogers, Ronald L. and Chandler Scott McMillin. *Relapse Traps: How to Avoid the 12 Most Common Pitfalls in Recovery,* New York: Bantam Books, 1991.

Rosellini, Gayle and Mark Worden. *Of Course you're Angry,* San Francisco: Harper & Row, 1985.

Rosellini, Gayle and Mark Worden. *Here Comes the Sun: Dealing with Depression,* Center City: Hazeldon, 1987.

Rowe, Kathleen. *Women's Issues,* Center City: Hazelden Foundation, 1986.

Roy, Maria. *Children in the Crossfire,* Deerfield Beach: Health Communications, Inc., 1988.

Rubin, Theodore Isaac, M.D. *The Angry Book,* New York: Macmillan Publishing Company, 1969.

S., Richard. *Releasing Anger,* Center City: Hazelden Foundation, 1985.

Salvatini, Frank G. "Clients or Students: An Educational Paradigm of Addictions Treatment." *The Counselor,* January/February 1994, pp. 35.

Sandmaier, Marian. *The Invisible Alcoholics: Women and Alcohol,* 2nd ed., Bradenton: Human Services Institute, 1992.

Sauser, William I. Jr. and Donald R. Self. "Alcoholism Treatment Philosophies and Theories: Basis for Service Strategies" Donald R. Self. ed. *Alcoholism Treatment Marketing Beyond TV Ads and Speeches,* New York: The Haworth Press Inc., 1989.

Schaef, Anne Wilson. *When Society Becomes an Addict,* San Francisco: Harper & Row, 1987.

------. *Women's Reality: An Emerging Female System in a White Male Society,* New York: Harper & Row, Publishers, Inc., 1981.

Schaef, Anne Wilson and Diane Fassel. *The Addictive Organization,* San Francisco: Harper & Row, 1988.

Schaefer, Susan and Sue Evans. "Women, Sexuality and the Process of Recovery" Eli Coleman. ed. *Chemical Dependency and Intimacy,* New York: Haworth Press Inc., 1988.

Schenkel, Susan, Ph.D. *Giving Away Success,* New York: HarperCollins Publishers, Inc., 1991.

Schmitt, Barton D., M.D., *Instructions for Pediatric Patients*, Adapted from Your Child's Health, New York: Bantam Books. 1991.

Schneider, Susan Weidman and Arthur B.C. Drache. *Head & Heart: A Woman's Guide to Financial Independence,* Pasadena: Trilogy Books, 1991.

Seixas, Judith S. and Geraldine Youcha. *Children of Alcoholism,* New York: Crown Publishers, Inc., 1985.

Shimberg, Elaine Fantle. *Depression: What Families Should Know,* New York: Ballantine Books, 1991.

Shukey, Harry C., *"Human Experiences Related to Adverse Drug Relations to the Fetus or Neonate From Some Maternally Administered Drugs" Advances in Experimental Medicine and Biology.Volume 27* New York: Phelum Press 1972.

Solberg, R.J. *The Dry Drunk Syndrome,* Center City: Hazelden Foundation, 1970.

Spence, W.R., M.D. *Today's Contraceptives: What's Good for You?,* Waco: W.R. Spence, M.D., 1991.

------. *AIDS: What You Don't Know Can Kill You,* Waco: W.R. Spence, M.D., 1991.

------. *Sexually Transmitted Diseases: Courting Disaster,* Waco: W.R. Spence, M.D., 1992.

Steinglass, Peter, M.D., Linda A. Bennett, PH.D., Steven J. Wolin, M.D., and David Reiss, M.D. *The Alcoholic Family,* USA: BasicBooks, 1987.

Stern, Ellen Sue. *The Indispensible Woman,* New York: Bantam Books, 1988.

Stewart, Felicia, M.D., Felicia Guest, Gary Stewart, M.D. and Gary Hatcher, M.D. *My Body, My Health: The Concered Women's Book of Gynecology,* New York: Bantam Books, Inc., 1979.

Stuart, Richard B. and Barbara Jacobson. *Weight, Sex & Marriage,* New York: Simon & Schuster, 1987.

Subby, Robert, M.A. Healing the Family Within, Deerfield Beach: Health Communications, Inc., 1990.

-----. *Lost in the Shuffle,* Deerfield Beach: Health Communications, Inc., 1987.

The 12 Steps For Adult Children, San Diego: Recovery Publications, 1987.

Trotter, Caryl. *Double Blind,* Independence: Herald House/Independence Press, 1992.

Turner, Diane Strauss, & Dudek, Felicia A.: *An analysis of alcoholism and its effects on sexual functioning.* Sexuality and Disability. 5(3), 143-157, 1982.

Walker, Lenore E. *The Battered Woman,* New York: Harper & Row, Publishers, Inc., 1979.

------ *Terrifying Love Why Battered Women Kill and How Society Responds,* New York: HarperPerennial Publishers, 1989.

Wegscheider, Sharon. *Another Chance: Hope and Health for the Alcoholic Family,* Palo Alto: Science and Behavior Books, Inc., 1981.

Wegscheider-Cruse, Sharon and Joseph Cruse, M.D. *Understanding Co-Dependency,* Deerfield Beach: Health Communications, Inc., 1990.

Weinberg, Jon R. *Interview Techniques for Diagnosing Alcoholism,* Center City: Hazelden, 1974.

Weiss, Lynn. *Attention Deficit Disorder in Adults,* Texas: Taylor Publishing Company, 1992.

Weiss, Gabrielle & Lily Trokenberg Hechtman. Hyperactive Children Grown Up, Second Edition. New York: The Guilford Press, 1993.

Wholey, Dennis,. *The Courage to Change,* New York: Warner Books, Inc., 1984.

Williamson, P. *Sex Addiction: Denial, Acceptance, Return to Sanity,* Center City: Hazelden Foundation, 1989.

Wills-Brandon, Carla, M.A. *Learning to Say No,* Deerfield Beach: Health Communications, Inc., 1990.

Wittenberg, Lynne, M.P.H. *Assessment of Perinatal Care Services in the San Francisco Bay Area,* Unpublished report: 1991.

-------. *Assessment of Perinatal Care Services in the South Bay Region,* Report prepared for the South Bay Chapter March of Dimes 1993.

Wittenberg, Lynne, M.P.H. Personal Interview September 14, 1996.

Woititz, Janet Geringer, Ed.D. *Adult Children of Alcoholics,* Deerfield Beach: Health Communications, Inc., 1983.

Woititz, Janet G., Ed.D. *Healthy Parenting: An Empowering Guide for Adult Children,* New York: Simon & Schuster, 1992.

-------. *Marriage on the rocks: learning to live with yourself and an alcoholic.* USA: Health Communications, 1979.

-------. *The Self Sabotage Syndrome: Adult Children in the Workplace,* Deerfield Beach: Health Communications, Inc., 1987.

Index

Recommended Reading

Although all of the books listed in the reference section are excellent resources, there are a few that stand out. These sources have been heavily referenced and quoted throughout the *Volume One: The Female Alcoholic* and deserve special mention. Stephanie Brown's work on alcoholics in her book *Treating the Alcoholic: A Developmental Model of Recovery* is remarkable in its detail of the disease and recovery process of alcoholism as well as its examination of the roles Alcoholics Anonymous and counseling plays in facilitating recovery. I highly recommend any book written by this woman.

Stephanie Covington has also done a fine job of exploring some of the recovery issues female alcoholics face in early sobriety in her book *Awakening Your Sexuality: A Guide for Recovering Women*. Katie Evans and J. Michael Sullivan's book *Dual Diagnosis Counseling the Mentally Ill Substance Abuser* is one of the best on this topic.

Getting Sober, Getting Well: A Treatment Guide for Caregivers Who Work with Women by Norma Finklestein and her colleagues is the only resource I am aware of that has extensive handouts and exercises developed specifically for women. This book is based on the treatment program for women, The Women's Alcoholism Program of Casper, and has provided information that can be used by healthcare professionals in their own programs. I can not stress enough the importance of this work.

Ann Jones' work, *Next Time She'll be Dead Battering & How to Stop It* and Lenore E. Walker's , *The Battered Woman* are incredible references for describing the battering cycle and the characteristics of the couple involved. Although I disagree with the premise that once a couple is involved in a battering relationship, they are unable to stop, it is probably more true than not. However, I work with alcoholic couples whose battering is frequently part of the alcoholism (though not always) and have witnessed recovery around these issues for many of them. Nevertheless, the information found in these books have proven to be accurate in my own clinical work with battered women.

Terence Gorski's work on relapse prevention, Joseph F, Perez's book on *Counseling the*

Alcoholic Woman, Marian Sandmaier's *The Invisible Alcoholics: Women and Alcohol*, and any of the books by Anne Wilson Schaef are highly recommended reading. Each author has a great deal to say on their particular area of expertise and have helped to guide my own work. Finally, Sharon Wegscheider, Janet Woititz and Robert Subby's books on adult children of alcoholics are definitely must reading.

All of the authors that I have listed here can be found in the reference section. If you are interested in learning more about women and alcoholism, I suggest you invest some time exploring these works.

Women and Addiction Counseling and Educational Services

111 Donna Court • Santa Cruz • CA • 95060 • (831) 426-6636 Ext. 4
www.women-addiction.com • fax # (831) 426-6636 • e-mail: info@women-addiction.com

BOOK ORDER FORM

Name_____

Address_____

City/State/Zip_____

Telephone #_____ e-mail _____

Qty	ISBN #	Title	*Price	Total
	0-9663144-0-9	Volume One: The Female Alcoholic	$25.00	
	0-9663144-1-7	Volume Two: Counseling the Female Alcoholic	$25.00	
		Subtotal		
		**CA residents sales tax		
		***Shipping & Handling		
		TOTAL		

* Prices subject to change without notice
**California sales tax ADD $2.00 per book.
***Add $5.00 Shipping & Handling for each book.   All orders shipped priority mail.

PAYMENT OPTIONS

[ ] Check or money order payable to Women and Addiction

Please charge my: [ ] Visa   [ ] MasterCard   Expiration Date: |__|__| |__|__|

Card Number: |__|__|__|__| |__|__|__|__| |__|__|__|__| |__|__|__|__|

Print Name on Card: _____

Signature of Cardholder: _____
(required on all credit card orders)

[ ] Order On-Line at: www.women-addiction.com

"Coming soon! *Volume Three: Recovery Issues of the Female Alcoholic*"

b:7/99

Women and Addiction

Women and Addiction is composed of several programs dedicated to addressing the concerns of women and their children. They are:

The Women and Addiction Home Study Program
Women and Addiction Internet Classes
Women and Addiction Counseling and Educational Services (WACES)
WACES Children's Books

All of the programs are committed to disseminating information about issues that specifically affect women. Of particular interest are issues related to relationships, parenting, step-parenting, health concerns, depression, attention deficit disorder (with or without hyperactivity), financial problems, domestic violence and divorce. In addition, both programs are particularly focused on female alcoholism, drug addiction (including prescription drug abuse), eating disorders, compulsive spending, smoking, and sexual dysfunction.

The Women and Addiction Home Study Program

The Women and Addiction Home Study Program offers provider approved courses written specifically for healthcare professionals in need of continuing education units for license and/or certification renewal. Courses can be completed in your home or office at your own pace. There are no deadlines! No travel expenses, missed work, lost revenue or childcare difficulties! Each course has an open-book format, includes all necessary materials/texts and comes with a 10 day money-back guarantee. Orders are processed and shipped the same day by priority mail.

Continuing education units made easy! Just read the course material, answer a few simple multiple-choice questions and then fax or mail in your answer sheet to receive your certificate. Certificates are mailed the same day via first class mail.

Women and Addiction Internet Classes

The Women and Addiction Home Study Program has Internet Classes that are provider approved for healthcare professionals in need of fast, easily available and inexpensive CEU's for license and/or certification renewal. Just choose a class from the course listings, read the on-line material and answer the questions. Certificates are mailed same day via first class mail.

Check out our web site at: www.women-addiction.com.

For a free brochure fax or call: (831) 426-6636, e-mail: info@women-addiction.com, or write to:
Dr. Judith Goodman at 111 Donna Court * Santa Cruz * CA * 95060-3105

Counseling and Educational Services (WACES)

WACES is dedicated to publishing books on topics of particular importance to women. Its mission is to address rarely talked about issues that, in fact, have a huge impact on women's lives such as issues related to relationships, parenting, step-parenting, health concerns, depression, attention deficit disorder (with or without hyperactivity), financial concerns, domestic violence and divorce. Of particular interest is female alcoholism, drug addiction (including prescription drug abuse), eating disorders, compulsive spending, smoking, and sexual dysfunction. Many of its books are used as textbooks for The Women and Addiction Home Study Program courses.

WACES Children's Books

The newest edition, WACES Children's Books publishes books for children that help explain some of the serious issues faced by today's youth. Parental alcoholism, divorce, step-parents, eating disorders and other family issues are explained in an easy to understand, age-appropriate manner. Most of the books are written for parents to share with their children.

Check out our web site at: www.women-addiction.com.

For a free brochure fax or call: (831) 426-6636, e-mail: info@women-addiction.com, or write to: Dr. Judith Goodman at 111 Donna Court * Santa Cruz * CA * 95060-3105